SPEAKING OF MURDER
VOLUME 2

Berkley Prime Crime Books Edited by Ed Gorman and Martin H. Greenberg

SPEAKING OF MURDER
SPEAKING OF MURDER, VOLUME 2

Speaking

OF MURDER VOLUME 2

INTERVIEWS WITH THE MASTERS OF MYSTERY AND SUSPENSE

Edited by

Ed Gorman and
Martin H. Greenberg

BERKLEY PRIME CRIME, NEW YORK

SPEAKING OF MURDER, Volume 2

A Berkley Prime Crime Book / published by arrangement with
Tekno-Books and Ed Gorman

PRINTING HISTORY
Berkley Prime Crime edition / February 1999

The Penguin Putnam Inc. World Wide Web address is
http://www.penguinputnam.com

ISBN: 0-425-16547-7

Berkley Prime Crime Books are published
by The Berkley Publishing Group,
a member of Penguin Putnam Inc.,
375 Hudson Street, New York, New York 10014.
The name BERKLEY PRIME CRIME and the BERKLEY PRIME CRIME
design are trademarks belonging to the Berkley Publishing Corporation.

PRINTED IN THE UNITED STATES OF AMERICA

10 9 8 7 6 5 4 3 2 1

Contents

Introduction

BY ED GORMAN & MARTIN H. GREENBERG

A reader recently asked why we liked printed interviews when most people had ready access to writers at bookstore signings and on television and radio.

The answer is simple, at least for us. A lot of writers are relatively shy people. In public appearances, they're a bit nervous. They sometimes say things they wish they hadn't, or spend their allotted time talking but saying very little at all. We certainly include ourselves in this group.

So, the printed interview becomes the forum of choice for many writers. Not only are they more relaxed when they're speaking—they also have the chance to revise themselves when the interviewer sends them the typescript. To say *exactly* what they mean to say.

Past generations of mystery writers have not left us abundant records of their time on this planet. Except for a handful of famous writers, for instance, there's almost no serious biographical material about the pulp writers. Or the generation that came after and started selling regularly to Hollywood and the slick magazines. Or worked in paperback originals in the sixties and seventies.

We started our magazine, *Mystery Scene,* sixteen years ago for just that reason—so that our generation of writers would leave behind a journal that was essentially a history of what writing and publishing was like in our time.

Speaking of Murder offers readers the same thing: an up-close and personal visit with some very popular writers. Few writers can tap dance, juggle or emote on cue. But they can talk genially, intelligently and entertainingly, as you're about to find out for yourself.

We had a great time putting this book together. We hope you have a great time reading it.

Dean Koontz

INTERVIEW BY BOB MORRISH

BM: You frequently mention the influence James M. Cain had on your writing. Could you tell us what that is?

DK: In spite of my overwhelmingly optimistic view of life and of basic human nature, I've occasionally been referred to as a *noir* writer. This always amazes me—yet I think I understand the comment. Perhaps because of my childhood and my relationship with my father, I do have a clear-eyed view of the dark side of human nature. I'm unsentimental about evil: I know that nurture isn't always or even usually the cause of it, that *nature* plays a fundamental role and that every savage bastard in the world isn't also a victim. Evil is real, and morality is *not* relative. We make our own damnation. *Noir* is in part an attitude, a *mood,* and in spite of their optimism and often happy endings, my books do frequently function in that mood.

But Cain's effect on me really had nothing to do with the *noir* quality of his writing. I find him a powerful and lasting writer because of two things. First, the great clarity of his writing gave his books—especially *The Postman Always Rings Twice, Double Indemnity,* and *Serenade,* even *Mildred Pierce*—the appearance of simplicity, the purity and swiftness of running water. Second, that clarity of the prose is like a magician's sleight-of-hand, because it leaves you dazzled by the effect while distracting you from the *source* of that effect. His work is only simple on the surface. If you stare into it long enough, reread it, you realize that you're not gazing down into a foot-deep stream but into a fearful depth, such a depth that, though the water remains clear, it ultimately fades into perfect darkness beyond the reach of light. Every sentence of Cain has more than one purpose, not just advancing the plot but setting the mood, revealing character, and weaving intricate currents of symbol and archetypal reference that resonate with the reader on a subconscious level. I seldom admire obviously dense writing, writing that wears its importance and its noble intentions for all to see, seven hundred pages of earnest striving. Often, books of that nature *are* all surface, a sun-spangled mist, bright as a sea of jewels, but with only a void beneath. Books with hidden depths, that achieve their effects through manipulation of the subconscious—they're harder to write. Sometimes they are not as admired by academic critics, but time brightens books like Cain's while leaving more self-important *tomes* riddled with mold.

BM: You also say that John D. MacDonald remains your favorite writer. What do you think made him tower above his peers?

DK: Much like Cain, MacDonald wrote prose that was easy to read, smooth and flowing, prose that looked simple on the surface but hid some pretty strange depths. I'm not even talking now about the Travis McGee books, one of the greatest series ever written, because as good as they were, the McGee books were not his best work. Books like *The Damned, The Only Girl in the Game, Cry Hard Cry Fast, The Last One Left.* MacDonald understood evil, truly understood it, as few mystery-suspense writers do. He didn't glamorize it. He didn't make it cozy. He didn't scratch at the festering wounds of Freudianism to come up with some putrescent justifications for human perfidy. He wrote about evil with a cold, clear perception—which resulted in some of the most reality-based and utterly chilling antagonists in all of fiction. MacDonald was writing about sociopaths decades before the word was invented, and in numerous of his villains beats the same heart that empowers Hannibal Lecter—except that, for my money and in spite of the fact that I very much like *The Silence of the Lambs,* some of MacDonald's antagonists make Lecter seem like a clown.

MacDonald also fascinates me because of his willingness to take huge narrative risks. He's done books with multiple first-person points of view, which is risky because each chapter, when you change to another "I" narrator, it's got to sound different from the others yet maintain the momentum of the story, the mood, and the reader's sus-

pension of disbelief. Or look at a book like *Cry Hard Cry Fast:*
Through the first third or half of a relatively short novel, he keeps
hitting us with new characters and new situations in each chapter,
which seem utterly unrelated—until suddenly we find the connection; this risks alienating the reader, who wants to know what kind of
story it is as soon as possible.

MacDonald was also brilliant with characters. He's one of the
few writers I've ever read who can stop a story dead in the water for
character—four or five or six pages of backstory—and make it so interesting that when he picks up the story and starts moving it again,
you find yourself saying, "No, no, wait, forget about the story for
awhile, and tell me *more* about this fascinating person."

Some mystery critics, to whom puzzle is everything or to whom
the essence of characterization is eccentricity piled on eccentricity,
did not like MacDonald. Some of the dumbest critical writing I've
ever read involved respected mystery critics savaging MacDonald—
wherein they revealed only that *they didn't get it* and perhaps didn't
have the *capacity* to get it. He was a great writer. He had his weakness, as we all do, one of which was a fondness for writing humor
that wasn't matched by a talent for it. I loved *The Girl, The Gold
Watch, and Everything* when I was twenty—and winced at the adolescent humor when I was forty. But virtually everything else he
could do better than anyone, and throughout his career he was top-
ping himself.

BM: Your penchant for mixing/crossing traditional genre boundaries
is well known. Which of your books do you feel are most successful
at blurring the genre lines?

DK: *Mr. Murder* was well-liked by mystery-suspense readers and
critics, yet at its core is a solid science-fiction premise, and many of
the ramifications of that premise are pretty horrific. Indeed, the recent sheep and monkey cloning has brought the moral and ethical issues to the attention of the general public. At the same time, there's
lots of humor in *Mr. Murder*—maybe not as much as Donald Westlake would work into one of his comic crime novels, but a lot. *Watchers* seemed to capture suspense, science-fiction, horror *and*
mainstream audiences, which wasn't as true of, say, *Hideaway* or
Dragon Tears. But there's an infinite number of ways to combine genres, and some are bound to please more people than others. The fun
for me is in the challenge of it, finding new forms of fiction, new
ways of telling stories, unexpected juxtapositions of mood and
material.

BM: Tell us about some of the resistance you met from publishers when you began mixing genre elements in your work.

DK: Tremendous resistance. When I delivered *Lightning,* my publisher wanted me to put it on the shelf for "seven years" because she was afraid it would destroy my career at the very time that I had finally begun hitting hardcover best-seller lists. We argued for six weeks, but finally she went ahead with the book. To her credit, she later acknowledged that I was right, that the public *was* ready for a novel that blended time travel with elements of the suspense novel, the adventure novel, the comic novel, and the biographical novel that spans a character's entire life. This publisher is a very savvy woman, right far more often than she is wrong, so I can't say I blamed her for trusting her instinct. There's *still* so much resistance to genre-bridging that I'd never recommend a young writer try it. You have to be very sure of your intentions and confident of your skills, because if you try to mix genres, you're going to be called upon to justify it book by book and to stand your ground even when everyone in your professional life is assuring you that you are wrecking your career. This can be exhausting—stealing time away from *writing.*

BM: In the last few years, you've begun using greater amounts of humor in your books. Can you trace the development back to any particular cause?

DK: Early in my career, I wrote a comic novel—*Hanging On*—that was well reviewed. But it didn't sell. I looked around and noticed that very damn few comic novelists made a living at it for any length of time. Being stubborn but not stupid, I gave up comic novels for suspense—but knew the time would come when I could start slipping comedy into the books and get away with it. *Watchers* had a storyline in which a thread of humor was not only justifiable but essential. I liked the experience so much that I incorporated more humor in *Lightning*—and even made one character a stand-up comic so her constant stream of funny lines seemed natural to her. I mean, there are a lot of funny accountants out there—well, maybe not a *lot,* maybe two or three—but readers would find it harder to believe these humorous lines springing from an accountant than from Thelma in *Lightning.* There wasn't much room for humor in *Intensity,* and only slightly more in *Sole Survivor,* but everything else since *Watchers* has included humor to one degree or another. Why? Because life is funny. The human experience is both a tragedy and a farce—and I can't imagine writing well if I didn't give voice to both aspects of that experience.

BM: You worked with two of crime fiction's greatest editors, Lee Wright and Barbara Norville. What made them so special?

DK: They were both *hugely* knowledgeable. They knew everything about mystery and suspense fiction and were passionate about it. They had read everything—to an extent I'm not always sure that current editors have. They knew when a book was building on the work of giants and didn't mistake imitative work for dazzling originality. Lee was a very warm, supportive, loving aunt who charmed your best work out of you. Barbara was wisecracking, street-smart, and quite humorous; her sometimes gruff, don't-bullshit-me attitude was as different from Lee's genteel approach as you could get, but it had the same effect of getting you to perform at your best level. Both were fine editors and I learned a lot from them.

BM: Some critics have noted the influence of Alfred Hitchcock on your novels. Is that an accurate impression?

DK: Well, I suppose they're talking about the mix of suspense and humor in books like *Mr. Murder, Cold Fire,* and *Dark Rivers of the Heart.* I've always felt that tension can be enhanced if the terror is seasoned with an occasional laugh, and that characters seem more well-rounded and dimensional if we see that they have a sense of humor, because in real life most of us deal with tragedy and horror with one degree of humor or another. Hitchcock was a master of this mix. There's also a sense of *adventure* in Hitchcock that is usually an element of my novels, and he keeps his characters on the move more than most filmmakers, which is something I do in novels. Think of the ceaseless movement of *North by Northwest.* While I've long enjoyed Hitchcock's best work, however, I can't say that I've been consciously influenced by it. I think I'm just predisposed to see the world through an angle similar to his in some regards; that the human experience is simultaneously a tragedy and a comedy.

BM: You use female protagonists extensively. Why did you decide to do so? Do you feel there's a particular book in which you have been most successful in creating a strong female protagonist?

DK: I began using female protagonists when they were virtually unknown in hard suspense (as opposed to romantic suspense, where people like Daphne du Maurier had been using them for years). Another writer once flabbergasted me by saying in print that I had a formula—always a female character as major as the male lead. Excuse me? Formula? This is *life*. There are *two* genders—well, three if you consider Dennis Rodman—in real life, and stories in which one sex or the other is relegated to the background never strike me as stories that could be *real*. Using women in roles equal to male roles, portraying them as equally smart and courageous and indomitable and tough—that's simple reality. Anyway, I don't always have equal male and female co-leads. *Intensity* has *no* male lead, only Chyna Shepherd and the villain! So there. Hah. And judging by reader response, I'd say Chyna is my most successful female character to date.

BM: You've written two "dog-centric" novels—*Watchers* and *Dragon Tears*. Why?

DK: Because I'm always fascinated with viewpoint in novels. Out of interesting and convincingly rendered viewpoints comes the plot, the theme, the very soul of the book, because stories are first and foremost about people. And when I say "people," I include dogs. My kind of dogs. Somewhat anthropomorphized but definitely not humans in costume. From a dog's viewpoint, I can say things about the human condition that might seem too harsh if said by a human character, because the dog's observation is colored by his innocence. In *Watchers,* I never really went wholesale into Einstein's viewpoint; there was never a scene done through his eyes. I just didn't feel confident enough to do that yet. By the time I got to *Dragon Tears,* the confidence was there, and I found the right note for Woofer's point of view almost at once. In spite of the highly simplified language, the viewpoint was so *rich*. I loved writing those scenes so much, creating the entire doggy perception and idiom, that I was tempted to bring Woofer back for an entire novel told in his voice. Now *that* would have driven my publisher right over the edge!

There's also Rocky, in *Dark Rivers of the Heart,* a totally different dog from any others I've done—and a mirror of some aspects of the hero. And Scootie in *Ticktock.* And I'm doing a novel—the first of those for Bantam—which involves a dog in a major role. I think I was a dog in another life. Maybe if I'm really lucky, I'll be a dog again some day.

BM: You've commented in the past about envy among writers: ". . . I discovered there are some writers who consider writing to be every bit as competitive an exercise as the Iditarod Dogsled Race." Do you still see a lot of this? Are there any anecdotes you'd care to share—with names censored?

DK: Many writers are fine people, honorable and well balanced. But as a profession, we have a higher than usual percentage of self-absorbed bastards with no sense of humor about themselves. One evening, reading the newspaper, I came across an article about a thirty-year study of 15,000 people who earned all or a significant part of their income through creative writing of one kind or another—and the headline of the piece was *Eighty Percent of Writers Exhibit Evidence of Schizophrenia and Megalomania.* I showed the headline to Gerda and jokingly said, "Can you believe it's only eighty percent?" But I was only half joking. A well-known writer once became so disturbed when my (now former) British publisher praised one of my books that he went out of his way to find a bad review of it and sent it to the publisher in London with a note to the effect that "not *everyone* liked it." My publisher was so startled by this that he sent me the other writer's correspondence with the advice that I better watch my back. I've got a hundred of these—but I'll save them for my memoirs. For my money, you can bet that when you see any author attacking another by name in interviews or with apparent casualness in essays or by the cowardly tactic of slipping disparaging remarks about other writers into the mouths of characters in his books, you are looking at an author who is desperately unhappy, deeply unsure of his own worth, and in need of building himself up by tearing others down. It's all stupid and sad. I have many close friends who are writers, but the majority of my friends are in the construction trades—masons, cabinetmakers, painters—largely as a result of the fact that Gerda and I have remodeled and built so many houses over the years. All of these people are craftsmen of real talent and some of them are artists by any definition, proud of what they do—but I have *never* heard one of them express an envious thought about a fellow tradesmen or attempt to enhance his own reputation by belittling the work of others. They make damn good friends.

BM: You've not yet been fortunate enough to have one of your books creatively and successfully adapted for film or television, and your frustrations with the filmmakers who've mutated your work is well-known. In your fiction career, your eventual success was seemingly due, in some part at least, to your dogged persistence and sheer force of will. Have you ever considered trying to bring that determination to bear on the Hollywood scene, in an effort to see one of your books successfully filmed? Or is the film industry just too political and too collaborative (and too avaricious) for any one writer to have that substantial of an impact?

DK: Well, I've just seen the director's cut of the miniseries based on *Intensity,* and it's quite wonderful. That was a case in which I got to choose the screenwriter—Stephen Tolkin—who did a phenomenal job. There are moments in the second night that I itch to change, but overall it is tremendous television. For the first time, filmmakers succeeded in capturing the essence of what I do—the thematic crosscurrents and especially the emotional content. They realize I'm not a horror writer. I've said I'm not a horror writer so often that no one even hears me say it anymore—but these people grasped that they were making psychological suspense with a spiritual element, and they did a knockout job. It airs in the autumn. Meanwhile, I wrote and exec produced *Phantoms* for Miramax/Dimension, with Peter O'Toole and Joanna Going and some other solid actors. I had total control of the shooting script, by contract. I've not seen a director's cut yet, but I've seen Joe Chappelle's assemblies of several primary sequences, and the picture looks as if it is going to be absolutely terrific. Again, I convinced Miramax to stop thinking of *Phantoms* as a horror story and to start thinking of it as science-fiction suspense. The moment I turned their heads around on that, everything fell into place, and now they are ecstatic with the dailies and the cut footage they're seeing. I'm sure we'll work together in the future. And when I finish the book for Bantam that I'm working on now, I intend to write the screenplay immediately and attempt to set up the production in such a way as to give me even more control than I had on *Phantoms.* I find that when I have a strong element of control, when I don't have to argue my way through endless—and generally useless—script-development meetings, film can be worth my time and energy. A strong element of control is the key—and hard to win, except when the studio badly wants the property and can get it no other way.

BM: Getting back to your "dogged persistence and sheer force of will": Discussing your novel *Twilight Eyes* and its character Slim MacKenzie, you've referred to "the iron will with which Slim has tried to bring order to—and make sense of—a world that he knows is infinitely bizarre and perhaps senseless." I thus can't help but wonder whether Slim is reflective of his creator. Do you think he is? Taking the point further, I'm sure there are bits of you strewn through all of your books (what an image!), but are there any particular characters that you feel are reflective of yourself, or that you especially identified with while creating them?

DK: I am not the Outsider, the monstrous killing machine from *Watchers*. Well, come to think of it . . . as a kid I was always an outsider, with a small "o," so I know what it feels like to be in the cold looking in on a place of warmth and laughter. So maybe I *am* the Outsider—which is why I could give the reader so much empathy with the beast at the end. There's certainly a lot of me in Regina, the disabled girl in *Hideaway,* in her wide-eyed sense of wonder about virtually everything in life and in her curious relationship with God. Marty Stillwater, the writer in *Mr. Murder,* shares many of my own attitudes, especially as to the meaning and purpose of fiction, which he expresses in a scene somewhere past the middle of the book. I am very much like Chyna Shepherd in *Intensity*—or would like to think I am. I identified so strongly with her and with her journey from an abusive childhood to a life of decency and hope that I could literally feel her terror and exhilaration and despair as she was struggling through that story. The characters who use humor to cope with life— Thelma in *Lightning,* Holly in *Cold Fire,* so many others—are all reflections of me. When people do hurtful things to me or when life throws me a really scary curve, I eventually turn the experience into an amusing anecdote—which has given me such a fund of funny anecdotes that Tom Snyder just asked me to do his show for the fourth time this year! So even terrible pain can become prime material for book publicity!

BM: You've mentioned that in the course of doing research for *Watchers* and other novels, you've done a lot of reading in the field of criminal psychology, and that you've found that many widely held notions are seemingly ill-founded: "the hard scientific data that is available seems to disprove most of the assumptions behind large areas of psychology. Antisocial behavior must not be caused primarily by social ills or childhood trauma because truly vicious criminal activities—the worst species of evil—don't correlate with those causes in any consistent manner." If that's the case, why do you think that such beliefs are widespread? Does the media serve to propagate this thinking? If so, why? Also, do you think your strong interest in this field is somewhat attributable to your own dysfunctional upbringing?

DK: Widespread beliefs are often ill-founded, even those that appear to be based on solid intellectual ground. After all, it was once rather unanimously held that the sun revolved around the earth. Or look at Darwin. I believe that large elements of his theories may be correct. But for a century and a half, his theory enjoyed largely unassailable status in the scientific community; it was "Theory" with a capital "T" and seemed as monumental as the Rocky Mountains, as timeless as the stars. Yet in the past couple of decades we've seen the Theory stood on its head by Steven Gould's "punctuated equilibria," which was desperately needed to explain the lack of any observable proof of random selection through gradual mutation—and such issues as irreducible complexity. Darwin believed—as did virtually all the scientists of his age—that the smallest unit of matter was the cell, which he called "carbonized albumen." Atomic and subatomic particles were unknown in 1858—which is one reason why Darwin's theory is now plagued by such thorny problems as irreducible complexity, which even the most brilliant of the hard Darwinists have not adequately answered. And in our own age, quantum physics and chaos theory have radically altered our previous perceptions of the fundamental nature of matter, energy, and time.

So if even the hardest of hard sciences are periodically forced by new discoveries to discard what seem to be absolute truths for new theories, why should it be surprising that in fields like psychology and other "soft sciences," a lot of what we think we know about human behavior and motivation is pure bunkum?

The facts are that ninety-nine percent of all violent career criminals are diagnosable sociopaths who lack the capacity for empathy, and there is no overwhelming or even halfway clear correlation between childhood abuse and sociopathy, poverty and sociopathy, or social-political oppression and sociopathy. Indeed, because most if not all violent sociopaths exhibit similar disturbing behavior by the age of three (torturing insects and then small animals), there's an unnerving amount of evidence that points toward a genetic cause. And boy does *that* possibility lead us into a tangle of moral and ethical questions, especially if the mapping of the human genome eventually allows us to determine the exact genetic damage that reliably identifies a sociopath. Anyway, there is not one case on record of a genuine sociopath being rehabilitated—yet our laws, our system of justice, even our fundamental political assumptions are predicated on the Freudian belief that *anyone,* given adequate therapy and led firmly enough to deep self-examination, can be rehabilitated. Even most of modern psychology has begun to distance itself from Freud and the religion of victimology that arises from his theories, yet our culture and society remain so saturated with Freudian attitudes that we persist in thinking of ourselves as victims, all victims of what our parents did to us, what our culture and society did to us. There is not a shred of proof that Freud's theories are correct, and much proof that they are not, yet as a culture we hold fast to them.

Because, as you ask, the media propagates them? No. The media *does* propagate them, but that's not why we embrace these untruths as truths. We embrace them because they excuse our worst behavior: If each of us lacks free will, if each of us is only a product of what his family, his culture, and his society did to him, then none of us is fundamentally to blame for what he does. What an enchanting idea! You can be a right bastard to others, lie and cheat and steal—and remain a victim. You and the Menendez brothers! Several years ago, I began to realize that *all* modern fiction uses Freudianism as the basis for character motivation, whether the authors of those works are always aware of it or not. When I look back at my own *Whispers,* for instance, I see the ultimate Freudian psychology at work in every character in the book—yet I was not aware of how slavishly I followed the Freudian faith while writing it. Some time ago, I made a conscious determination to stop using Freudian psychology as the underpinning of characterization. Since then my characters are defined and given depth by their actions, their reactions, and attitudes; they are possessed of free will and the power to make moral decisions; they are not defined solely by their backstories, by childhood trauma and the limitations of their socioeconomic status and whether they suffered bed-wetting episodes when they were nine. Some critics don't get this at all. In their postmodern hipness, they are ironically reactionary and dogmatic: They feel a character *must* be defined by the psychological damage he sustained as a child and adolescent. This psychological background detail, lathered on, is the only thing they recognize as characterization! Tedious. If you think about it, the best characters ever to walk through the pages of fiction—those of Dickens, for instance—were created before anyone had ever heard of Freud.

As for whether I am interested in psychology in general and aberrant psychology in particular because of a dysfunctional upbringing . . . You bet! My father was a violent alcoholic who held forty-four jobs in thirty-four years, who was later diagnosed as sociopathic, and who made two attempts on my life, the second in front of a lot of witnesses, which landed him in a psychiatric ward. After growing up under the thumb of a deeply disturbed man, I'd have to be brain dead not to be interested in the source of sociopathic behavior, the issues of nature versus nurture.

BM: Unlike a lot of people who've undergone such weirdness and trauma as a kid, you seem to have turned out fairly . . . well, *normal.*

Do you ever see reflections of your father's behavior in your own behavior?

DK: Normal? Well, yes, relatively normal. For a number of years I did believe that Betty Crocker was the secret master of the universe and a figure of towering evil. But I'm better now.

I know Betty Crocker is not the secret master of the universe. The secret master of the universe is Richard Simmons. All hail his name. All hail his name.

My father was sociopathic. You have to understand what this means: He completely lacked the ability to empathize with the feelings and needs of others. Like all sociopaths, he was convinced that love, honor, courage, and all the better human feelings were a hoax, that no one really felt these things any more than he did, that everyone simply faked these things in order to manipulate others. Sociopaths recognize no needs but their own and are narcissistic in the extreme. Were I to exhibit behavior like this, my wife would smack me upside the head.

BM: One other childhood question: When was the last time you returned to Bedford, PA? Do you know if the house you grew up in is still standing?

DK: I returned in 1989 for various reasons. The house I grew up in was not much of a house: four tiny rooms, a tar-paper roof and no indoor plumbing until I was about eleven. But it was still standing. Relatives thought it would be interesting for me to go back and see the place, to remind myself how far I'd come. They had even arranged with the folks living there to let me make a visit. We pulled up in front of the place, and I was so overcome with a sense of oppression that I could not go inside. I could think only of my mother, of what she had endured there, and I couldn't bear to walk through the door again. In fact, I never got out of the car. We stopped—and then drove almost immediately away. That is the past. Life is about the future.

BM: You've been quoted as saying that ". . . my editor at Putnam has said that all of my books, in one way or another, are about the remaking of families, some of them unconventional but nonetheless happy." Given the central role that families play in much of your work, I can't help but wonder why you've never had children of your own. Any comment?

DK: Two of my father's brothers committed suicide. I believed I saw elements of my father's mental condition reflected in others in his family. My wife and I wanted children . . . but when we were first married we had a hundred and fifty bucks, a used car, and low-paying jobs. We were too poor to afford a family. By the time we could consider having children, we had endured so much from my father (because he continued to play a role in my life as an adult) that we seriously had to assess the risk that any child of ours might be like him. If sociopathy can be genetic, then it might conceivably skip a generation. We did not want to be responsible for bringing into the world anyone who, regardless of upbringing, might be a danger to others.

BM: You've described your religious beliefs over the years as "Protestant, then Catholic, then agnostic, now firmly back in the believing camp again, though with no firm idea of the nature of God." What prompted these changes, most particularly the recent change back to believing?

DK: The move back into the camp of believers has actually been taking place since before I began writing *Strangers* and has progressed steadily since—and one of the motors driving me, oddly enough, is my lifelong interest in science. I read a lot of science, much of it obscurely published, and if you have been following much of the work in molecular biology, quantum physics, and chaos theory over the past decade plus, you will be aware that some scientists—a minority but with quite a few of the best and brightest on its side—believe that they are seeing powerful evidence not merely of an ordered universe but of a created universe. This is a hot debate in some quarters. But even Francis Crick, who won the Nobel Prize for discovering the double-helix structure of the DNA molecule, has found it difficult, if not impossible, to explain the diversity and complexity of life on earth with the standard theories—and thus suggested that all life here was probably engineered and seeded by an extraterrestrial intelligence! Begs the issue, doesn't it? If life here was created by ETs— who created the ETs? The older I get and the more observant I become, I am also further convinced of a meaning and purpose to existence simply because life is so full of fascinating *patterns*, complexities, subtle connections that I was too self-centered or preoccupied to notice when I was younger. There's the odd *synchronicity* of life, which Jung explored at length but never adequately explained, and year by year I become ever more aware of it. If I ever get the chance to meet Richard Simmons, I know everything will be explained. All hail his name.

BM: When asked about writing sequels, you've said, "The only novel to which I've contemplated writing a sequel is *Watchers,* but even that might never happen. There are two basic reasons for not doing it. First, new ideas grip me, and I'm more excited about those than I am about returning to older ideas." This makes perfect sense to me. *However,* I'm intrigued that you have taken the time to revise some of your older works—most notably *Invasion* and *Demon Seed*—before re-releasing them. What does revising an older work amount to, if not "returning to older ideas?" How do you distinguish your tendency toward revision from your aversion toward sequels? Finally, what about a *Watchers 2.* Are you any closer to someday writing such a book?

DK: Generally sequels are boring because the characters in the subsequent books do not grow and change the way they did in the first novel. Their natures freeze, and they become less like real people; they mutate into collections of eccentricities—because that's easier for the writer and because readers often *want* to see precisely the same traits and behaviors exhibited by characters that have become old friends. It's comfortable fiction. As a reader, I'm guilty of it, too. I loved Rex Stout's series of Nero Wolfe mysteries—but over literally dozens of books, Nero Wolfe and Archie Goodwin and all the characters in Stout's milieu remained *exactly* the same, unchanged by their experiences. This is true in 99 percent of sequels. One of the few series in which repeating characters underwent fundamental— often subtle—psychological change was in John D. MacDonald's Travis McGee books. I'm not nuts enough or vain enough to think that I could easily step into MacDonald's shoes.

Revising an old book is an utterly different exercise from writing a sequel. You look at a book written in your twenties and wince at the naiveté, the clumsy use of language, the themes inadequately explored. Yet . . . there's something in the concept or the characters that still intrigues, that begs to be revisited, reworked. Sometimes this leads to a *totally* new novel like *Winter Moon* (which, nominally, started with *Invasion*), and sometimes it results in the very same story so utterly recast that it *seems* like a new book, as in *Demon Seed.* None of us can go back in time and undo a terrible mistake that has affected his whole life or be gentler and kinder to someone whom we treated poorly back then—but a writer can revisit early books that were not well done (either because of financial pressure or inadequate technical skills) and remake the past a little. It's fun. But I'd never write a *sequel* to any of those books, having revised them.

That said . . . I will reveal that I am launched on a trilogy that features the same lead character. I found a premise of such interest to me and a character with so much capacity for depth and growth and change that I became excited about seeing if I possessed the ability to wring the full potential from the material. The idea is that the books could be read in any order, each standing entirely alone, yet the central character has a major character arc within each book and is not the same person at the end of each that he was at the beginning. It's easier to announce this intention than it is to effectuate it!

As for *Watchers* . . . if I ever come up with a story that feels like the equal to the first, I might write the sequel. But I would not want to toss out a continuation that is a pale reflection of the original.

BM: What do you like about today's crime fiction?

DK: More writers make an honest effort to get the details right than used to be the case. Police procedure and forensic pathology, for instance, are more often written about in a factual manner than in the old days. We still see the amateur detective who is infinitely smarter than the cops, who smugly saves the day when the authorities fumble, but there's a lot less of that and more acknowledgment of reality. Also, more of today's writers seem to make an effort to give the reader a poignant sense of the *effects* of crime, of the monstrousness of murder. Light murder mysteries—in which the whole purpose of the story is to work up and then solve a puzzle through the offices of a detective with a signature array of eccentricities—have always made me uneasy, because they almost seem to make a joke of murder, not unlike the way in which pornography denies the sacred aspect of sex.

BM: What *don't* you like about today's crime fiction?

DK: Maybe I'm just getting older and crankier. *Maybe?!?* But it seems to me that crime writers these days—actually writers in *all* the genres, including literary fiction, which is just one more genre—care less about style, about using the language well and with flair. So much of what's published is written in flat declarative sentences, as if everyone totally misunderstood Hemingway. It's possible to read book after book and never encounter an engaging metaphor—or *any* metaphor. And there seems to be more impenetrably tangled syntax than previously. And there are some writers—well, I just don't like their shoes, or their taste in neckwear. I told you I'm getting cranky.

Donald Westlake

INTERVIEW BY LEE SERVER

Donald E. Westlake is the Great American Crime Writer. For nearly forty years he has been turning out brilliant and original works across the mystery spectrum, from the toughest Hammett-like thrillers to delirious comic capers. The Fugitive Pigeon. The Mercenaries. Pity Him Afterwards. The Hot Rock. Dancing Aztecs. Good Behavior. Two Much. Kahawa. Baby, Would I Lie? The Ax. *And dozens more. Not to mention his managing the careers of "Richard Stark" and "Tucker Coe." If there is another novelist around with Westlake's skill and range and inventiveness then that person has been keeping a very low profile.*

When Westlake first saw his name in print Raymond Chandler and Sax Rohmer were still scribbling and yet his latest novels are as fresh— and often as hilarious—as the morning news. His newest, What's The Worst That Could Happen?, *the ninth misadventure of born-to-lose thief John Dortmunder, and such recent efforts as* Smoke, Trust Me On This, *and* Humans *give continuing proof of the writer's limitless creative resources. His mantel is loaded with the trophies of institutional approval, the various Edgars, Grand Master and Lifetime Achievement honors, the Oscar nomination for screenwriting, tributes from around the world. But in talking with Westlake one gets the impression that his most coveted award remains the opportunity to sit behind his Smith-Corona Super*

Silent and write. *"The absolute pleasure in it,"* he says, *"has never, never dimmed. It was and is a whole lot of fun."*

LS: As a kid growing up in Albany, was there a moment you can look back to when you realized that writing, storytelling was what you wanted to do?

DW: I was reading all the time, and I loved fiction more than fact, always . . . And it was a feeling of wanting to go through the looking glass, how to get into the story myself . . . And the only way was to do it myself . . . Let me tell you mine instead of somebody else tell his. I first tried to write a short story when I was eleven . . . I don't even know if I finished that one. But I went along and kept writing these short stories, and after awhile I would send them out to magazines . . . and they would send them back.

LS: Which magazines were you sending to?

DW: Everything . . . I wrote mysteries, science fiction, there were still western pulps and I wrote westerns—though I'd never been any farther west than Troy, New York.

LS: Did you make any sales?

DW: No! None . . . no, no, everything came back! And you always got the rejection slip. And I saved every rejection slip, I couldn't bring myself to throw them away . . .

LS: They were your contact with the world of publishing.

DW: That's right! So I put them up on the wall over my desk and I had all these rejection slips and I thought, "I'm gonna throw them away when I finally make a sale." And I'm . . . God . . . I was doing everything . . . I was writing "slices of life" . . . I was sending to the *New Yorker,* the *Atlantic,* the pulps, *Sewanee Review*! I was aiming high, low, and in between. And the rejection slips were coming in left and right. I had in my mind, my goal in life was to be a published teenaged writer. And I missed it by four months! [Laughing]

LS: So you were a published twenty-year-old writer. What was that first sale?

DW: A science fiction thing to a little magazine called *Universe.*

LS: Pretty soon after the first sale you went into the service, the Air Force. Was that a pleasant experience?

DW: No! [laughing] We agreed to disagree. I'm still rather disorganized and I was certainly too disorganized for the Air Force when I got in there. I did meet a lot of interesting people in there, and liked some of them. The good thing about military service, I think, is that it really does show you that there's a whole lot of other kinds of people around that your high school told you nothing about!

LS: Did you get to go overseas?

DW: Yes, to Germany for a year and a half, and that was a very interesting experience. But . . . the military stuff itself I never did . . . *close with*. [more and mysterious laughter]

SEX AND SCOTT MEREDITH . . .

LS: So you came back to New York, I guess certain that the service was not going to be your career.

DW: Yeah. I went back to school, G.I. Bill, up to Binghamton, it was then Harper College, a year-and-a-half, got married, then came down to New York where I went to work for Scott Meredith as a "fee reader." Do you know what that was?

LS: Actually, I worked there, too . . . for a few months.

DW: You did? I was there for six months—I think that was the max for anyone!

LS: Were the conditions any more humane in your era?

DW: A science fiction writer named Damon Knight, who worked there before either of us, wrote the line, "For three months once I was chained to an oar at a literary agency."

LS: [Laughs mirthlessly] So it was your job to write reviews of the manuscripts by fee-paying clients, unpublished writers. Memoirs of a pharmacist, that sort of thing?

DW: Yeah! And all of these hopeless short stories, and you had to write the letter back in "Scott Meredith form." But . . . it was another learning experience. About the third day I was there a sweet, touching short story came in from some woman in the Midwest. Very well written and horribly non-commercial, not a market on earth for it. And the only thing I was permitted to do at this point is lie to this woman! You know, write and tell her how close she was to selling and write another story and send it in with some more money, and then just denigrate the story in every way . . . It was the decisive moment at this job. And there were always people at that place who left the first day or went out to lunch and never came back, they couldn't handle it. And I had to make up my mind—I couldn't use the Eichmann defense, "I'm only obeying orders," or tell myself, "If I don't do it someone else will." And I thought, "Well, the only defense that I have is that I'm here because I want to play with the Big Boys, and if I want to play with the Big Boys I do this . . . So I stayed.

LS: You figured the agency was a way of getting your foot in the door as an aspiring writer?

DW: Yeah. When I went to work there Hal—Hal Dresner—was there, and he was another fee reader. And he said to me, "You see that guy there—Henry?" It was Henry Morrison, who now has his own agency, but he was Scott's assistant then. And Hal said, "If Henry comes over to you and says 'Do you know anything about—' and mentions any kind of writing, horror stories, whatever, say 'Yes' and you'll get an assignment."

LS: These were, like, quickie assignments the Meredith agency would field from publishers?

DW: The Scott Meredith Agency always had a relationship with these schlock publishers who would call up and . . . order by the yard. I remember when I was first there, there was *Manhunt* magazine that only bought from Scott.

LS: Ha! Do you know why?

DW: It was cheaper for them—they didn't need to have an editorial department!

LS: So Scott Meredith was the de facto editor of *Manhunt*!

DW: Yeah, *Manhunt* and another magazine they had. So the publishers said, "What the hell, we get all this shit from Meredith anyway, let him do it!"

LS: Every agent's dream, to cut out the middle man!

DW: There's more! If you were a striving freelancer and you sent a short story to *Manhunt*—this was happening while I was there—the envelopes would not be opened, they'd be packed up and sent over to Scott in clusters, each submission taken out of the envelope, put in the stamped, self-addressed return envelope, mailed back without having been read by anybody, but the return address would be copied down and a Scott Meredith brochure would be sent to the person . . . there was such . . . cruddiness . . . everywhere you turned over there . . .

LS: And so, did Henry Morrison give you an assignment?

DW: Yes.

LS: What did he ask you if you "knew anything about?"

DW: Sex!

LS: He wanted you to write some "erotica?"

DW: He asked if I could write a sex novel and I said yes and he said, "Good, give me 10,000 words and an outline by Monday." I said "All right." But I had no idea what he was talking about. This was the morning so I waited till the afternoon—I figured I'd let the assignment settle before I exposed my ignorance. So I went over and I said, "Henry, when I was a kid there were these little staple-bound books, they looked like *TV Guide,* is that what you're talking about?" And he said, "No." And he reached behind him and grabbed three books, two of which it later turned out were written by Larry Block and one by Bob Silverberg. And he said, "Read these." And what they were, they were paperback originals that belonged to a market that only lasted about seven, eight years . . . they were what I call "euphemism novels."

LS: No dirty words.

DW: Yeah, nothing explicit—"Passion . . . pulsating, pulsating deeper . . ." And they weren't genre . . . they weren't mystery, or historical, nothing, just . . . stories with some sex . . .

LS: They didn't even have to be very melodramatic, right? Just contemporary novels. Two women in Greenwich Village slowly discover they are attracted to each other . . .

DW: That sort of thing, yeah. That's what it was. So I read these three books and I thought, "Heck, I can do that." You know, it's no problem writing 50,000 words if you can't call anything by its rightful name!

So I did it and it was accepted. They were paying $600 for a novel. And I wound up doing . . . well, I did eight of them and Larry and I did three in collaboration—where the collaborative method was, no discussion beforehand, one of us does a chapter and hands it to the other guy, who does a chapter and who tries to end a chapter in such a way that the other guy can't go forward . . . We did three books that way, which was amusing. God knows what the books were like!

LS: Were you feeling thrilled to be writing books and getting paid . . . or were the special circumstances working against that?

DW: Early on there was some satisfaction, but it didn't last . . . somehow being at Scott Meredith and doing sex novels . . .

LS: Wasn't there a sex book publisher you worked for who edited the books "for length?" Was it Newsstand Library?

DW: Oh yeah . . . Nightstand Library. Yes, right! I can't remember the guy's name, a publisher out of Chicago. He had some paperback lines, and a *Playboy* imitation called *Rogue*. And these sex books came out and the last chapter or two chapters, they would just not make sense. I hadn't looked at them but a guy who wanted to try writing this stuff read some of mine and said, "Your stuff gets really weird at the end there!" And I looked and they made no sense. The actual last page with "The End" written on it was still there but many of the pages before that were just missing. And I said something to Henry Morrison, I said, "Henry, I know this is just schlock, but the endings of these books make no sense, aren't they going to alienate their readers?" And Henry said, "Yes. This doesn't make any sense!" And he called the publisher and found that the publisher had turned the sex line over to his nephew. And the nephew determined that the books had to be exactly 244 pages or whatever it was, and if they went a page over that they would have to print another signature and it cost more.

LS: At which point a conventional editor would line edit the manuscript to fit.

DW: Yeah, but this nephew just grabbed a chunk of pages from the book . . . to the point where one sentence would blend into another sentence from twenty pages down the road.

LS: Like a William Burroughs "cut-up"!

DW: Totally incoherent. And Henry had the publisher look at one of the books while he was on the phone. And there was silence while the publisher at the other end in Chicago is looking at the book . . . And finally Henry hears him shout, "What shit is this! What shit is this!" And Henry said to me, "I think the nephew's out."

LS: Your official "first novel" was *The Mercenaries,* a tough gangster mystery. That sold to Random House, the big time.

DW: That was very strange, actually. I had written the book and I was represented by Scott Meredith and took the book in to Henry Morrison. And he said, "All right, we'll send it over to Gold Medal." I said, "Aw, gee, I thought it was a hardcover." He said, "You don't want a hardcover, there's no money in hardcover." And I said, "Yeah, I do! I want it . . ." He said, "All right, I'll make a deal with you. There's only two hardcover houses that are worth it, that pay any money at all and they are Simon and Schuster and Random House." The rest just paid minimal amounts. He said, "If you want to waste your time, I'll send it to those two, and then I'll sell it to Gold Medal." All right. So he sent it to Simon and Schuster, and the mystery editor there was a guy who was a writer also, by the name of Clayton Rawson.

LS: The guy who wrote The Great Merlini books in the '30s, the magician detective?

DW: Yeah, right. And he was a real traditionalist. He liked real traditional locked-room kind of stuff. And this book of mine was . . . I didn't know the word *consigliere* at that point but that was what it was, the Mob guy's right-hand man solving a murder. A switch. It's a Mob story but with a murder mystery inside the Mob. And Rawson sent it back with an *angry* letter. He was angry! "How dare you send me a piece of trash like this! This is a serious house ... I thought you respected my taste better than that!" Really an angry letter. Well, that got Henry excited a little bit and he said, "All right, we'll teach this guy; let's send it to Random House." And Lee Wright, a wonderful editor, called Henry and said, "This is a pretty good book. But it's not good enough, so I'm sending it back. But I wish the author lived in New York because I'd like to talk to him." Henry said, "He lives in New York." So, all right, set up an appointment. And Henry told me Lee Wright rejected the book but wanted to talk to me about it. "So go there and listen, then bring the manuscript back and we'll send it to Gold Medal." So I went and we talked for an hour and a half and in the end Lee Wright agreed to look at the manuscript again if I made certain changes. I carried it home and called Henry and said, "Wright wants to see it again." All right. And they took it. Terrific. Random House. And the following year Lee Wright took another one. And I kept selling books to them.

ENTER RICHARD STARK ...

LS: You wrote *Killing Time* and *361* for Random House, then branched out with a series at Pocket Books.

DW: Random House would only take one book a year and I thought, "I can write faster than that." And I was thinking, "I'd really like to sell a book to Gold Medal."

LS: You'd been a fan of their crime novels.

DW: Yes! I was a real steady reader of the Gold Medal crime novels and enjoyed a lot of those writers.

LS: MacDonald, Peter Rabe, Lionel White ...

DW: Yeah, all of them. And I wanted to ... I thought I could do that. So I wrote a book, thinking Gold Medal, and I gave it to Henry to send to Gold Medal under this pen name. And they sent it back. And I was really taken aback by that because I thought I'd done it right.

LS: We're talking about *The Hunter*, the first book as Richard Stark. Any significance to the pseudonym you chose?

DW: The name Richard Stark came from Richard Widmark playing Tommy Udo in *Kiss of Death,* and Stark because I wanted to remind myself that that's what I wanted the language to be . . . that those who need adverbs will starve to death here.

LS: So Gold Medal rejected it—

DW: Then Henry sent it to Pocket Books, and the editor, Bucklyn Moon, said, "Can the guy get away at the end . . . and can you give me three books a year about him?"

LS: What was the original ending? Does Parker get killed?

DW: Near the end . . . it's been a while since I've thought about it . . . Parker had gone into a bodega and there was a guy he knew there who was involved in smuggling, and the police had the place staked out, nothing to do with Parker, but as a result of that they had now been following Parker and they've got the goods on him. It was just at the moment when he's done everything and it's all clear, nothing to worry about, and he walks into a hotel and the cops arrest him . . . And I'd only done that because I thought you *had to* . . . the bad guy has to get caught at the end! So when Buck said, "Can you let him get away?" I said, "Oh, *very easily!*" So . . . a small change and a little addition on the end and Parker was ready to go . . .

LS: The first three seem vaguely like a trilogy, all concerning the repercussions of the fallout with Mal—

DW: Well, actually, the first five all do that. And after that, the sixth book was the first one that didn't come out of everything that had started with the first book . . . I've always thought the sixth book was the least successful one in the series.

LS: Which was the sixth title? *The Jugger?*

DW: *The Jugger.* And I made a mistake . . . Either I didn't yet know who the character was, though I should have, or I forgot . . . And it was based on a false premise. This old guy who Parker knows, a message bearer, calls him and says "I've got trouble here—" in this little town in the Midwest, "and I need help." And Parker goes there and the old guy's dead. Then, everything follows from that . . . Well, the problem is, Parker *wouldn't go there.* Parker doesn't help people! It was basically the wrong character. I was writing some other guy.

LS: Parker's criminal code is practicality—

DW: Right. He does "what's needed now."

LS: When did you decide that *The Jugger* was screwed up?

DW: It was screwed up from the beginning. I could sense it as I was going along. But I had to turn in a book . . . Buck at Pocket had always liked the books, the first five books he liked a lot. He read *The Jugger* and he called and he didn't like it. He called and he said, "Come on in, I think we can fix it." And by the time we were done, something under twenty, maybe sixteen pages of the original manuscript were still left when we finished with it. Every other page of the manuscript was changed drastically . . . But . . . it never worked . . . whatever I did, I was still . . . If you've started in the wrong direction on the first footstep it really doesn't matter what you do after that.

LS: You were writing so quickly in this period, did you never consider just putting it aside and cranking out a replacement?

DW: No, I really wanted to solve the problem! And I really wanted to get past it and on to something else . . . The next one I got Parker on track and then it was all right. But it was a horrible learning experience of, you know, don't ask a horse to give milk . . . Basically I think it's best if a writer has no idea what he's doing. Self-consciousness is bad for writers. But after awhile you have to know something about what you're doing. I finally decided that the Parker novels are novels about work, and that the ideal workman is somebody who does the job at hand with the tools at hand. And that that's what those books are about.

LS: The Richard Stark books have this feeling of effortless authenticity. Was this imagination, research, experience?

DW: I never did any sort of "Folk Song Collector" type research. Nor did I pal around with bank robbers. But in my teens and into my twenties there were some troubled people that I was "hanging out" with, and I shouldn't have been hanging out with them . . . "Dutch" Leonard has these people down pat. I'm thinking about the Crowe family in *Maximum Bob*. And I knew people like that. Hard and mean and stupid and absolutely requiring that luck be with them or they're not going to get through the day. And I was around them and got a . . . got a sense of a worldview really, more than expertise in how do you bust into a safe. And then some of that other stuff I would find along the way. I might read in a newspaper that some burglars did this when they were breaking in and I'd say, "Oh, that's interesting . . ." and remember it later.

LS: Didn't the Parker novels get the seal of approval from real-life criminals?

DW: Richard Stark got fan mail from prisons. They felt that I— Richard Stark—was somebody they could talk shop with. I'd get letters, and if I responded I got more letters. And they'd tell me about jobs, and busted jobs.

LS: You let Parker's happy-go-lucky colleague Grofield grow from a sidekick to the star of his own series.

DW: In the fifth and the eighth book there was this other character named Grofield and he was sort of amusing to me and I thought, every once in a while there has been in popular fiction or in newspaper comic strips a series character where something will happen and the series will continue without that character for awhile. So I thought, "Let's try it, the next book in the Parker series, Parker won't be in it." The eighth book [*The Handle*] ended in Mexico and Parker's going back to the States, leaving Grofield behind, wounded, in a hotel room in Mexico City, with a suitcase full of money in the closet. We'll start there. What if he opens his eyes and there's a girl climbing in the window? Now what happens? But as I was finishing this book—timing is everything—Pocket Books changed their distributor. And the new distributor told Pocket Books they were better at distributing science fiction than mysteries. At that time Pocket Books had, I don't know, six or seven or eight mystery series. And they dropped the whole lot, all their paperback original crime novel series, and they made a deal with Ballantine in order to get some science fiction on board. So that's when we took the series to Gold Medal—Knox Burger was the editor there, and I couldn't say, "Here is the next book in the Parker series and the character isn't in the book." And so Grofield became his own series and was sold in hardcovers to Macmillan. And the next Parker novel became something else entirely.

LS: So, finally, you were a Gold Medal author. But you didn't stay there. Parker then jumped to hardcovers.

DW: There was at Gold Medal a man whose name was Ralph Dey, who was not an editor but whatever is above editors. And he was never very comfortable with the Parker series. He didn't like anti-heroes. He wanted the good guys to be good guys. He was sort of annoying Knox Burger, who was my editor, and annoying me, and messing around with the covers all the time, and trying to get changes in what I wrote. So after four books it was just too uncomfortable and I had talked about it with Lee Wright at Random House and when I had another one done I showed it to her and she took it. And the last four were done with her—three before she retired and someone else took over the last one.

THE BIRTH OF DORTMUNDER

LS: Dortmunder came into existence out of what had started as a Parker novel, right?

DW: Yeah. Around 1970. I wanted to do another Parker and so I began thinking about the character. I thought, "One thing about Parker is that he does not suffer fools gladly and he's a bad guy when frustrated." I thought, "What would happen if I frustrated him? Would that give me the story? What if he had to steal the same thing several times? That would probably really irritate the man." So I started to work it out a little bit and described it to my wife and while I was describing it, I was laughing. And then my wife was laughing, and then I started to describe it to my agent, Henry Morrison—he had his own agency by then—and the two of us were laughing. I said, "I've really got to be careful with this, because the worst thing you can do with a tough guy is have him be inadvertently funny. It drains all the menace out of him. And all of the interest out of him. I don't know about this." But I liked the idea and I kept fiddling with it. Is Parker going to do this? He just isn't going to do this. And since I had already made that mistake once with *The Jugger* of forcing him through a story that he really wouldn't have done, I decided I couldn't do it. But gee, I like the story, maybe I can do it with somebody else. And that's where Dortmunder and *The Hot Rock* came from. And that was supposed to be a one-shot, never going to be a series. Then, two years later, there was this bank in New Jersey . . . I had a weekend house in New Jersey and twice a week I'd drive past where this construction was going on. They were tearing down the old bank and putting up a new bank in the spot and they were operating out of a mobile home next door during the construction. And finally I thought, "You know, an enterprising guy could back up a truck to that bank and drive it away. I think I know the people to do it." And Dortmunder came back for *Bank Shot* because that was just the perfect job for him.

LS: Is *The Hot Rock* the only time you ever sort of cannibalized a book that hadn't worked out?

DW: Another Dortmunder called *Good Behavior* had the concept of knocking over an entire office building, cutting out their alarm system so you can go in and out of whatever offices have valuables. And they have a mail-order business in the building, so everything that's stolen is taken to the mail-order business and mailed out. Well, that was originally a Parker novel that I got sixty pages into and failed. So I not only borrowed that concept for Dortmunder but the woman who runs the mail-order business existed in the Parker. Pulled her back and cleaned up her language a little bit for Dortmunder. So there's been a certain amount of cannibalization.

LS: And then there was the cross-pollenizing in *Jimmy the Kid*, where the Dortmunder gang themselves take their cue from a Richard Stark book—studying at the foot of the master.

DW: Yes. And at the end of that, where the kid's now sold his story to the movies, they've made a movie out of it, and Richard Stark sues the movie people. And I called my lawyer and said, "Have you by any chance ever used a pen name in your work?" And it turned out he had, I forget why, some pro bono job. And he used a pseudonym. I said, "Great, do you mind if I use it?" And so Richard Stark's lawyer is my lawyer's pseudonym. That was about as far through the looking glass as you could get on that one.

LS: When you wrote *Jimmy the Kid* were you aware of the actual case where the kidnappers had been basing their plan on an old Gold Medal story by Lionel White?

DW: Yes, sure, that's the derivation of it. It was the Peugeot grandchild, you know, Peugeot automobiles. This Lionel White novel [*The Snatchers*, 1953] was read in France by this really minor league Parisian crook who took it around to friends of his and said, "Look, it's a blueprint. If we do what the book says, we're going to make out like gangbusters!" And they did everything the book says. Kidnap a baby because a baby can't identify you. So they kidnapped a baby. And the book said, "Do not kill the baby, return the baby alive, because if you just steal money, eventually they'll stop looking for you, but if you kill the baby, they'll never stop looking for you." So they carefully returned the baby. They did everything the book said and it worked out. They made all this money. But . . . *they ran out of book.* They began doing stupid things, getting drunk and talking—"I bet you don't know who kidnapped that Peugeot kid . . ."—and spending money they weren't supposed to have, and they all got caught. And a friend of mine said they should have sent some of the ransom money to Lionel White to write a sequel and tell them how to get away.

WESTLAKE AT THE MOVIES . . .

LS: Can we talk about the movies for a bit? I would say the best adaptation of your work to date is still *Point Blank.* What do you think?

DW: Yes, yes . . . I just saw it on the big screen here for the first time in many years. Up here they have a little film festival every summer and try to show some things that have a connection with local people involved in film. So this year they did *Point Blank* and it was terrific to see it on the big screen again. I think it's very good. A film critic friend of mine said, "That's a watershed film. It's a movie the next thousand movies come out of."

LS: The post-modern gangster film.

DW: Yeah. And it wasn't thought of very highly when it came out. It got very mixed reviews.

LS: Did you have any involvement in it?

DW: No. It was a drawn-out thing, the rights bought by one company who sold it to another, and another, a whole lot of people involved and I was long out of it.

LS: Did they track you down to invite you to the premiere or anything like that?

DW: Oh yeah, I was invited. I met the two producers, Chartoff and Winkler. I met them, they were very decent, nice guys actually. The book was the first thing of mine that was ever sold to the movies and it was back when I was still at Scott Meredith and it was sold for no money at all, just ridiculous.

LS: Like . . . under ten grand?

DW: Well, two thousand.

LS: Two thousand dollars?

DW: Yes. And I met the producers and they said, "This is some kind of strange deal you had here." And so they made an offer to incorporate sequel rights into a contract and they would pay $50,000 if they did a sequel. And they would pay me ahead. One way or another they couldn't pay me more for *Point Blank* because it had already been paid for with the $2000. But they wanted to have an ongoing relationship or whatever, and in the light of a movie budget it was a gesture they could well afford. But the fact that they did it was very nice, I thought.

LS: How about the other Stark filmings? *The Outfit, The Split . . .*

DW: *The Outfit* I think is very good. *Point Blank* is very poetic and mythic and all that, but *The Outfit* is closer to what the book is like. And Robert Duvall is great. In fact, the thing is full of all these wonderful B-movie people—Richard Jaeckel, Sheree North, Anita O'Day singing in the bar. So that's very good. *The Split* I thought was interesting here and there, some good people, Julie Harris, Ernest Borgnine, but essentially is dull and didn't show a helluva lot of talent in the writing or the direction. And as for Jim Brown and Diahann Carroll, a friend of mine said, now we know the sound of two blocks of wood making love.

LS: What about *Made in USA,* directed by Jean-Luc Godard, with a woman, Anna Karina, ostensibly playing Parker? It's pretty scarce, have you ever seen it?

DW: Yes, I had to, because we sued them. I had to watch it a few times!

LS: Why did you sue them?

DW: A French producer named Beauregard was in the process of buying the rights, paying it off in monthly installments. He had sunk all of his money into a movie, *La Religieuse* . . . it was about either a whore becoming a nun, or a nun becoming a whore, I don't know. But the French government banned it and wouldn't give it an export license. So he was stuck. And Godard was a friend of his and said, "Let me help you out. What can I do?" He said, "Well, I have this book—" It was *The Jugger.*

LS: *The Jugger* again!

DW: Godard at that time was shooting *Two or Three Things I Know About Her.* So he had all the film equipment and everything. And on twelve afternoons while he was shooting *Two or Three Things* he shot *Made in USA* with Anna Karina, to help out his friend. When Beauregard saw what he had shot, he figured, well, that certainly doesn't look like the book, so I don't have to pay the man for the rights. And we said, "You stopped paying—that means you don't have the rights." But we didn't know that he had made the movie, we said he no longer had rights to the book. Then he didn't tell Godard what he was up to. And when Godard told an interviewer what he was working on, a *serie noire* thriller by Richard Stark, a friend told me, "Hey, Godard's making a movie from a book of yours." I said, "No he isn't." And it went on from there.

LS: You had to prove in court the movie was derived from your book?

DW: Once you make the switch—it's not a boy robber, it's a girl reporter—every other scene is taken from the book. There's one scene in it in which Godard himself goes into a bar and there's a mailman and a bartender and they get into a conversation on the meaning of words. "If I say 'pancake' does it have to mean 'pancake?' Could it perhaps mean 'umbrella?'"

LS: A "Godardian" scene.

DW: A Godardian scene. That, I'm happy to say, is not in the book. But everything else in that movie is in that book. It's a mess.

LS: How was the suit resolved?

DW: It's my only international lawsuit. Happily, I won. But I didn't win anything. All I could sue for was copyright infringement. This guy didn't have any money, so forget that. With copyright infringement the cure is that all infringing material is destroyed. So now technically I can say, "Destroy all prints and negatives of *Made in USA*." So, instead of destroying everything, we said, "Give me North American distribution rights." So I have the North American distribution rights if you ever know anybody wants to see it. Ha!

LS: So that's why it's been so scarce! I saw it once at the Thalia in Manhattan in the '80s. It was made in, what, '65, and this was billed as the American premiere.

DW: Yeah, I think I got about twenty-five dollars out of that.

LS: Well, let's move on to *The Hot Rock*. That was another very good adaptation, I thought.

DW: Yes. Bill Goldman did the screenplay on that. He is wonderful. I think he's the best. We had not met and he called me, said, "I got the job to do this, and I want to have lunch with you. I want you to tell me everything you know about those characters that you didn't put in the book." And I thought, "This is a smart man." And we met, and became friends. It was a real learning experience. Bill extended the ending from the book, a scene at Kennedy Airport with Robert Redford, who's a long distance runner, running across Kennedy with this young African diplomat who's also an Olympic runner, chasing him. And it begins as a chase and ends as a race. And they forget the diamond and get into a conversation about running—it's very funny and very sweet and there's more to it than that. So Peter Yates came in as the director very late in the process. The movie he had done before that was *Bullitt*. And *Bullitt* ends at the airport in San Francisco. And Peter Yates came on and said, "I can't do two movies in a row that end in airports!" Well, we didn't know the movie was about *him*. So he wanted a different ending, and Bill said, "No, I'm happy with what I did, and I've done what I'm contractually required to do. I don't want to think of a new ending because you don't want to go to the airport." On the day they started shooting, Bill went to Paris, and nobody else could do anything so if you ever see that movie you'll notice it doesn't end, it just stops. He goes and gets the diamond out of the bank and walks down the street and some dixieland jazz plays. And the camera goes out of focus. The end.

LS: And now the world will never be made to see two airport scenes at a Peter Yates Film Festival.

DW: Ha! Exactly.

LS: Had you ever imagined Dortmunder looking like Robert Redford?

DW: No. I thought he did an honorable acting job. There was no way on earth anyone was going to look at him and say, "There's a loser." But other than that, he did a good job.

LS: Who would you cast as Dortmunder if given the task?

DW: I've never written a book with an actor in mind, but a few times the movie people have said, "Do you have anybody in mind for Dortmunder? Do you know who he looks like?" I tell them he looks like Harry Dean Stanton and they say, "That's nice. He can't carry a movie." I say, "You didn't ask me that."

LS: What about Parker? Lee Marvin was pretty great, of course.

DW: When I was first writing way back in the beginning I thought Parker looked like Jack Palance.

LS: Your first credited screenplay is for *Cops and Robbers*. Did you have any problems working in that format?

DW: Actually I had done one script before that and I didn't know anything. It was not a high budget thing, everybody had eleven dollars and they were trying to get something going. The director was the one who said to me, "You're telling us everything, all the dialogue. Please give me a chance to show them something." And I learned then that you can lose a helluva lot of dialogue. Let the actors do their job, let the director do his job . . . So having that horrible experience behind me, when I got to do *Cops and Robbers* it was easy. I had already done my messed-up screenplay.

LS: How did you come to do the screenplay for *The Grifters*?

DW: The German director, Volker Schlondorff, and I had been working on an Eric Ambler novel called *Passage of Arms* for Orion Pictures, just as Orion was dropping dead, so that didn't get made. Volker ran into Stephen Frears, who said he was about to make his first American film and was looking for an American writer. Volker said, "Well, I've been having fun with Don Westlake." And Stephen said, "Fun? Oh, yes, he used to write those tough things as Richard Stark, but now he only does comedy, does he?" Frears kept looking at writers, but then he saw that I'd done this thing called *The Stepfather*. And he looked at that film and decided that Richard Stark was still alive and that *he* had written *The Stepfather*. So through the agents I was offered this and I had read the Jim Thompson book years before. And I said no. I thought it was too much of a downer and there was no way to do it and make it interesting. About a week later the phone rang. "This is Stephen Frears calling from London. Why don't you want to make my film?" We talked. And Stephen said, "If you see it as the son's story, then it is a story about death. But if you see it as the mother's story, it is a story about survival, and the price of survival, but at least it's about survival." Okay, that's actually very interesting. The problem is, of the three principal characters, the mother comes in third after the son and the girlfriend. How do you tell an audience—never mind about the person you saw first, never mind about the person you saw second, concentrate on the third person who comes in much later? Frears said, "I don't know. You're the writer." I said, "Give me a week to figure out a way to say it's the mother's story, or at least make a level playing field. If I can't, there's no way." He said okay. Five or six days later he called and I said, "How about a triptych? We divide the screen in three, three characters in three locations going through doors into their lives, each doing something. And at least we've got the mother in up front, and we can sort it out later on." And he said, "Fine, do that." And it was very complicated to shoot for a split screen, timed so exactly to get everything coordinated, always a script girl on the side counting 23, 24, 25, and they had screwups and had to do it all over a few times. And Stephen would say, "You and your triptych!" But that solved it. It made the thing possible. And then it was a pleasure to do.

THE RETURN OF DORTMUNDER AND PARKER . . .

LS: You've said the Parker novels were about "work." What would you say the Dortmunder series is "about"?

DW: I think the Dortmunder series is about one's worst expectations. When I thought of that title, *What's the Worst That Could Happen?* I thought, "This is not the title for the book, this is the title for the whole series."

LS: Dortmunder has disdain for modern technology. In the new book he looks at a fax machine like it's from outer space. Do you still work on a manual typewriter?

DW: Yes. But I love the fax machine, myself! Dortmunder's a bit more of a Luddite. Ha-ha.

LS: Fax machines aside, to what extent is he an alter ego?

DW: I am a bit of a pessimist, and all of my pessimistic beliefs are embodied in John. Damon Runyon said all of life is 6-to-5 against, and Dortmunder would kill for those odds.

LS: Would it be accurate if I said that, with a few exceptions, you've never cared to inject a lot of explicitly autobiographical elements into your work?

DW: I think it's just natural with me to do that.

LS: A lot of writers use a series character as a mouthpiece . . . so they can tell us all about their opinion of everything, their politics, their favorite breakfast cereal. It doesn't interest you?

DW: No. It's like . . . you're in a bar with a boring drunk. I would try not to do that. John D. MacDonald got to doing that in the Travis McGees and I was sorry to see him do it because he was such a taut, solid storyteller and that has to get in the way . . . Also, most of my opinions are subversive. No one is going to listen to them anyway, so I might as well keep quiet.

LS: *What's the Worst That Could Happen?* is the ninth Dortmunder since 1970. Has your approach to the series changed any in the twenty-six years since it began?

DW: Not very much. Only to the extent that . . . inevitably it has become an ensemble company. In the first couple of books it was Dortmunder and Kelp, really. Murch and Murch's mom and a couple of people would be around. But now . . . there are certain things that kind of have to be in there. They have to go visit the O.J. Bar and Grill. Tiny Bulcher, who wasn't in the first books, has to be there. I think the readers expect certain things from the books. Stations of the Cross. Not that it's a strain, I enjoy it. But I feel there are these signposts now, and that's the only difference.

LS: You don't do one every year. That must help to keep them fresh.

DW: Yeah. Every third book is a Dortmunder and I have no idea what's going to happen in the next one. That way I don't get self-indulgent. There are people who do a series and after a while they just do schtick. I have time so that the new book will be well out of my head when I start to do the next one.

LS: I'm sure a lot of people have asked you this, but will there ever be another Parker novel?

DW: Yes. I've done it. Warner Books is going to publish it next year.

LS: That's great . . . How . . . I mean, it's been over twenty years since the last one. What brought Richard Stark out of retirement?

DW: The fact is that I tried several times over the years . . . I tried four different times to write another Stark book. Finally, I just gave up. I don't know, I thought, "He's left me, for whatever reason." And then in '89, around the time I was writing the screenplay for *The Grifters,* I started another one. And I got half of it done, and it just stopped. I had like 124 pages, and stopped. And then in '91 I showed it to Otto Penzler at Mysterious Press and I said, "Will you tell me, one, does this read like a Richard Stark novel, you know, or does it read like a pastiche, somebody imitating himself? And number two, do you have any suggestions for me as to where the hell the thing goes from here?" And he read it and said, "Yeah, it sounds exactly like a Richard Stark novel." And he had a couple of suggestions about ways in which I had overly complicated the story in the first half, and if I got rid of this and that it might make it clearer. I said, "Yeah, that's great." I went ahead and redid it and still couldn't do it any farther. And then when I finished *What's the Worst That Could Happen?* I said to my wife, Abby, "You know, it's an odd thing, usually I know what I'm going to be doing next. A screenplay assignment or another book, a short story. But I have no idea what I'm going to do next and it's a funny feeling." And she said, "Why not take a look at that Richard Stark novel?" So, alright. I read it over, the portion that was there and I went, "Oh well, wait a minute, I know where this is going, another two chapters anyway. Let me try it." And it went on, and I did it, finished it. And Mysterious Press is going to do it next October.

LS: Can you tell a little bit of the premise? Is it a caper?

DW: It begins with—actually I don't want to talk about it a lot . . . but just to say that one of the problems that Parker begins to face is that there are fewer and fewer places in the world where there's cash. You know, computer crime is not his style . . . You know, he might hit you with a computer, but that's about it. And one of the last places where there's lots of cash is the big evangelistic preacher revival meetings. People make the "love offerings" and it's all in cash, a ton of it. And I suspected that Parker would not be a respecter of such places. So that's the setup: there's a stadium over there and there's an awful lot of cash in it.

LS: Do you have a title?

DW: *Comeback.*

LS: Will there be more?

DW: We made a three-book deal. And I've started the next one.

LS: That's wonderful news . . . And not a bad place for us to stop.

Janet Evanovich

INTERVIEW BY ADRIAN MULLER

J anet Evanovich burst onto the crime writing scene in 1994 with the
highly acclaimed One for the Money. *The book won various awards
and it marked the start of a series featuring Stephanie Plum, a young
New Jersey woman who decides to take up bounty hunting after losing
her job in a downmarket lingerie store. The film rights to the central character were sold shortly before* Two for the Dough *was published, and
since then Stephanie has made two further appearances in* Three to Get
Deadly *and* Four to Score.

After majoring in Art at Douglas College, New Jersey's State
University, Janet Evanovich initially put her efforts into a career as an
artist. After she married she stopped painting and took "a whole
bunch of really terrible jobs like Stephanie" to help finance her husband's university education. Then she became pregnant, had a
daughter, and later a son, and concentrated on being a mother. As the
children became older she started having more time to herself and
once again began looking for an artistic outlet.

Looking back Evanovich says, "In the interim of not actually
having a career I discovered it wasn't that I loved painting so much,
but that I just loved creating things. This was very enlightening to
me because it meant that, whilst looking forward to a career, I really
didn't need to restrict myself to being a painter."

Janet decided to try writing because she liked the idea of having a big audience. "When you do a painting a limited number of people will see this piece in the life of it. I had too much ego for that, I wanted to reach millions!" She chuckles before continuing, "I tried a lot of things and failed. I tried writing children's books, and I wasn't any good at that; I tried journalism, and I was really crummy at that; and then I decided—it was a bizarre idea—I would write a novel! I wrote this very strange book about a fairy who was living in this scary forest in Eastern Pennsylvania." Unsurprisingly that manuscript was turned down, as was her following one.

Knowing their children were looking forward to going to college, Janet realized that her husband's occupation, good as it was, would not be enough to pay the college fees. Unwilling to give up her writing for jobs she was not interested in, she did some research and came to the conclusion that she might break through by writing romantic novelettes. The market had a huge turnover and it was not necessary to have an agent.

"I had never read any romance novels because as an art major you don't read 'trash'. I went out and literally bought and read about a hundred romance novels, finding I liked them because they were fun, they were very positive, and they had a lot of good qualities. I analyzed them, trying to figure which ones I liked, which I didn't like, and what I wanted my book to be about. That was before deciding that I was going to try writing the short contemporary romances. Then I sat down, wrote one, and sold it!" Smiling at the memory of how easy it was she says, "I had become a romance writer."

Janet says it was a good place to start because, having no literary background, it gave her the chance to work with a lot of editors, thereby learning and improving her writing skills. She also gained maturity as an author and, by the time she started work on *One for the Money* five years later, she felt she had found her voice as a writer.

Working on her ninth romance—she wrote twelve—Janet became bored and wanted to branch out. Believing her style did not suit a long novel, she decided to continue writing genre fiction, which she felt was more appropriate for a shorter book. She had recently started reading crime fiction, discovering Robert Parker and Elmore Leonard, and realized it met many of her requirements.

"I was really influenced by Robert Parker because what I wanted to do was write a very fast, entertaining read, which is exactly what he was doing. He was writing these very simple, linear books, with snappy dialogue and an irreverent voice. I liked that. The other thing that appealed to me was that the PI novel is one of the few areas where it is acceptable to write in the first person. I really wanted to write in the first person because it was a good vehicle for my kind of humor, which has this very conversational tone."

With a grin Janet grudgingly admits that, in the expanding market of crime fiction, a further attraction was the prospect of her book reaching a very large audience. "Apart from good writing skills, finding a gap in the marketplace is what ultimately makes you a success. I felt like I could move into crime fiction, take some of the things that I knew I did really well as a romance writer, like sexual tension and physical humor, and use them in a mystery novel."

By now Janet had acquired an agent who suggested that, for her first crime novel, she write a police procedural. Feeling it would require specialist knowledge she did not have, Janet searched for over a year before finding a concept that suited her abilities. "My intention was to try to find something where I could come up to speed with my protagonist. I wanted to have some honesty in this character, just in terms of understanding her. Then, one day I walked through the den and my husband was watching *Midnight Run,* a movie about a bounty hunter starring Robert de Niro and Charles Grodin. I just immediately knew that's what I could do."

After finding out bounty hunters really existed, Janet managed to meet and talk to some of them but did not do any active research, "Because," she says, "nobody wanted to drag this middle-aged housewife around, chasing some guy who had shot people. I got to be friends with a couple of bounty hunters and tried to figure out what kind of people they were. It turned out that they fly by the seat of their pants, responding to all sorts of situations. They look at a bond agreement, see who's put up the bond, or trace people who are important to the felon. Then they start from there. They stake that person and wait for this guy to come visit his girlfriend."

Janet also went to Trenton, New Jersey, the location of the Plum books, and spent some time with the police. Apparently the area is not as crime-riddled as it is in her novels, and the author admits to having fictionalized some of the settings as well. "You don't want to invade people's privacy, and I also wanted to create my own world, but some things are pretty spot on. I get fan mail from people in New Jersey all the time saying they recognize places, so there must be something there."

Apart from *Midnight Run,* Janet also wanted to use some of the things that she liked best on television, and when borrowing from television she borrowed from the best! Most prominent is probably the influence of *Moonlighting.* "I looked at *Moonlighting* and I felt it just had a great formula. It looked like a mystery, it had all the structure of a mystery, but it was actually a romantic comedy. I loved the love/hate relationship between the two characters and that was one of the things that I set out to do in my book."

The love/hate relationship in the Plum series is between Stephanie and Joe Morelli. It all started when Stephanie was six years old and was not allowed to be the train when playing "choo-choo" with eight-year-old Joseph Morelli (it is worse than it sounds). Ten years later Joe strolled back into Stephanie's life and into the bakery where she worked, just long enough to take her virginity behind a case of chocolate eclairs. Her revenge came three years later when, driving her father's Buick, she clipped Joe and broke his leg. Stephanie's excuse that it was an accident has never been accepted because she jumped the curb in the car and followed Joe down the sidewalk.

When Joe jumps bail in *One for the Money*, he becomes one of Stephanie's first cases, hardly improving their relationship. Yet mutual lust is a hard thing to ignore, so surely it can only be a matter of time before they hit the sheets again?

"Well, I'm going to delay it as long as I can because I think that's the fun of it. What I discovered as a romance reader was that as soon as they actually did 'it', the tension was all over for me. The chase is what I like. So even if Stephanie and Joe ultimately do the deed it's not going to be a romance, something's going to go wrong somewhere along the line."

Further inspiration for the books comes from *Barney Miller*, *M*A*S*H*, and *Cheers*, not only for the humor, but for structure as well. "One of the things I realized was that these programs had a very large cast of characters which they could draw from. I looked at writers like Sue Grafton and Sara Paretsky, and I love their books, but they have their protagonist out there almost all by themselves. I thought this would make writing an arduous job. I couldn't imagine myself being so talented that I could carry a long-term series exclusively with this one person."

Apart from establishing the series' characters like Stephanie's parents, Grandma Mazur, (ex)prostitute Lula, and Stephanie's mentor Ranger ("This here's gonna be like Professor Higgins and Eliza Doolittle Does Trenton"), *One for the Money* focuses on Stephanie and Joe. The importance of the supporting characters becomes more apparent in *Two for the Dough* when Grandma Mazur has her moment in the limelight. Armed and ready, she knows how to draw attention.

"By using these characters, it helps me to make each book just a little bit different," the author explains. "I really was worried about making it boring for the reader, concerned that they would feel like they were reading the same book over and over again but with a different crime. I didn't want that to happen. So book number two, in losing some of the emotional impact of scenes in the first book, doesn't have some of the grit that the first one had, but I think it is very funny. Only time will tell if I'm successful, but I thought that by bringing out these different characters the whole tone of the books would reflect that, keeping the series fresh."

Stephanie & Co made their third appearance in *Three to Get Deadly*, published in the U.S. in 1996. In it, it is the reformed Lula who comes to the forefront, and Janet calls it her 'street book.' "The humor comes from Lula and her street mentality. She sort of puts Stephanie to shame with her bravado. She's just out there with her chest out front, when in reality she knows she's even less competent at bounty hunting than Stephanie is."

As the title indicates, *Four to Score* is the fourth in the Plum series. It finds Stephanie trying to track down a bail-jumping waitress while attempting to keep one step ahead of archenemy and rival bounty hunter Joyce Bernhardt. Not only is Lula back, but so is Grandma Mazur. If all of this is not troublesome enough, circumstances also force Stephanie to move in with Joe Morelli.

In the first two books some of the violent scenes felt very menacing and real, yet the author does not necessarily agree that female writers are better at portraying violence and its disturbing effects. "A lot of the people who have reviewed my books have said that they felt there was a theme running through them of violence against women," she says. "In fact it was not an intentional theme for me. I think maybe women are more vulnerable to violence, or maybe I should say that we look at them as being more vulnerable."

Turning to her male colleagues she says, "My two favorite authors right now are Robert Crais and Michael Connolly, and I frequently have a very strong sense of the danger when their protagonists are in jeopardy. Robert Crais had a fight scene in *Sunset Express* that has got to be the best I've ever read. I definitely was worried about this guy. So I'm not so sure if it's a gender thing rather than a male or a female writer being really good at their craft."

Stephanie is a big lover of junk food, frequently indulging in greasy take-outs, chocolate, and Rice Krispie Marshmallow Treats. Because of her appetite, it appears that Ms. Plum does gain the odd pound. "Stephanie has a hard time buttoning the snap on her pants, but she does keep pretty active." As for aging her characters, the author says Parker's Spenser was never the same for her from the moment he started wearing bifocals. "I'm not aging Stephanie at the rate that the books appear. There was a year and a half between the first book and second book, but in the storyline it's only months. I'm going to continue with that because I like this 'thirty' age. There's a lot of vitality to it. Stephanie still has all of these things in front of her so that she can be brash and have all of this bravado."

By now Janet Evanovich has a firmly established routine when writing her books. Getting up at around seven o'clock, she will have breakfast before walking her dogs. Saying her best time for writing is in the morning, she then works at her computer for four to five hours before breaking for lunch. Then she works out, or walks the dogs again, getting a little exercise before writing for the rest of the afternoon. In the evening she will help cook a meal with her husband and her son. If she is on schedule she will take the night off, but more often than not she has fan mail to answer. Plotting a book is equally well-established. "It takes me about a month to think about the plot, doodling and outlining it in my mind. By that time I know what the crime is going to be—that's the first decision I make. Then I decide who the bad guy is. At this stage I can usually see the beginning and the ending of the book. What I do then is to make a little time line. I know that my book is going to have approximately seventeen chapters, and about twenty pages to each chapter. Then, on a pad, I write maybe three or four sentences about each chapter. This is what I start from, and I revise as I go along. If I have real good quality writing time, where I'm not interrupted, then I think it takes me about five to six months to write one of the books."

One for the Money has been optioned for a feature film—and not inappropriately—the person working on the screenplay was a long-time scriptwriter for *Cheers*. Despite horror stories like *V.I. Warshawski*, Janet is not overly concerned about how the end product might look.

"My feeling is that nothing but good can come from a movie. I don't care if they change Stephanie Plum to a man or some little old lady. The book will still get all of the exposure that a movie gives. Then people go out and they buy the book and judge it on its own merit."

As to who might play her heroine, the author is unsure. Of the various actresses who have been suggested might play Stephanie— Michelle Pfeiffer (think *Married to the Mob*), Elizabeth Perkins, Marisa Tomei, and Sandra Bullock—only the latter strikes a cord, despite the fact that Bullock might be too young to play the thirty-year-old Stephanie. "Sandra Bullock might be a little young now, but by the time they get to make the movie she could be forty!" Janet Evanovich says, laughing.

In the meantime fans can kick back with the back-list of the Plum series and look forward to installment number five.

J. A. Jance

INTERVIEW BY RYLLA GOLDBERG

J. A. (Judy) Jance and I are definitely an odd couple, if one judges by appearances. She is tall, elegant, blonde; I'm short, no longer thin, and am learning to like gray hair. So much for looks. In the ways that matter, Judy and I have several things in common: we love stories (she tells them, I read them); we love hats and wear them often; and we both know what it's like to survive loving someone who is an alcoholic.

I met Judy nearly five years ago when I was working at an alcohol and drug abuse outpatient treatment center in Seattle. I was invited to be a guest co-host on "Straight Talk," a new radio talk show on the subject of recovery. The producer, a Philip Marlowe wannabe, accepted my idea of doing a piece about alcoholic fictional detectives who enter a recovery program. I suggested we start with J. A. Jance, whose protagonist, Seattle homicide detective J. P. Beaumont, was in treatment at an Arizona alcohol rehab ranch in Minor in Possession. I hoped she would talk about Beau's addiction and recovery. Happily, she was entertaining and articulate on the air (many people become monosyllabic when the mike is turned on) and the show was a wonderful success.

In the eleven years since Judy's first Beaumont book was published, her repertoire of mysteries has grown to include short stories in magazines and anthologies, three novels in her Arizona series featuring Joanna Brady, *and a baker's dozen of Beau's adventures (number thirteen,* Name With-held, *was released in January 1995).*

PS: Beau is still in recovery.

RG: You seem to enjoy the business side of producing books, and you participate in a variety of marketing and promotion activities here and elsewhere. Members of your family pitch in to help and they seem to enjoy it, too. Was it difficult at first for you to make the transition from writer to marketer? Since at any given time you are working ahead of—or even in a different series from—the book being promoted, do you have to remind yourself sometimes that *it's Tuesday so I must be in Rome?*

JJ: Actually, after ten years in life insurance sales, the initial transition was from marketer to writer and then back. I grew up in a large family, the daughter of a life insurance salesman and a full-time homemaker. I started in sales early—homemade jewelry, Girl Scout cookies, newspaper subscriptions, and all occasion greeting cards. In our family, selling was everybody's business with my mother dishing out the "leads" about new folks in town over the breakfast table. Once my first book was published, I took up where my mother left off. I'd do signings with my two kids—nine and ten—handing out brochures on the sidewalk or in the parking lot. To this day, either I or some member of the family calls our list—a two thousand-name data base—to announce the arrival of a new book and to invite people to the grand opening event.

And as far as juggling multiple balls, my ability to do that also comes from growing up in a large family. Living in a household with two parents and seven children with only one two-doored bathroom teaches focus in a way nothing else can.

RG: Speaking of promotion and travel, how much of the year do you spend thinking about, researching and writing a book compared to the amount of time required to market it? When your first book was published did you think it would be like this eleven years later, that so much time and energy would be spent to sell a book after all you went through to create it?

JJ: I think a lot of new authors come to this business thinking their responsibility ends once the writing and rewriting are all done. At the time my first book was published I had no idea how much of the selling job would be mine as well. For the first nine books, there was almost no publisher paid touring, and only one out-of-state trip to

L.A. Nonetheless, every book still had a minimum of thirty signings. Many of those were in the local Puget Sound area. The ones that weren't—Arizona, California, Oregon, and Idaho—were accomplished on our own time and our own nickel, often making use of my husband's hard-earned frequent flyer miles. The bottom line is that those initial signings, publisher supported or not, helped create my very local fan base.

Early on, the job was 50/50—fifty percent writing and fifty percent promoting, including speaking to any number of civic groups. Now, as the publisher picks up more and more of the slack, I'd say the division is more like sixty percent writing/forty percent spending time with my fans.

RG: Computer technology allows you to keep writing almost anywhere. How about the times when the plane is late, a road is closed, or some other obstacle forces a change in plans?

JJ: I have a little laptop that goes in and out with me. Actually, I was a very early adopter of laptop technology, starting with a dual floppy that I bought second hand from a real estate appraiser who wanted to unload the computer in favor of a pickup truck. Since then I've worn out three Toshiba laptops and have used them everywhere. When I bought my first computer in 1983, I could look up words in my dictionary faster than I could do it with the computer since I had to exit one program and call up another in order to use either the spell-checker or the thesaurus. In twelve short years, we really have come a long way, baby.

RG: Are you planning to distribute your books electronically, perhaps via a network or on CD-ROM? Do you think this method of distribution will be the norm in the future? Aside from copyright protection, which is a prime concern, do you think electronic distribution will open the flood gates to poor writing and leave better quality writing and paper publishers scrambling for markets and readers?

JJ: At this point, other than audiotaped versions of my books, I have no plans of stepping onto the information highway where I would no doubt end up as cyber roadkill. I use computers all the time, but right now I can't see how CD-ROMS will ever compete with an ordinary book for ease of use, privacy, and plain old convenience. I went on a weekend trip to a cabin once, expecting to do some last-minute editing on a manuscript. It turned out, though, that the cabin ran on propane and my computer did not. So, rather than working on my manuscript, what did I do instead? I read somebody else's book. The propane lights didn't make any difference when it came to reading words on the printed page.

RG: How do you manage your writing, family, and social schedules? Is this easier or harder to do now than it was when all or some of your children were home?

JJ: Friends and family are very important. Both my husband and I had first spouses who died in their early forties. We came away from those tough experiences with absolute knowledge that life is not forever, so if it comes to a choice between doing something with family and friends and doing work, family and friends are going to win every time. Between us Bill and I had five children when we married in 1985, and four of them were still at home. Now that they're all out on their own, scheduling—and mealtimes—are much easier to manage, but there were any number of books that were written in a household that contained a husband, four kids, three dogs, and no fence. Once again, growing up in a large family saved my life. I learned to concentrate by doing homework on a bench at the kitchen table with the ebb and flow of life swirling around me.

RG: You are very much a public figure in our community. Do you wish sometimes that you could be anonymous when you and Bill go out in public? For example, do restaurant owners or other merchants respect your privacy?

JJ: It is a little disconcerting to run into the grocery store in a pair of sweats and have people pointing me out over the stacks of fresh vegetables. It happened in Costco just this last weekend. Still, to have perfect strangers come up to you in the store aisle to tell you how much they love what you do is a real blessing. After all, there are lots of jobs where that *never* happens. For instance, whoever stopped a parking enforcement officer on the street to tell them how much they appreciate what the officer does?

RG: *Writer's Digest* recently asked a panel of published writers to name the "most influential writer of our time." A majority chose Ernest Hemingway. Which four or five writers have influenced you the most? Has that list changed in the years you've been writing fiction full time?

JJ: Reading Frank Baum's *Wizard of Oz* in second grade was enough to convince me that I wanted to be a writer. I was a voracious reader as a child, racing through the Nancy Drew, Hardy Boys, and Judy Bolton mysteries as well as every Zane Grey Western I could lay my hands on. I eventually went on to Mickey Spillane and John D. MacDonald. In terms of writing a series, I'd have to say that J. P. Beaumont owes a whole lot to MacDonald's Travis Magee.

RG: What books or which writers do you read now, compared to what you read before Beau entered your life?

JJ: James Lee Burke, Lawrence Block, Lindsey Davis. Right now, though, I'm lost in an eight-hundred-page Rosamund Pilcher. I think writing a series allows the same kind of connection to the characters that you get from one of those long family sagas. The only difference is, if you read in bed and fall asleep in the process of reading one of my books, you don't risk hurting your nose the way I might with Pilcher's *Coming Home*.

RG: Speaking of writers, were there other writers in your family before you? Are any of your children writing or being published?

JJ: I was the first person in my family to go to the university. My father attended a teacher's college for a year. One of his instructors encouraged him to consider doing some writing, but the Depression and any number of children precluded his following that advice. So perhaps, then, the genetic inclination was there, but so far none of my children is showing any particular bent in that direction.

RG: Who, besides writers, have been heroes to you or exerted the greatest influence on your life?

JJ: Because her vision was so poor and the family could not afford to pay for glasses, my mother was forced to drop out of school in seventh grade to go to work as a maid in Minneapolis. Despite her own lack of formal education, she encouraged me to get all I could out of school, including offering to let me skip some of the household chores in favor of taking extra classes in high school. Without necessarily realizing what she was doing, that tactic put me on a college prep track, and it's paid big dividends in the long run.

RG: Along with many of your readers, I believe *Hour of the Hunter* is the best novel you've written so far. Are you planning any other non-series books? If yes, when? If no, why not? How about writing in another form, such as a screen or stage play?

JJ: *Hour of the Hunter* was a real departure, and it's also my personal favorite. I've written a sequel, *Kiss of the Bees,* that is currently in a publishing scheduling limbo, but it will be out eventually. Meantime, both the Beaumont and Brady books continue apace, letting me do what I've always wanted to do, which is write books. As for screenplays or plays? I don't do windows and I don't do screenplays, either.

RG: The poems published in *After the Fire* are offered to anyone who is going or has gone through emotional trauma. The rage and pain were very real to you when you wrote them. (They have a healing effect on me.) But that was a dark time in your life. What about now? Do you use poetry to express the emotional highs, too? If yes, are you planning to publish any of these poems?

JJ: "I'll live with nothing rather than with less. The flame is out. There's nothing left but ash."

The emotional desolation in those words from the title poem speak to anyone who has loved and lost. You're right, the poetry was written at a very dark time in my life. Those bits of verse, jotted off on spare scraps of paper in the dark of night, acted as little pressure valves for me as I dealt with the grim realities of being married to a man who was dying of chronic alcoholism.

However, it was doing a poetry reading of *After the Fire* at a widowed retreat where I met Bill, my second husband. He and I have just celebrated our tenth anniversary, so I can assure you that the poetry had a very healing effect on my life as well. Writing poetry was a way of pouring out my soul at a time when no one was listening. Now, living a life that can best be described as happy as a clam with a loving, listening partner, I find that someone has turned off the poetry switch in my heart. I, for one, think that's just as well.

Margaret Yorke

INTERVIEW BY MICHAEL STOTTER

MS: I'd be interested to hear about your original motivation for writing.

MY: Telling stories. I always wanted to, even as a little girl of nine, scribbling in a notebook. I always wanted to be a novelist, and I am one! Not everybody grows up to be a train driver or whatever it is they wanted to do when they were nine years old. I had a certain facility with words, and I read a lot, and I always wanted to be a writer.

MS: Can you pinpoint a time with something you wrote which you thought, right, this is good enough to send to a publisher?

MY: Oh, no. I settled down and wrote a novel. I had written one novel which I have never submitted to a publisher because I had used people I knew in it to trigger off the idea and I was only about twenty-two when I wrote it. And I wouldn't dig that out now, because I don't suppose it's much good. I started to write a novel, which was eventually published as my second novel, in which I was trying to do something rather ambitious because it covered a span of years—these weren't crime novels. So I gave that up and wrote a book which was eventually published as *Summer Flight* but originally it was called *The Flower Show*. It was all about an escaped convict hiding in a village over the Bank Holiday weekend, at the time when they had the village flower show, and I thought that it would be rather amusing writing about the village flower show and what happened and all that. I also had the idea about the escaped convict hiding in the cellar of a house. In a very inexperienced, juvenile way it's the sort of thing I do now. I have several themes which I plait together but, of course, it was a suspense novel. It wasn't a whodunit. Then I went back to the other one I had begun and it was published, all of them published as romances, which they weren't, and I was very upset about this. If you've read any of them you'll discover that they are not, there may be a love story—it's not sentimental, definitely not Mills and Boon, and so they didn't meet the people who might have appreciated them. I sent *Summer Flight* to nine publishers and they turned it down, then my marriage broke up and I had a period of sorting myself out. Robert Hale took it, then of course I was under contract with them and they put me into this romantic slot, and I have to say that many, many years later John Hale was nice enough to say to me that was one of the worst mistakes he'd ever made. I didn't want to be put in this pigeonhole but I suppose he thought it wasn't strong enough to be put in the crime section. At that time they had Westerns, romance, and crime—so he put me into romance with a terrible jacket with some woman falling out of her shirt and a leering man, Rochester-like, in the background. Mortifying, because I had had so many rejections, but then they took the next three. I wrote *The China Doll*, which was a romantic thriller (it was romantic but definitely a thriller) and I tried to get that accepted under another name. After two or three rebuffs I decided to send it to Hale as my next novel because I needed the money. I was bringing up my children on my own. So again, that appeared as a romance but I think that was the last one I did with Hale. I went to Hutchinson, who had turned down *Summer Flight* with a very nice letter when I originally sent it to them. I sent it to the person who had signed that letter, and they took me on with *Once A Stranger*. But I wasn't any better off because they didn't publish me under the Hutchinson imprint, but under the Hurst and Brackett imprint, which was the romantic imprint of the day. I gave myself little exercises to do: I wrote books in the first person, or books taking place in the space of only a day. In one called *The Birthday*, the whole of the action took place on the birthday of this woman but by the end of the book you knew about everybody else involved. And that had a terrific review in the *Daily Mirror*, and a friend phoned and started reading it to me and I thought she was fooling. Not at all! Anyway, I continued like this until *The China Doll* was serialized in Norway and Sweden in two magazines and I got cheques for as much as two hundred pounds from those countries. A lot of money in those days. I then began to wonder if crime might pay. But I didn't think I could write a detective story because I thought you had to be very mathematical, which I'm not, but I thought, "I'll have a go," and so I wrote *Dead in the Morning*, which was the first crime novel.

MS: This was the first to feature Doctor Patrick Grant.

MY: I wrote it in 1969 and it was published in 1970. I thought if I write detective fiction I must have a sleuth who was someone I would like and whose work I could understand and identify with and all that. Also, I could not have a police sleuth because I am a great realist (at least I consider I am) and I wasn't going to write about something I didn't understand. My police procedure would have been hopeless because I wouldn't know what would happen to the body in the library. So I had my don—I had been working in various college libraries and was involved with Oxford life at the time, and I decided to write about it.

MS: Was he an amalgam of people you knew?

MY: Oh, no. Not at all. He's a total invention. I'm not saying that one doesn't do that, but it's a subconscious process when you create a character. I'm not saying that having met Jim Smith thirty years ago, the character in the book may not be like Jim Smith but it isn't a conscious process. I think that everything goes into a sort of mincing machine and out it comes at the other end. No, I was going to have an Oxford don because I knew about them; his subject had to be one I was very keen on, so he had to be a Shakespearean scholar, because I was very keen on Shakespeare but of course he was always one or two jumps ahead of me because he was an expert and I was just an enthusiast. I made him look like Gregory Peck in *To Kill a Mockingbird*—have you seen that? Yes, well from a female point of view you can look no further than Gregory Peck. His name came to me as Patrick just out of the blue, then I had to think what his surname was going to be and my eye fell on the bottle of Grant's whiskey, so he became Patrick Grant. Then I checked that there wasn't a Patrick Grant of that age on the Oxford list and went ahead with him.

MS: And he survived for five books.

MY: Yes, he still survives. I gave him up and it was very lucky that I did. I was absolutely entranced by him, he was great company for me when I was writing the books. There I was starting a book, and there was Patrick looking like Gregory Peck to be my companion throughout the book. What more could you ask? But he started off as about thirty-four or thirty-five, Dean of St. Mark's College, Oxford; what was going to happen when he got older? He had a sister who had a little son and eventually had a daughter; they grew older and so did the sister but what about Patrick? He didn't seem to be getting any older, and his love life seemed troubled, and I didn't want to marry him off to anybody because that was the knell of death for a hero like that. But I also found it very limiting; when I finished a Patrick Grant book I felt thoroughly stimulated, like someone who had completed the whole crossword, not one word missing. Whereas now I feel rather wrung out because my characters have had such an awful time and I've suffered all the way with them. Because I was doing a whodunit I had to conform to the pattern with the red herrings, and the four or five suspects, which in real life is very improbable. Because I was really interested in writing about people, which I had wanted to do when I was this little girl filling up her notebooks, and thought I'd been doing in my earlier novels; I didn't like this juggling you had to do to make people act out of character in order to prop up the plot. Several of the Patrick Grant books concentrated on a particular setting because as a don off he could go to Greece and other nice places and he'd go skiing and so on. The stories were contrived. Then I got the idea for *No Medals for the Major.*

MS: That was a change in your style. I found that the Patrick Grants were very dialogue-driven and now there was a change to being narrative-driven.

MY: That would be a fair assessment. I had the idea of somebody like Major Johnson living in a village, like this village, walking down a street, like this street which is typically English with cottages and all that. He had come to live in the village having retired from the army, wanting to make his mark, settle in, and be a pillar of the community. And he perceived himself as quite a dapper chap still, quite a smart-looking man walking through the village but what the observer saw was an elderly man, short and rather plump and not this dashing figure he perceived himself to be.

MS: There's this perception of how we would like people to see us.

MY: Yes, and also people act a role. For instance, if I'm giving a talk, I'm Margaret Yorke, and on this platform I'm this writer woman standing there. I used to be very nervous, and I had to get myself into this gear, hair done, as nicely dressed as possible, but now it's automatic because I'm so ancient . . .

MS: You're more relaxed with yourself.

MY: Well, yes. It's not as though it's not a challenge and you don't get a little rush of adrenaline because you do. You've got to do your best because they've come to hear you, and you want them to be interested and so on. It's rather like driving a car, you've done it before so you can do it again, sort of thing. But when you get in that car, you are the driver of that car, not someone pushing a shopping trolley down the street or wheelbarrow down the garden. You are in a role—even if it's just as a car driver. But if it's a more demanding role, like the president of a company, when you get into the office you are that president, not the father who's just left his children and his wife at home. In different sections of your life, different parts of you are called on to fulfill the role you are asked to do at that particular time. So I write about that a certain amount. An awful lot of it is automatic. I don't really analyze very much what I do, I don't think.

MS: Is that something you leave to other people?

MY: Yes. Anthony Price doesn't analyze his work either. He says it's rather like taking a watch to bits to see how it works. You can't put it together again.

MS: What fascinates you about writing about rural crime rather than urban?

MY: Because it's what I know. Except for living in the suburbs of Dublin as a child and in Solihull for a bit when I was first married, I have always lived in the country. And I just don't know enough about urban life. I do believe in "write what you know." Some people are successful in writing about what they don't know, they seem to be able to do it. But if I were to set a whole book in an inner city I would make a mess of it because I'm not familiar enough with that culture.

MS: Do you think your story lines would change if you lived in town?

MY: Yes, I do. But I wouldn't be happy living in town. Yes, they would have to because I am restricted by the fact that I don't have a day job, and I don't have anybody coming home who's got a day job.

I've got a son and a daughter who are both working, my son's in business and my daughter's a teacher, and I've got four grandchildren. My grandchildren keep me abreast of what goes on with young people and I can ask them anything. And if they know, they'll tell me. They range in age from nearly thirteen up to twenty. Which is very useful because to a certain extent it keeps me up with the times.

MS: I find that your characters are a mix 'n' match between the generations.

MY: I do deliberately try for that. I don't think I settle down and work out that I've got to have an oldie, middle-aged, younger, and a child. I don't do that. I think of my plot and my central characters and might think, "Have I got somebody in such-and-such an age group, and if not should I put somebody in who is not going to be superfluous and who will contribute to the plot?" But that's a minor consideration. After all, if you're reading a book about a child, for instance, think of *Oliver Twist* or something like that, you can identify perfectly well with the little boy even though you are an adult. If you're reading about a character who's in a different age group than yourself, and if it's well done, although you won't be personally identifying with that person, you will identify with them because you'll say this is what it must be like to be this old man or something. I had this illness, an overactive thyroid, during which I suffered from very severe muscular failure. I was only about fifty-two or fifty-three. I couldn't nip out of the way of traffic in the road and I had an awful job going upstairs and so on. I thought, this must be what it's like to be really old and dilapidated. In the book I was writing at the time, *The Scent of Fear*, I was able to describe the lack of mobility of this elderly person because although I was much younger myself, I was experiencing it.

MS: Again, this is going back to writing about what you know.

MY: Yes, but you can make a huge imaginative leap and it may work. But there are certain imaginative leaps that you can't make. For example, if I set a book in Central Africa, where I've never been, what a failure it would be! Then you can point a finger at me and tell me about Harry Keating, we all know that. Also long, long ago there was a woman named Elizabeth Goudge who wrote about New Zealand. They were historical novels with a slightly romantic tinge, and they were very, very good. And she had never been to New Zealand in her life, she had read it all up. You can say that Ellis Peters hadn't lived in medieval days. It's imagination linked to a great deal of research. Possibly if I immured myself in a library with twenty books about Central Africa and some films and stuff, I might be able to do it.

MS: From meeting your readers over the years have you considered why they find the crime novel so interesting?

MY: I think readers like crime novels because they tell a story. You have to have a beginning, middle, and end. Whereas lots of modern novels don't tell a story at all, they're all about the inner meditations of their characters, and pretty boring some of them are. Full of self-pity and self-analysis and stuff. I mean, you get some of that in a crime novel, but you've got to have a story that moves on. You can write a couple of wonderful pages of description, then you look at it and you think, "What a splendid piece I wrote there." But is it necessary? Is it moving the story along? Or is it necessary because it's contributing to the background of our comprehension of these people? If the answer to the second question is yes, then keep it. But if it isn't serving a function and you are just having fun, cut it out.

MS: Do you find yourself being ruthless on editing?

MY: I used to find it difficult at first. Then there was a period when I was being published by Hutchinson when they wouldn't let me write more than 60,000 words. Mine ran out to 75,000 and I had to cut them. In the end I was probably allowed 63,000. Which I thought was wrong of them but on the other hand people comment on my spare style. Well, that's where I got it from, I expect. Everything that wasn't strictly germane had to come out. But now I can be as long as I like. But the sort of thing I write you can't sustain for more than 90,000 words, I think. You know when you're repeating or waffling; or there may be a subplot which you don't need because it's taking away from your main plot. Of course you can have several subplots, but you've got to decide if you want this little one you've just thought up, or keep it for another book.

MS: You've been quoted as being perpetually on the lookout for interesting aspects of contemporary life to explore. What is the key that hooks you into this?

MY: I might read something in the paper, or someone might tell me something about an experience they knew of. Or I might see a television documentary. I do try, always (without sounding pompous), to have a serious thought, some theme, some subtext that I want my readers to have pass through their heads, whilst at the same time I hope they are absorbed by the story. For quite a while I had one of the deadly sins in each book; that kept me going. Because I have my ingredients, you see. I start off with these various strands; for example, in *Intimate Kill* I had the strand of sloth, because Marcia was very slothful and was murdered as a result. And I had the frivolous idea about the garden gnomes because I couldn't think of anything much to write about and at that time the garden gnomes had just demonstrated outside the Chelsea Flower Show because they weren't allowed in! Ah, you do laugh! I often use that in my talks. So I thought I'd find out about gnomes. So there was my research under way, Stephen was in prison for murdering his wife. This book was a watershed. I then started getting interested in penology because the book was going to begin when Stephen got out of prison. But I suddenly realized that I would have to know what had happened to him in prison, and what the release system would be and all this before I could start. That led me into the anomalies in the law (we can think of several without trying too hard). In *Almost the Truth* I picked up on the very inequitable system of sentencing rapists. Although they are tightening up now, it is quite usual for someone who committed rape to get a lighter sentence than his fellow burglar.

MS: If they get sentenced at all.

MY: Yes. Equally at the same time there is the converse where false accusations of rape are hard to disprove, and I take that up in *A Question of Belief.*

MS: With those two novels you are seeing two sides of the same story. When you were writing *Almost the Truth* it was from the female point of view and its effects on the victim, and in *A Question of Belief* it is Philip's viewpoint.

MY: But I didn't think of them at the beginning as a pair that I was going to do like that. I'd written *Serious Intent* in between, and in that I wanted to write about the question of children being brought up by men who are not their natural fathers. In *Serious Intent* I have four boys, none of whom is living with his natural father. One is the child of a single mother; he knows nothing about his father. Two are a pair of brothers with a very kind stepfather, and they resent him and make his life absolute hell. The fourth boy's widowed father marries a very nice woman, so he has a very kind stepmother. Then his own natural father dies, he's left with his kind stepmother but he is angry because he has lost both of his natural parents. And he's the one who is on a bit of a slippery path. Then somebody who's been in prison comes into the district and that's the criminal trigger, the catalyst in the lives of all the other people in the story. You asked about the popularity of crime fiction. I think it is a very moral form of writing. I regard that as very important. If you glorify an antihero and hold up someone who is a rapist, a torturer, a really bad person as a hero, you are doing an immoral thing, in my view. Some fellow practitioners don't share that opinion but I couldn't go on writing if I didn't take a moral stance. You can have a frightful, violent person as the central character in the plot but the fact that the author thinks this is a bad idea has to shine through—in my view. I can try to explain why it may be happening but I must not be seen to be extolling it. Anyone who reads a book by me will know that at the end, in one way or the other, justice will be done. The villain, male or female, will go down, maybe not caught by the police, but in some way. I'm not saying that everyone will be happy ever after because that's not what life is all about. I am merely trying to illustrate certain things about life that concern me today. For instance, I think it's distressing about divorced families and the problems they have, but in many, many cases a good job is being made of the rearranged family. In other cases, it isn't. I think a lot of people don't realize how difficult it is when they embark on a new pairing. They think everybody's children will muck in together. Why should they? It's the parents who have taken to one another, not the children. If the children just happen to get along they are very lucky. Then you get all these single girls and their babies and it's so distressing. I don't think it's fair to say that they get themselves pregnant to get themselves a flat, but I'm sure some of them do.

MS: Something you share with Harry Keating and others is the violence, or rather non-violence, whereby you are not interested in describing it. There are other modern writers who love going into the minutiae of wounds.

MY: I don't think this is necessary. I don't think my readers want to read this. I don't want to write it. If someone had been murdered and they've been stabbed, unless it's internal bleeding, there's going to be a terrible lot of blood all over the place. I'm not in the business of shocking somebody, it's the consequences of this that I want to show you. That it's the horror of what has happened, not just to the victim that's been killed, but their family, everyone that's associated with them. The shock to the police. Maybe it's the young constable who happened to be first on the scene who's got to get used to all this. If either you or I happen to be the first on the scene, even I, tough old girl that I am, I think I would find it quite horrifying. Later on I think I'd like to be given a nice glass of brandy, thank you. I think we'd find it very distressing.

MS: I had to admire the way you write on the ripple effects of crime, of how it affects other people. Like a stone being dropped in a pond, the ripples are wide-spreading rather than insular.

MY: That sentence, about dropping the stone into the pool and the ripples going out, was in one of my novels at the end of one of those very early books. For a grown-up person, to be earning her living by writing horror is not on. My eldest grandson when he was about ten said, "Why do you write horror stories?" I said, "But I don't." I told him the story of *No Medals for the Major* in simple terms, and then I said, "Now that's not a horror story, is it?" And he said, "No." So I said, "Well, that's the sort of thing I write." The ending is quite dramatic; Harry Keating thought I'd made a mistake about the ending and Elizabeth Ferrars did, too. But it was the only ending I saw I could have at the time.

MS: To tell you the truth, I was surprised, too.

MY: You see his honor—the Major's—had been impugned. Elizabeth Ferrars thought he was a brave man and he wouldn't have done this. If I wrote that book today, I don't know if I would take such a stance at the end. At the time, it seemed to me that is what he would do. And I think that same man now might not take the same way out. Written as it was, more than twenty years ago, that seemed to be the way it had to be. But writing that book was very exciting because all those minor characters took on their lives and they just told me what to do. But it was very simple compared with what I'm doing now.

MS: Do you believe that your characters actually lead you through your stories?

MY: Yes, I do. I would think, "What would so-and-so do now?" And then he or she would tell me. So they just simply reveal their lives to me. I just set them up in the beginning.

MS: Do you ever compile a character profile?

MY: No, I know them. Of course I write down their names, and if they have children their children's names and so on. They're real people. I sit there and I meet that person. They're terribly real to me. I never profile—I'm not doing an ice cream cornet with a bit of chocolate and a bit of strawberry and a bit of vanilla.

MS: Once you've got your main idea of a book together, you always weave in a sub-theme of something that is of interest to you, don't you? In *A Question of Belief* it was about animal rights; is this something that worries you?

MY: The rent-a-mob bit worries me very much, yes. I don't question the sincerity of some people but, as with the road-protesters, you get this group of genuine protesters—whether you agree with what they are doing or not, you have to respect that they are sincere, but you get the rent-a-mob who really have nothing much to do, so they go and live in a tree. I can see that if the alternative is sleeping rough under a bridge at Waterloo or something, it's better to be up a tree. I'd prefer to be up a tree, too. I think society has become very confrontational now and if you have a point you wish to raise with somebody, instead of discussing it in a calm manner one side or another may become pugilistic. I think we get it from the radio, every interview, people aren't allowed to give their views, they are interrupted, they're shouted down. This permeates into every area of society. If you are against hunting or whatever, and you injure the horses or the hounds, who are you considering? A fox is being chased and you've got every right to be against that but not to the extent of hurting the hounds, horses, or most of all, the humans.

MS: That was brought up by Dennis, the town boy character.

MY: Yes, you see he was fascinated by the country. He's never really been there and suddenly he sees all this space around him. I got very fond of him. His friend Biff gets carried away by all the excitement of the moment (and a few beers) and Dennis can't understand why it's okay to hurt the horses when you're supposed to be concerned about the fox.

MS: There is a similarity here with the criminal in *Almost the Truth*. Where he is bundled up in the boot of the car and the line there is that he had never been to the seaside before. And here he was on a cliff edge! It seems a recurring theme, that your urban criminal hasn't been around as much as he thought he had. He may be streetwise but not countrywise.

MY: Of course you would notice that probably having read my books close together, in a way I wouldn't have because I write them further apart. Of course I repeat ideas, and someone'll say I'm awfully keen on the outdoors, which I am! Fortunately I'm active still, I love the country and I would hate to live in town.

MS: That's reflected in your characters with their love of gardening or antiques.

MY: I'm not very knowledgeable about antiques. I've got people I can ask about them. But you can see where I live, it's a lovely village and I've lived in this house for twenty-five years, and before that for five years in another house at the end of this village. Then before that nine years in a neighboring village. I did a lot to those houses, I improved the gardens. Then when I came to this house I reckoned on staying here, which I have.

MS: What are your main worries when you start a book?

MY: Oh, what am I going to write about? Panic! Panic! One day you have to sit there with a blank piece of paper and you've got to start.

MS: Do you start off with a detailed synopsis?

MY: No. I tend not to have a synopsis at all. No, no synopsis at all because I don't know what's going to happen. As I think of them, I write down who the people are. It's fun finding out, you see.

MS: And you find out through your characters and situations.

MY: Yes. Sometimes you're totally stuck and you think, "Well, have we got the police involved? What would they do now, or is it the moment to bring them in?" Or if I'm stuck with one lot of characters, I go to another group, and maybe the second group of characters will react on my first group, and I'll know what they will do next. But I'm just at the end of the first draft of the book I'm doing now and I don't know how it's going to end. I think I've got about twenty pages or so to do. Very exciting.

MS: Does this way of writing create writer's block?

MY: Oh, yes. I expect I get blocked all the time! I don't go around tragically mopping my brow saying I've got writer's block! Every year I get quite down until I've got quite a lot of pages piling up and my family ask how's it going and I say I don't know what it's going to be about, and they say you always say that and you always manage to do it. And I do. As long as that can carry on, that's all right. When you've written as many books as I have, I don't want to repeat myself. Of course my attitudes will be repeated, and you mentioned the one-liners and my attitude to the country and all that. That is bound to be repeated because that is me. That's how I am. I can only write the sort of book I am capable of writing because my experiences are limited. You get younger writers (because nobody very young ever writes crime novels) and they've had their day job, which is more dramatic than working in a library, which I did. I was still at school when the war began. Then I was in the Wrens for three years. I've got the experience of the war. I do realize that I have a tendency to have elderly people in the books who have been very much affected by their war experiences, and I think I must watch this and cut it down a bit because it's going to be boring for the young. You have to accept that for anyone who went through the war, as I did, in whatever capacity, their entire life afterwards has been affected. And the same with the people in the Falklands. When that happened I got very depressed, and I discovered that a lot of people of my generation were very, very dispirited over all that because we'd seen it all before. We'd seen those ships sailing out, we knew that people were going to be killed, we just knew. Looking back, my mother was a young woman in the First World War and how on earth did she cope with this a second time? When she was a young woman practically every young man she knew was killed.

MS: I believe that's reflected in the different generations of writers. You're writing about what you know and the younger generation are writing about what they know. Writers around thirty or forty are just beginning to live and have different ideals as well.

MY: Yes, absolutely, and young writers have such expertise. Take Francis Fyfield, who is a lawyer; that's a very big area for writing crime novels. Because it's all there—you've got cases you've dealt with, you know how the law works, all the things I have to find out. And you get policemen turning into thriller writers—with the same advantage. There's Dick Francis with his horse racing expertise that he's used to great effect. I'm sure crime novels will go on and they will evolve because the people who write them will have a different sort of experience. Take Kate Charles, her experiences with the Church. She's very expert in her novels, and D.M. Greenwood does the same sort of thing. You get dons writing novels because they know about college life and all that. One is restricted; it's a bit late for me to sign on with the police and have a few years' experience!

MS: You mention that you have researched the anomalies with our legal system and have been active in gathering information to a previous murder case. I can see this in *A Question of Belief* with the Philip Winter character—unjustly accused of rape and the consequences involved.

MY: Yes, that's right. You've only got the evidence of that woman, and in that case she was advised not to bring the case because the police thought it was a bit iffy. What triggered that off was that a man I knew was accused of sexual harassment and lost his job, and I thought it can't be right, he couldn't possibly be sexually harassing these people, I don't believe it for a moment. I met that person later, after it had been in the paper, and he was absolutely a shadow, I scarcely knew him. He had been totally destroyed. I was haunted by this, I knew I had to write about this. And this was just harassment. I knew it was no good just having sexual harassment, I had to have something stronger, so it had to be a rape case for the book.

MS: Quite a few of your viewpoints, or your characters' viewpoints, are women's observations rather than a male's point of view. I might be good at describing a car but no good at describing a woman's attitude. Do you find that there is a difference between women and men crime writers?

MY: Yes, of course there is. I think women have an eye for detail, maybe domestic detail and that sort of thing. It would be a fair statement to say that I don't have enough dominant male characters in my books. But I have a lot of young males in the books. Because I've lived on my own for a long time, I don't have a big circle of middle-aged men who work in offices whose knowledge I could tap into. I wish I did know more about how business operates so that I could take you into an office and have several men reacting. But I can't do that and I might get it wrong and so I don't. I actually write a lot about cars because I like cars. I was a driver in the Wrens. Again you might find a man might fall down over some aspect of female characterization. However well he got on in women's company, how much he thought he knew about women, there could be a weakness. It's foolish to write about something you think you're going to make a hash of—so don't write about it. I enjoy researching, but the difficulty is the time factor. You get interested in the subject. For example, I've got some books on dolls' houses because someone in the book I'm writing at the moment has got an old dolls' house. I haven't got enough about dolls' houses in it at the moment. I'll probably put more in when I revise, but at the same time it's only a side issue, rather like decoupage for Marigold Darwin in *Serious Intent* because I thought, "She's got to have a hobby, what should she do?" A friend of mine said make her do decoupage, and that seemed a good idea. I had to read up on that, you see.

MS: It lends authenticity to the novel. As long as you know about that character and you are confident about writing on the character it will come through.

MY: It's like an iceberg. Only a little shows on top; much more is hidden. You know more than you tell. At the same time, you mustn't get so carried away by what you've been researching that it takes over the whole book. Then you'll start writing a different book. Also, if I pick up a legal theme, I must check on it, but I mustn't belabor the poor reader with it. I must give them just enough. If they don't pick it up—it's all right.

MS: What is your personal favorite book?

MY: *No Medals* and *The Scent of Fear.* I was so fond of Major Johnson and so fond of Mrs. Anderson.

MS: Do you have a typical working day?

MY: It all depends on what stage of the book I'm at. If I'm revising then I can put a lot of time in at the desk and do twenty pages a day. But if it's new work, I used to do 3,000 words a day—I don't do that now. If I've done 2,000 I consider that to be a good day. I find now that I spend far longer on the first draft than I used to and the revision goes much more quickly. This pattern has changed very much in the last seven or eight years. I used to do the first draft in five or six weeks because I had this feeling that I had to keep going because I'd lose my idea and I'd lose the immediacy of it. Somehow or other now I put it right as I go along instead of waiting to do it at the revision stage. If I anticipate research I do it at first, of course, but then things crop up. In the book I'm doing now there are one or two things to look into before I can finish. A few phone calls, maybe a trip to the library. A call to the coroner's office will answer one question.

MS: And do some of your friends come to the rescue?

MY: Yes, I was having problems researching the regulations for a research establishment in *A Question of Belief.* A doctor friend gave me the information I needed. The research labs are strictly controlled and I had got it totally wrong and I had to rewrite whole chunks of the book.

MS: I've asked Harry Keating and Michael Gilbert about the future of crime writing and they're saying it's moving into a more psychological field but you're there already. Are you staying there or . . .

MY: I'm staying there! If I get a sudden idea of something new, I would do it. Oh, yes. But I think it's unlikely that I'll get such an idea now because I expect my thinking is slightly channelled into a certain way. I might suddenly wake up one morning and want to write a book about so-and-so, and if I thought it was a good idea, and strong enough, I would do it. Just as I did with *No Medals* all those years ago.

Carl Hiaasen

INTERVIEW BY CHARLES L. P. SILET

I n his introduction to Fawcett's republication of John D. MacDonald's
first novel, The Deep Blue Good-By, *Carl Hiaasen admitted a kinship with MacDonald's bittersweet view of South Florida and Mac-
Donald's passion for inveighing against "the runaway exploitation of
this rare and dying paradise." For anyone familiar with the work of both
writers it is easy to see why Hiaasen responded positively to MacDonald's
passion and to understand why he has taken up MacDonald's mantel. Hiaasen's books are more humorous and less sexist, of course, and deal with
up-to-date environmental problems, and moreover, they do not have an
on-going series character like Travis Magee, but the indignation is still
there, as is the sorrow over the human despoliation and waste of what was
once truly a paradise.*

*Carl Hiaasen began his writing career as a high school journalist who
published an underground newsletter that took on the high school administration and provided an alternative to the local school paper's preoccupa-
tion with fluffy social gossip. He continued to report the unpopular news
(especially about the Vietnam War and the Nixon Presidency) for the university newspaper at Emory and later at the University of Florida. While
a freshman he was asked by his writing instructor to help a local doctor
ghost write his reminiscences into novel form, and Hiaasen got his first
taste of fiction writing. One of the books was later made into a popular
film,* Doc Hollywood.

Once he was out of school he began his apprenticeship as a reporter, eventually landing a job with Florida's premier newspaper, the Miami Herald, *where he now writes a widely syndicated column that often rather savagely attacks the same despoilers of Florida's natural wonders that so incensed John D. MacDonald. In his early days at the* Herald *Hiaasen collaborated on three other novels, books he has described as "conventional thrillers," with a colleague on the paper. By the time he came to do the first of his Florida books, Hiaasen already had considerable novel writing experience.*

Since the publication of Tourist Season *(1986), Carl Hiaasen has written six very funny, often very dark, even at times splenetic books, about the various ways Florida's natural wonders have been violated. Many of his plot ideas come directly from his columns, although he admits that some of the news material is frankly just too bizarre even for his fiction. Hiaasen's novels, for all their humor, also carry a serious message, and like such satirists as Swift and Twain before him, the humor often masks a deeply and passionately held anger over human folly. On a national morning talk show he once remarked that there was nothing wrong with South Florida that a good force-five hurricane couldn't cure.*

CLPS: I want to talk a little bit about how you got into writing fiction. You wrote a couple of novels with Dr. Neil Shulman and collaborated on some thrillers before your current run of crime books.

CH: Well, Shulman and I worked together. When I was a freshman at Emory, one of my professors said, "Look, there's a doctor here who has written a bunch of stories and chapters plus little anecdotes about what happened in his life, and he's not a writer but he wants to get the material organized and put into novel form with a narrative thread and a story line." I'd never done anything like that before, but I always loved books and I always knew I wanted to write novels so I helped Neil with that first book. We organized the material and added some characters, just really made a novel out of it instead of sort of a collection of yarns. His name is on the book. They're his stories. I did another book with him just a couple of years later and again his name is on it. The second one was made into the movie *Doc Hollywood,* which came out a few years ago. Then I did three novels a few years later with a reporter friend, Bill Montalbano, when I was with the *Herald,* which were really conventional potboilers as they would have to be since they were written in a collaboration. They're very tightly plotted, and we wrote different sections of the book, sort of alternating eight or nine chapters each. To do that you have to have it plotted pretty well. Because Bill was a foreign correspondent, he was often traveling and it was a real tricky deal, but we did three together, they were all published and did pretty well. I learned a whole lot about plot and characters and also about the publishing business. I've been very lucky they've been all good experiences for me.

CLPS: Why did you decide to branch out on your own as a novelist?

CH: The novels I did with Bill were fine, but they involved a continuous compromise. We have different writing styles, but we have similar editing sensibilities so it wasn't hard to work the manuscript into a single voice. We were a success when nobody knew us or knew who wrote what. Bill and I knew but nobody else did, nobody could tell. But you want to write your own stories and novels, and I wanted to do much more personal books and I think Bill had the same feeling. You have to get your own voice and you can't get that collaborating with someone. Maybe nonfiction is not quite so difficult but in fiction it's extremely difficult. We were lucky because we were friends and we had a newspaper background, which gave us thick hides so we could edit each other rather brutally without any consequence, but not everyone is capable of that. I would not recommend it.

CLPS: Where did *Tourist Season* come from?

CH: It was a kind of story I wanted to tell and a lot of it had been building up I think. I just really wanted to cut loose and have some fun, and it seemed logical to make the main characters newspaper people, or ex-newspaper people, although I wasn't writing a column at the time. I invented the character Skip Wiley, who is central to that book. I was still on the investigations' team when I began the book and halfway through it the paper gave me the column. It was interesting because people are always asking, "Did you model the crazy columnist in *Tourist Season* after yourself?" I try to tell them that he was introduced as a columnist before I was. If anything I maybe modeled myself after him.

CLPS: But Brian Keyes is an ex-reporter.

CH: He's an ex-reporter and he's sort of the flip side of Skip, in a sense. I've seen people go many ways after many years in journalism. I can identify with someone who goes around the bend, especially someone, like Skip, who really loves Florida and just can't stand the way it is being exploited anymore. I can also identify with the guy that just can't stand walking up to the house, knocking on the door and telling someone that their kid just got killed, that kind of thing. I can understand why someone would walk away from that, and it doesn't have anything to do with guts or spine, it's just some people aren't suited for that nasty work and that's Brian, that's the other side of Skip.

CLPS: How about the eco-terrorism?

CH: That was just a young Floridian's fantasy: Anything to get the cars headed the other way on I95 would be lovely. It was just a great way to work that into a suspense plot. It was a little extreme for its time, but it certainly is an idea or a notion that a lot of Floridians are vicariously plugged into.

CLPS: In *Double Whammy* you take on big-time bass sport-fishing and land developers.

CH: I'd been getting clippings on all the scandals and cheating and even, in one case, a homicide that were involved in professional bass fishing tournaments. I grew up bass fishing the Everglades out of inner tubes, in little John boats, but now they have these $20,000 rigs and the ESPN Saturday Morning Fishing Show. They are just hilarious. My son, who loves to fish, and I always used to watch the shows, and they were just outrageous. Sponsorships were turning the sport into the NASCAR circuit. I just thought it was a suitable allegory for what was happening in the country in the eighties. There's incredible lust, greed, backstabbing, cheating, and skullduggery all over a stupid fish. It was wonderful, and I had to do it. It was just quite logical. I knew that it wasn't very commercial at the time, but it was the sort of thing that was perverse enough to appeal to me. I mean, bass fishing? The book really wasn't about bass fishing, but the publishers didn't have any idea how to promote a book like that. I was proud of getting that one published, that was a tough book to get out. It was a hard story line to sell, really. So that's where that one came from. When I began writing I knew that I wanted each of the books to be very distinct from the others. They've all been set in Florida obviously because that's the only place I know, but the setting of them (I don't want to use the word target) would be different whether it was cosmetic surgery, theme parks, bass fishing or whatever. I wanted them to be different enough so that the books wouldn't blur together in people's minds which is so typical when you have a continuing detective, a Joe Blow character, and you're cranking out a book a year, which I never intended to do anyway. It's real easy to lose track of the books and your readers start to lose track, too, and they become sort of a blur for the readers. "Did I read this one, didn't he just have one out?" I know this even from reading writers that I'm crazy about, when I find that I'm swamped and I've lost track of what I've read and what I haven't read.

CLPS: Tell me a little bit about Skink and Jim Tile.

CH: Skink started as a character who was only going to be around for a couple of chapters in *Double Whammy*. I didn't really think I'd use him again, and then I liked him so much, and he said things and did things that I liked so I decided to keep him around. And the more he was around the more I liked him. Very selfishly I decided that he really had a bigger role to play, and then I got such an incredible response to him from the people. But I resisted the idea initially of ever bringing him back. He was useful to me in *Double Whammy* and especially in sort of the environmental and conservation mode, because he could get away with things, say things, do things either I haven't been able to or would like to be able to do. And also coming from him, if I was careful in the writing, there wasn't so much preaching and crusading in the books; it was more indignation and outrage. He got his message across without really stomping up on his soap box too often, which I liked. Readers liked him. They plugged in right away, I guess, because of his militant side or at least his craziness. There's such affection for him, more than for any other character I've written, and I like him, too. I've got to admit I like it when he's around. He's in *Stormy Weather* but I honestly don't know if I'm going to bring him back again. I thought I couldn't very well have a hurricane without this guy. This is an event he's probably been waiting and dreaming about for a long time, and I really like the idea of him getting strapped to the tallest bridge of the Keys waiting for the storm to hit, just to experience it. Again, I'm not making a comparison for my skills and Melville's skills, but I thought of it almost in the way that Ahab was lashed to the whale. Skink wants experience, up close and personal, of a really big hurricane. The scary thing is that I understand that feeling totally. A hurricane is a majestic thing if you can divorce yourself from fears and worrying about your homeowners insurance and power lines coming down. If you could just look at it as a force of nature, it's an extraordinary thing. It's an incredible engine of water and wind which comes up out of the Caribbean. We've been watching them all year long sort of hover and dash by Florida, and they've torn up the Islands pretty good. It is something to be respected. That was the message in *Stormy Weather*. Put five million people in the tip of Florida with the arrogance that only the human species possesses, more or less daring nature to stop doing what it's been doing for thousands of years. "We're here now, please don't send a hurricane." We're going to build these houses with popsicle sticks, and we're going to lie to people and tell them that they're going to stand up in the storm, but it would be nice if nature just didn't send a hurricane, thank you very much.

CLPS: So Floridians prefer just not to think about hurricanes?

CH: It's astonishing. In a sense Andrew was a real lesson for a lot of people, and most of them had never been through a storm. They were newcomers, and it had been thirty years since a really big storm. Andrew provided a whole new experience for them, and they were just flabbergasted by it. They should have been, it was just an awesome thing to see.

CLPS: In *Stormy Weather* you write that a hurricane is an eviction notice from God.

CH: An eviction notice from God, yeah. A lot of people did leave. Unfortunately, they were replaced by a lot of lowlifes who had come down to take advantage of the disaster and cash in. These are elements I didn't even think about anticipating a big storm, but I should have being a reporter and knowing human nature. There were sixteen billion dollars of insurance claims; it was the most expensive natural disaster in the history of the country. And those were all insurance checks headed for South Florida. People went flying down to get a piece of that action. Some of the people, frankly, who were victimized by the storm, who did lose a roof or a wall or something, were not shy about ripping off their insurance companies either, by claiming more damages than they actually had. Swimming pools appeared after the storm which were not there before, that kind of thing. So there was greed all the way around. It's distressing but it's true, that's what happened.

CLPS: Let's talk a little about *Skin Tight*. What motivated you to take on plastic surgery?

CH: Again, it was a trend and was extremely popular. It still is. That book was written on the wave of everybody going in to get a nose job, a boob job. My wife worked for a plastic surgeon; I knew some plastic surgeons. I'd written about some bad ones in South Florida. *Skin Tight* was about vanity. It was about what people will do to each other, do to themselves, to try to fix things with a scalpel that they can't fix with Prozac. It had a lot of the elements that I like, especially hypocrisy. I'd worked on a series for the paper called "Dangerous Doctors," about physicians who had committed some horrible things and were still allowed to practice, plus I'd always wanted to get a bad doctor in a novel. My friends are obviously very good doctors, but I heard some stories from them that were just appalling, stories about how hard it was to get rid of bad colleagues, how hard it was to get bad doctors off the hospital staff, how hard it was to shut them down. I heard again and again that they almost have to kill somebody before anybody notices how bad these guys are. So I had Rudy do just that in that book. Also I got to work in the whole P. I. lawyers thing. You know the guys with the big billboards: "If you've been hurt call me up." That started in Florida before anywhere else and now it's all over the country, of course. You can't go anywhere without seeing these ads on TV and the billboards but the first bunch of that stuff began here. My dad and grandfather were appalled and mortified with the whole idea, but to me it was a satiric opportunity, it was too good to pass up. Some of the billboards actually had the advertisements I had in that novel, which I thought were so arched that people would understand the obvious satire. They've been surpassed long ago. Some of the ones I thought so outrageous wouldn't even draw a whisper these days.

CLPS: *Native Tongue* is a novel that deals with all of the crazy people who work in a theme park called the Amazing Kingdom of Thrills. You seem to have a very dismal view of theme parks.

CH: Well, I've obviously written some news stories about them. I did a series one time on all the lawsuits filed against Disneyworld. This has been years ago, and it was great fun because you had people obviously trying to rip off Disneyworld and they make up phony injuries and then you have some real serious things that have happened there that the Disney people didn't want anybody to know about. Also, against my will, I've been there on a number of stories. It was not my favorite place but I'd gotten a flavor of the thing. Nice people work there, everybody's nice. They're sickeningly nice. Part of the thing that always bothered me about Disneyworld was that it could be anywhere; it could be Scottsdale, Arizona; it could be in Grand

Rapids, Michigan. It didn't have to be in Florida. They had gone out of their way to make it so generic, to purge any local associations. I thought this was marvelous. You're in Florida, one of the prettiest states in the union, and they're such control freaks that no animal ever crawled across the property that wasn't a robot. I mean they didn't know how to handle nature; they weren't equipped for it. Everything had to be on a computer, you know what I'm saying. It was such a hermetic environment that I thought it would be nice to create a competing theme park where things really did go wrong, which would provide a lot more suspense and, for my part, a lot more fun. I was needling them a little bit, and it was fun. Also watching theme park behavior among humans is quite something to see. Sort of like watching lemmings, the lemmings we become when we go through this turnstile and the things we do for our kids. These are all little things and moments that I wanted to recapture and I had fun with it. And also if anybody in South Florida started a theme park to compete with Disneyworld, they would never do it as well as Disney. They could never possibly have that kind of control, and I thought it would be fun to satirize South Florida, where anyone with money (and they don't care where you get your money) gets the red carpet treatment if they walk in with cash and a crazy idea. This is especially true if they think it'll help tourism. So that's why I like the idea of Francis Kingsbury, who's in the Federal Witness Protection Program, being embraced by civic leaders. That's happened down there, and people live down there recognize immediately this kind of behavior. I like that idea so I just ran with it.

CLPS: In *Strip Tease*, why did you decide to use strip clubs as a way of talking about Big Sugar?

CH: I don't know how I made that connection except that the events actually happened. In 1976 or 1977 my congressman from Ft. Lauderdale got arrested in a real dive of a strip joint near the Ft. Lauderdale airport for being drunk and disorderly and grabbing the dancers. This was long before Wilbur Mills, long before Gary Hart, long before Bob Packwood. I remembered the picture in the newspapers of this old guy getting led out of the Torch Club, or whatever it was called, with his jacket over his head and the dancers all saying what a sleazebag he was. It was the end of his political career. That stayed with me and from that I developed the story. What would happen if you had a congressman who is so obsessed with a topless dancer, the way Wilbur was with Fanny, that it jeopardized all the special interests that put him in office because it was such a potential embarrassment. My character's fascination with these women, these clubs, was really the premise of the book. Big Sugar was logical for me because I had been writing about it extensively. Sugar subsidies are a big issue down here as is the continued pissing into the Everglades by the sugar industry, which basically I've been writing about for years. So to me it was a springboard into writing about my sleazy congressman and who he is in the pocket of. It was that simple. I also wanted a good strong female heroine in this book, and I did spend some time in the clubs talking to the dancers. Particularly, I was trying to talk to single mothers who are dancing. I felt it's got to be a tough life. So that's why I was pretty pleased when Demi Moore got the part [in the movie] because she's a mom, and among one of her first questions and thoughts and ideas about the character in the script were along maternal lines. Would a mother do this kind of thing? That kind of pleased me.

CLPS: What was it like having *Strip Tease* appear on film? Were you pleased with the results? Have any more of your books been optioned?

CH: The filming of *Strip Tease* was an entertaining experience, and I was proud that some of the most depraved moments in the novel (the yogurt scene, the Vaseline scene, etc.) made it to the big screen. I've got nothing but sympathy for Andy Bergman, who wrote and directed the movie, because my novels are so difficult to adapt to film. Currently, both *Skin Tight* and *Stormy Weather* are in some vague stage of development, but that's not to say they'll ever actually get made. The new book, *Lucky You*, was bought while I was still writing it, and a couple drafts of a script are already done, or so I've heard.

CLPS: Why did you decide to feature a strong central female in *Strip Tease*?

CH: I just try to do something different every time I write a novel. I really want to work on that. Some of my characters I liked a lot, but I hadn't yet done a central female figure. I was hesitant and I don't feel comfortable writing from a woman's point of view. Most male writers, if they're honest, tell you they don't. It was just another challenge and I really wanted to bring her to life and I wanted to like her and I wanted her to be strong. I mean, I always made the female characters in my books much smarter than the male characters. But they weren't as dominant as the males, and they weren't in the center of the action much. But if you look at the aerobics instructor in *Tourist Season*, she is pretty much ahead of poor old Brian. I find that's true in life. I think women are way ahead of the men and pick up on things, not just through intuition but ingenuity. I've always tried to show that in characters, but I really wanted Erin to be not just very strong and smart but also central to the plot. I hate to jump through the same hoop every time in these books so I try to change every one of them. In the hurricane book, *Stormy Weather*, I had to have a little larger cast of characters, larger than the usual bunch, because I wanted to capture the chaos which happens after a big storm like that, where on every street corner there's a little drama going on. There are people beating each other up over bags of ice, there are monkeys running all over the place, that sort of thing. To capture all of that I needed a few more faces on the scene and juggling them was tough, because you don't know if you can pull it off and bring them all together in a way that makes any sense. But I was just trying to do something a little different each time out and that's where she came from.

CLPS: Is *Stormy Weather* the kind of book which bears out of your rather infamous comment about South Florida needing a force-five hurricane to cleanse itself?

CH: I always wanted to do a hurricane book, but that was wishful thinking. For one thing Andrew was only a category-four hurricane. So I think my comment still stands. Without getting into it, you don't want to see people die and you don't wish for the misery and suffering that happened after Andrew, but it was unnecessary. The houses didn't have to be built so poorly, people could have been fine in that storm. But you need nature to remind you occasionally of human frailty. I certainly don't mind seeing the skyline rearranged a little bit by a big storm. It wouldn't bother me in the least because that's nature.

CLPS: Does the humor in your books detract from them being taken more seriously?

CH: Well, I don't know. Satire is tricky, some people get it and some people don't. There's one school that says that people who don't get it aren't the people you're writing for anyway. There's another that says that you should broaden it and maybe make it a little less subtle, a little less pointed to try to get more readers. I just write in a narrative voice that's really, truly my own, and I don't have any control over it. I can't calibrate whether this one is going to be more commercial than the last one. Most of the reviews of my books, certainly the good reviews, talk about the satire and the humor first and foremost and that's very gratifying. So I don't think it's hurt me at all. People really like to laugh. They like to be turning the pages, and they like to get caught up in the suspense, but they also like to laugh a little along the way. So I don't think it's hurt me, but even if it does, I don't know how else to write.

CLPS: Tell me a bit about *Naked Came the Manatee*. What is it and why did you do it?

CH: *Naked Came the Manatee* was basically a group novel that was published serially in the *Miami Herald* by thirteen Florida writers, including myself, Jim Hall, Elmore Leonard and Dave Barry. Each of us took a chapter—Dave got the first, I got the last. Since nobody knew what anybody else was writing, the plot zigzagged all over the place. To our astonishment, Putnam asked to put the thing out as an actual novel. We agreed on the condition that all author royalties and advances would go to charity. As it turned out, the book (and I use the term loosely) did very well.

CLPS: Let's talk about your latest book, *Lucky You*. What's it about?

CH: *Lucky You* is about a woman who wins the Florida lottery but loses her prize ticket to a pair of slimeball robbers. She can't collect the jackpot without the ticket, so she decides to chase these guys down and steal it back. Along the way, the robbers take a hostage— a Hooter's waitress—who complicated matters immensely.

CLPS: Most of your novels have a central social theme of one kind or another. What is central to *Lucky You*?

CH: Like my other novels, *Lucky You* is pure venomous satire disguised as a mystery thriller. The heroine is a black woman, and the bad guys are would-be founders of a white militia group. I wanted to write about the new culture of hate in this country—the shallowness and aimlessness and unoriginality of it. If you read some of the crap from these skinheads and racists, it's clear they're only looking for somebody to blame—Jews, Blacks, Catholics, *anybody*—for their own failures. It's pathetic, and the guys in my novel are pathetic. Occasionally very funny, but still pathetic.

CLPS: Are you working on a new novel now?

CH: At the moment, I'm starting a short book about how Disney is taking over the entire planet. It's my first stab at the horror genre, and also at nonfiction.

Nevada Barr

INTERVIEW BY CHARLES L. P. SILET

*N*evada Barr grew up in the West in Susanville, California, where
her parents operated a small mountain airport. After receiving her
master's degree in Acting from the University of California in
Irvine, she went to New York and appeared off-Broadway at the
New Classic Stage Company. During the early eighties Nevada Barr
began commuting between New York and Minneapolis where she worked
successfully in repertory theater and doing radio voice-overs, television
commercials, and industrial training films. While in Minneapolis she became active in the environmental movement which eventually lead to her
working as a park ranger during her off-season in the summers.

   In 1979 she wrote her first novel, which she never sold but it did get
her an agent. She placed her second novel, a Western, Bittersweet, and
began her career as a writer. Bittersweet was an historical novel about
two women who ran a stage stop in the Smoke Creek Desert in Nevada,
just after the Civil War. She followed Bittersweet with two more books:
one about the 1913 Colorado coal strike in Ludlow which erupted in violence when the militia clashed with striking miners and their families,
and another set during World War II about a woman pilot who ferried
planes for the military. Neither book sold, although Barr is thinking about
revising the Colorado book for publication now.

   Nevada Barr turned to mystery fiction with the first Anna Pigeon
book, Track of the Cat (1993), which came out of her experiences work-

ing as a ranger at the Guadalupe National Park in Texas. Her first novel was very successful, receiving both the 1994 Anthony and Agatha for Best First Novel of 1993, although she wrote most of the second book in the series, A Superior Death (1994), before the first was accepted by Putnam. Since then she has published four more Anna Pigeon novels, each featuring a different national park locale: Ill Wind (1995) is set in Mesa Verde in Colorado, Firestorm (1996) in California's Lassen Volcanic National Park, Endangered Species (1997) in Cumberland Island National Seashore off the Georgia coast, and the latest, Blind Descent (1998) set in New Mexico's Carlsbad Caverns National Park.

CLPS: Why did you first join the Park Service?

NB: I had an interest in the environmental movement, and the man I was married to at the time had dropped out of the theater and become a National Park interpreter during the summer, and I got caught up in it with him. I had talked to a law enforcement officer when I was visiting my husband on Isle Royale, and found out that *they* got to do the interesting things: fighting fire, search and rescue, emergency medicine.

CLPS: How did your Park Service experience suggest a crime novel?

NB: Well, I was down in Guadalupe in Texas, and I was doing a lot of back country which was very isolated. You wouldn't see people for days, and I was fantasizing about how to kill people (there were certain persons in the park that I thought should be killed) and get away with it. I came up on the idea of doing a murder mystery based in the park with this sleuth based loosely on myself. It was the first time, I think, in all of my years writing that I found my voice.

CLPS: Tell me a little bit about Anna. Who is she?

NB: She is a widow and a park ranger; she is kind of running from her past—simply the grief of it. She's a bit of a loner, cares deeply about the wilderness. She is moderately distrustful of people but has several very close female friends; she has not yet established a long-term relationship with a man; she's grouchy and quite intelligent. She's based emotionally on a pastiche of myself and the women in my life and the things that we're concerned with and think about. She's a very good ranger, much better than myself, and she has great physical courage, but emotionally she's a bit of a coward.

CLPS: How did the idea for *Track of the Cat* develop?

NB: There were radio-collared mountain lions in Guadalupe and some of them had been killed by hunters. I was tracking them, and I'd done some reading on game poaching, and that provided the germ of the idea. As I wrote the plot fleshed itself out. But I didn't set this up to be a series. I had no idea that it would be; I was just writing this one book.

CLPS: Tell me how Anna's sister, Molly, works in the books.

NB: Well, my sister's name is Molly, and we're very close. The character started out as a combination of my sister and my aunt Peg. In the books she was something of a device. You have someone to call and to discuss all of these things as a way to bring Anna out and to move the mystery along. I liked the idea that Molly was there to help us solve the mystery of Anna Pigeon's personality. To me, women calling each other and talking is a part of life. I can't imagine what women do who don't have sisters and telephones.

CLPS: Let's talk a little bit about the ending of *Track of the Cat.*

NB: That's my favorite ending. If I ever write another ending that good I'll be pleased. Anna just leaves Harland there. There is some discussion as to whether she actually repents and goes back and saves him. I never thought she did, but the book was over. Fictional characters do what they do, but in my mind, why would she go back? He's a slime. I wanted to leave the ending open.

CLPS: Had you read much crime fiction before you started writing it?

NB: None, and when I wanted to do this murder mystery, I thought, "You don't know how." So I went to Carlsbad, which was the closest town to Guadalupe, and I checked out dozens of murder mysteries: P. D. James, Dick Francis, Agatha Christie, Dorothy L. Sayers, everybody I could possibly get my sticky little paws on. I read them as fast as I could and then I would outline them, like you do in grammar school. I did that until I kind of got the idea.

CLPS: The first book did very well, you got an Agatha and an Anthony for a best first novel. Have the critics in general been kind?

NB: They've treated me very well, but I'm not an overnight success; I've been kicking around for fourteen years. I was surprised to be getting the attention and delighted. Some of it was because it was a good book, but a huge amount of it was also timing and luck. A character in a national park setting was a good thing to do at that moment. And of course Sara Paretsky and Sue Grafton and the gang had paved the way. If I'd done it ten years before, it probably wouldn't have worked.

CLPS: *A Superior Death* is set on Isle Royale, Michigan, on Lake Superior.

NB: I worked at Isle Royale. It's a wonderful, mysterious place. So after I had written *Track of the Cat*, and decided I wanted to do a second Anna Pigeon, I set it there because of all the sunken ships and the fog and the cold water. Also the number of sunken ships at Isle Royale attracts divers, but the water is so cold and inhospitable. Because the sunken ships are so hard to get to and the diving is so dangerous, they've retained a lot of their natural character and haven't been vandalized. A cold-water dive just scared the pants off of me. Having that marvelous cold, scary, claustrophobic place worked for me.

CLPS: You write primarily out of your own experience but with the diving sequences you had to rely on your imagination.

NB: I have never cold-water dived, but as a ranger I wrote permits to divers, so I talked to them and saw their videos—a lot of them had video cameras. Then, I got in touch with the head of the submerged cultural resources unit for the National Park Service and talked to someone who had dived to *The Kamloops*. He worked on the book with me. And also I got a lot of insight gossiping with the guys that dive for a living. They talked about the danger and the mindset. It helped me to imagine the experience.

CLPS: Tell me about Frederick Stanton, Anna's friend from the F.B.I., who has a bigger role in the second novel.

NB: I needed someone for Anna to relate to and so Frederick showed up again. Frederick wasn't going to come back, but I kind of got fond of him. He was so weird. He's following his own agenda and seems very comfortable doing it. There's not much about himself that he gives away. A lot of the things he does are affectations, like the dressing funny and the bad haircut. You don't know if he has no taste or if he's putting you on or if he's doing it to set you off guard; his motives were murky enough that I got interested in him.

CLPS: You use both male and female antagonists; how do you decide?

NB: I decide first who dies and how they die, and who did it and why, and I don't pick a boy or a girl for any gender-specific reasons, but as the story's forming in my mind I will usually seize upon an image of someone that works for me. I think that women predominate in my books because I am one, and I come from a long line of strong, active women. A lot of the people in my life that have shaped it have been female. They just naturally come to mind. So it runs about fifty/fifty.

CLPS: You write about park visitors a lot. Is there something that bothers you about people who visit parks?

NB: As always with your customers and your clients, it is a love/hate relationship. The only reason you're there as a park ranger is because they're there, and you're there to preserve something that belongs to them, not to you. But it's sort of like museum curator; you don't want people coming in and looking at your stuff, and you get sort of an ownership feeling when you work in the parks. There's a lot of us, and the parks are finite and so I guess wanting to control the flow into the parks came out a bit, to keep us from trampling them to death.

CLPS: Tell me a little bit about Anasazi culture in Mesa Verde National Park, which is featured in *Ill Wind*.

NB: I went to Mesa Verde partly because I had moved with my husband to Colorado, and it was the nearest park. I was interested in wilderness, and the Anasazi, even though they're dead, were still people and I didn't have much interest in human history. After hanging out there for a couple summers the mystery of the place crept up on me. Although I'm not an expert on the Anasazi, I lived with interpreters who knew what they were talking about and I read books. I became fascinated with the aura of history and mystery that they left behind them. The Anasazi vanished—using the word vanished lightly here—about seven hundred years ago. The mystery of the Anasazi in Mesa Verde and in most of the ruins in the Southwest, is that they were a bustling and, to all appearances, wealthy, busy, prosperous culture that just suddenly stopped being. There are many differences of opinion about why they deserted these intricate cities and dwellings that they'd built. I liked the fact that we didn't know anything much about them. That human beings don't know something, I think, puts us in our place.

CLPS: There are a lot of ghosts in *Ill Wind*.

NB: There really were. It was kind of funny because I don't believe in ghosts, I've never seen a ghost. I'd go out on one of my midnight tours and suddenly I'd start thinking about ghosts, the kind of Navajo ghosts that Tony Hillerman writes about. I'd just scare myself to death. I love ghost stories and stories of the paranormal. I think it adds an interesting dimension to things. You were talking about the closed feeling of parks that make for good mysteries. I don't know if I'll ever write one for the Natchez Trace because it's not closed; it's a parkway. But I'd love to write a ghost story set in Mississippi. The South is full of ghosts. Even for those of us who don't believe.

CLPS: Of all your books, *Firestorm* is the most driven by action.

NB: Yes, it is an action mystery. I used to fight quite a bit of fire, but I haven't done it in a couple of years, and I was fascinated by fire camps. They spring up like Brigadoon in the middle of nowhere and disappear the same way. Then when I came up with the idea for the murder, I liked it because the fire camp provided a perfect setting for a Victorian locked-room mystery. It was a difficult book to write, because I narrowed things and narrowed things until the plot is unfolding almost in real time, but I couldn't have it any longer because there's no way the fire fighters could remain unrescued any longer. I pushed the maximum amount of time you could get stranded in the wilderness by the weather and keep it credible. Since it was in real time it became action-driven. When I was about halfway through it I thought, "I've written myself into a corner here. I can't get out—I don't know what to do." I had the characters on a ridge, a handful of people and a dead body. I mean, what's going to happen next? You can't be going off and discovering things; you can't be calling people on the phone. A lot of the things that I usually do to weave a story and get in all the red herrings and the mysterious happenings were cut off from me. Anna's just basically out there with a canteen and a flashlight. I thought that might be too limiting. So I started writing from Frederick's point of view, partly because I wanted to do something different. I wanted to get away and look back at Anna. I also wanted to give the reader a place they could go where their feet were dry and get a cup of coffee. The discomfort of that ridge needed to be broken up.

CLPS: In some ways this is Frederick's book. Suddenly he is a large presence in this book in a way he's never been before.

NB: He gets five chapters from his point of view. I wanted to move his and Anna's relationship along. He becomes a real person, instead of just a friend of Anna's. He factors in quite a significant way in the book that I am working on now. And then I'm not quite sure what I'm going to do with him. I might kill him; I might marry him. I haven't decided.

CLPS: *Firestorm* strikes me as being a more political book, because it deals with the Park Service and involves leasing public land rights and exploiting its resources.

NB: I'm not a highly political person and so the politics in my books are viewed narrowly from my point of view and used for the plot. But politics did factor more heavily in *Firestorm*, partly for plot needs and partly because in this one for the first time I mixed my agencies. I had the Forest Service and the Bureau of Land Management and the Park Service; three major agencies struggling over turf. I also had some experience with the oil industry living in Colorado and hearing the gossip from various people who worked in it. Usually they were people who were annoyed that the gas companies were being allowed to dig and drill. It seemed to work into a good motivator. So I used it.

CLPS: What about the problems of working a series character through a number of books, dealing with aging, relationships and so on.

NB: It's kind of tricky because I would just keep her my age, but unfortunately, I age faster than I write. She's got her own chronology going and I have to pay attention to it. The editors don't want her to get too old, but I'm going to let her get as old as I want. The big problem writing the series is keeping Anna fresh for me, and therefore interesting for other people. You get to a point where you think, "I have said everything I have to say about this woman; I explored her neuroses and so on and so forth, and I'm done." But you're still signed up to write some more books. I think that's where you either get really creative or you burn out. Series can be restricting in many ways, but I wrote a number of books that didn't sell, and I am delighted to be employed doing something people like to read. There are restrictions, though. On one hand there is the restriction of people not wanting you to do anything else, locking you into a type, but on the other hand, I'm selling books, and that wasn't happening before, so I'm a pretty happy camper.

CLPS: What do you do to keep the series fresh?

NB: I don't know how long I can maintain it, but so far I have changed locations in each book, which forces me to change a lot of other stuff. I try to find something in Anna that is unresolved. It can be personal or professional, anything to make me think a new line of thought for her so that she doesn't just become like a tape recording coming on over and over. I try to introduce a new crime to fit with the new external challenges as well so she is not always just scaling cliffs. Also I try to bring in characters that she has not met before and that I have not written before in other books to keep us both on our toes.

CLPS: You set *Endangered Species* in Cumberland Island National Seashore. What attracted you to that locale?

NB: I was sent there on a sixteen-day, pre-suppression assignment. Just like Anna was. The thing that attracted me most was the dichotomy of developed areas mixed with wilderness areas, of old money and politics mixed in with new conservation and Park Service regulations, the sea meeting the land, and the desert meeting the swamp. The island is just full of interfaces, human and natural. I loved that. Also it is beautiful.

CLPS: What is a pre-suppression assignment?

NB: When it looks like something might burn in a park, the Service sends in a fire crew to hang around just in case. It is the most boring job in the world. You find yourself hoping that the natural resources will go up in flames, because you are so bored, you want something to do. They had a terrible drought on Cumberland Island and so that was what we were doing there.

CLPS: You seem to like to use the national parks for their isolation, and there is nothing more isolated than an island.

NB: I guess I like that kind of environment partly because of my addiction to Victorian closed-house mysteries and partly because it is easier for me to work the mystery my way if I can get a distance from all of the machinery of law enforcement. That allows Anna her own freedom, and for me not to have to get into the techno aspects of investigation, which don't excite me as much as the psychological aspects and the abilities of a real person to figure something out.

CLPS: What did you want to do with *Endangered Species*?

NB: It started out with me wanting to do something on Cumberland Island. I wanted to get Anna into a new place, and I wanted to get a new environmental and psychological crime, which required a new setting. In that book I also wanted Anna to move on personally from a lot of relationships that needed to be culminated in one way or another.

CLPS: Talk a little about the new kind of crime in *Endangered Species*.

NB: It is more a people crime where the land is used inappropriately as opposed to an environmental crime in which the land or the resources are actually damaged by human use. It is a little further from animals and more toward the human animal.

CLPS: What's Anna's particular challenge in this novel?

NB: She ended up challenging her own personal weaknesses as she has done in the other books. In that respect there wasn't anything new or different about this book, particularly.

CLPS: You mentioned Anna getting away from other relationships. How is she evolving through the books?

NB: I want her to evolve because, like Woody Allen's sharks, if Anna stops evolving, she will die, become this paper doll puppet that I trot through various plot sequences. That is of no interest to me. It will be interesting to see how long I can keep her evolving before we both get kind of dull. So far so good.

CLPS: You introduce a new character in *Endangered Species*. Tell me something about Lynette.

NB: Lynette was based on a girlfriend of mine whom I worked with and found absolutely charming. I used the character in the book because I wanted Anna to be faced with someone who she would customarily not respect or like. Lynette is a Christian, almost a fundamentalist. I wanted Anna to see and know and like her even though she was a fundamentalist Christian, feminine, a flirt. She is in the book to bring out some different things in Anna and for my entertainment in writing about her, whom I love.

CLPS: What does she bring out in Anna?

NB: I think a little bit of the concept of faith and softness, the acceptance and friendship between women, and their unquestioning support. There were just lots of tiny little things that floated in, but that I thought were an aspect of women I like and Anna needed at that moment.

CLPS: Tell me a little about the newest book, *Blind Descent*.

NB: It turned out wonderfully. Do you know about Lechugilla Cave in Carlsbad? It is possibly the biggest cave in the world. They've only mapped ninety miles of it, but there are hints that it may be more than three hundred miles. It is full of incredible decorations: stalagmites, stalactites, chandeliers that look like giant white marble ferns, crystal clear pools with pedestals in the bottom, formations that look like clouds, and formations so delicate that if you walk by them too quickly you break them just like angel hair. Incredible stuff. About seven years ago a woman caver was down there mapping the cave and she broke a leg and they had to carry her out. It took them four days because there are 180 foot ascents, crawls, anything you can think of. I got fascinated with the concept of the double fear of being underground, being helpless, and then maybe having someone who wants to kill you. So I got in touch with the guy who actually led that rescue, and we went caving in New Mexico for a few weeks and I evolved the story from there. It is very like *Firestorm* in the sense that it is about a contained, terrifying space and incident. For a while there I was calling it my dirt monograph, because Anna is underground for so long. If the Eskimos have thirty-two words for snow, I came up with forty-eight words for dirt.

CLPS: How does Anna handle her claustrophobia?

NB: In various ways. Denying it, compartmentalizing it, working as hard as she can to get through it. One of the problems of the book was to make an event compelling enough that she'd even go in the cave. A theme running through the book is all the different ways you bring up for dealing with an instinctual terror.

CLPS: You move in your last two books from the tropics of a Georgia sea island to the desert of New Mexico. Why did you make that shift?

NB: I basically did it because I follow what tickles my fancy and because a new story came into my head. Making such a shift for me is always refreshing. Once you've done sultry nights for eight months, you need a new vocabulary, a new vision, and changing locations is a very pleasant way to do that.

CLPS: Are you going to continue the Anna Pigeon series?

NB: I'm contracted for three more to come out in the spring of 1998, 1999, and the year 2000. So if I don't drop the ball I have remunerative employment until the turn of the century.

CLPS: What are you working on now?

NB: I'm writing an Anna book set on Ellis Island in New York. I have a girlfriend who works in the park there, and I go stay with her. In the book Anna is back in New York to be with her sister, who is quite ill. It is the closest Anna is going to get to an urban mystery. I fell in love with Ellis Island. It is just marvelously bizarre. The Registry Hall has been magnificently restored to perfection. I went through the whole thing where the immigrants came in, but was bored, bored, bored. Then there are the other two parts of the island that have the old hospitals which have been let go completely to hell because there is no money to restore them. I loved them. They are like the world's biggest haunted house, full of incredible things. They provided the perfect setting for a new Anna adventure.

Walter Mosley

INTERVIEW BY CHARLES L. P. SILET

Walter Mosley *achieved instant recognition with the publication of his first Easy Rawlins book,* Devil in a Blue Dress *(1990). The critics loved his historical recreation of post–war Los Angeles, and the unique voice he had captured with his characters. A* Red Death *(1991) was equally well-received. With this novel Mosley moved the time frame forward into the early nineteen-fifties as he once again explored the Afro-American world of L.A. Even though Easy, a black man, walked down mean streets not explored before, Mosley was placed squarely in the hard-boiled tradition of Hammett, Chandler, and Cain.*

With the publication of White Butterfly *(1992), Mosley arrived. It did not hurt his sales when then-presidential candidate Bill Clinton was seen carrying copies of his books on the campaign trail or when he told reporters that Mosley was his favorite mystery writer. By then the paperback editions of the first two were on the stands and selling. Easy's world had become better known, and Mouse, Jesus, Mofass, the locale of the "other" Los Angeles were familiar to a growing number of mystery readers.*

Walter Mosley has said he hopes that his success will have a positive effect on young black writers and encourage them to write genre fiction. His books so far have opened up the world of crime writing not only to a new voice but also to a new perspective. As Mosley works his way forward in history, he is presenting his readers with a uniquely ethnic vision, one that brings favorably to mind the writings of Chester Himes, until now the best-known black writer of crime fiction. Like Himes, Mosley celebrates his heritage, warts and all.

CLPS: Let me begin by asking for some background information, where you were born, something about your family.

WM: I was born in Los Angeles in 1952 of a black father and a white Jewish mother. For quite a while we lived in Watts in south central L.A., and then moved to west Los Angeles into that great vast middle-class ocean. Then, as soon as I possibly could, I left and went back East, first to Vermont, then to Massachusetts, and finally to New York.

CLPS: You said that your father was black and your mother was Jewish. Did this present problems? Was it an enriching experience?

WM: One of the interesting things which most people who are white don't understand is that the black community is pretty accepting in general. So there was really no problem. I had a white mother, but it was just different, nobody made a big deal out of it. In the middle class I was in the lower end and that was interesting, and the neighborhood I was in was half-black and half-Jewish, just like me.

CLPS: Tell me something about your schooling.

WM: Actually elementary school was very important for me. I went to a place called Victory Baptist Bay School which was the only private black elementary school in Los Angeles. It was a very poor school where mainly the teachers just loved you to death. I went back there some time ago and the school is exactly the same. Everybody is new, but it hasn't changed one bit. The principal was walking through the schoolyard, and she knew every little boy and every little girl and what all their issues were. One of the interesting things about education for children is children can't help but learn. They always want to learn; they can't stop learning. The problems are mostly of an emotional kind. In that school we felt so loved in a real way. I think it was a great experience for me, a really wonderful experience.

CLPS: Then you went on to high school?

WM: Yeah, I went on to junior high school and then high school. They were public schools, predominantly Jewish, where I learned a great deal, but I wasn't very happy in those schools because it was more like a factory education.

CLPS: Were you interested in writing at this point?

WM: Nope.

CLPS: What about college?

WM: I went to a place called Goddard College in Vermont, where I was actually asked to leave. It's almost impossible to be asked to leave Goddard but they did. Then I went to Johnson State College, some years later. I studied political science, and then I went to political theory school at the University of Massachusetts at Amherst. I finally decided, "Hey, this isn't making any sense." So I returned to computer programming, that was the big thing in my life, returning to programming.

CLPS: How did you get into programming?

WM: I had been in Europe with a friend of mine when I was about nineteen or twenty and we were staying with his relatives who were very wealthy, and I realized that not only did I not have as much money as his relatives, but I didn't have as much money as the people they hired to work for them! On the way back to L.A., I was thinking, "Ok, now, I have to have a job. I don't really want a profession; I don't want to be a doctor or a lawyer because I don't have any commitment to that stuff. So I need a craft." I thought of all these possible things to be, and finally it got down to nurse or programmer, because you could move around a lot with either one of those jobs. Then I thought, "Oh, God, I can't stand the sight of blood!" So, programmer.

CLPS: How did you get from computer programmer to author?

WM: My first book was *Gone Fishin'*. I sent it out and nobody bought it. So, then, I started writing something else that turned out to be *Devil in a Blue Dress*. My plan was that I was going to go to school, get a degree, and after the degree get a job somewhere, not in New York, as a teacher of creative writing, and I would keep writing and one day I would be accepted as a writer. But I wrote this book, *Devil in a Blue Dress*, which I kept in the closet. The head of the writing program, Frederick Tuten, said, "Why don't you let me take a look at that?" This is abbreviated, but it's not much. So I did and I went away for the weekend, and when I came back, he said his agent, Gloria Loomis, was going to represent me. She told me, "This is a good book, this is good literature, and we're going to do something." And I've never been happier.

CLPS: Why did you decide to set the books back in time?

WM: It's a migration, only rather than through space it's through time. The first book, *Gone Fishin'*, happens in 1939. Also it just turns out to be important because the books are really about black life in Los Angeles, how the people got there, what they were up to. The big influx, not only for black people but for everyone, was right after World War II. Then there are all these important events since World War II, contemporary historical events which black people have been edited out of. I'm talking about, for instance, in *A Red Death*, the juxtaposition of the lives of black people and the lives of those people who were destroyed by McCarthy. So there's all this important history. Because real history, it seems to me, is held in literature not in history books; people simply don't read history books. The history as it appears in novels is always flawed but emotionally true.

CLPS: Let's talk a little bit about some of the individual books. *Devil in a Blue Dress* was your first. What did you want to do with that?

WM: It's very interesting. The subtext of it is jazz language. The period of the book was a time of incredible hope. All of these very poor people from the deep South had left the South, which was even worse than the war, and had come to L.A. This was a time of absolute possibility. We were going to make it. But there were built-in problems. There was the racism of the world around them and the limitations in themselves that they were carrying with them. That's how I went with Easy. I wanted to talk about him as this incredible, complex psyche who comes out of the deep South into L.A. with all of these hopes and aspirations and what he can and cannot do for both external and internal reasons. That was the dynamics I was talking about.

CLPS: One of the early Chester Himes novels is about working in a war plant, and it deals with thwarted aspirations.

WM: But that is very different from my characters. One of the things about Richard Wright, James Baldwin, and Chester Himes is that all of the characters at the end of their novels end up in Paris. Easy is not the kind of guy who would end up in Paris. He wouldn't know how to end up in Paris. So he does make it here in America. But how he makes it is flawed and scarred. I mean he gets money, he buys property, but he pays for it. It's such a complex thing that I can't break it down to any kind of social, political, or racial level. If you push against life, if you try to make it in life, then you create even more tragedy. It's not that you don't make it, it's that you realize that getting there wasn't what you thought it would be. And that really comes out of the *noir* genre, that whole idea of you can't really get what you want.

CLPS: *Devil in a Blue Dress* was made into a Hollywood movie. What did you think about it?

WM: I thought *Devil in a Blue Dress* was a very good film. I liked it very much. And *Always Outnumbered Always Outgunned* is being shot as an HBO movie now and will be out in March.

CLPS: What do you explore in *A Red Death*?

WM: *A Red Death* has several things going on. One is the concept of friendship in this modern, civilized world. Easy finds himself working for the IRS and the FBI, and he hates them and they hate him. And he is working against his best friend's mom. The other thing is, of course, the McCarthy period itself. Most black people were poor and working-class and had nothing to do with Communist organizers. They were black already. You don't need to be on a blacklist if you're black. I just want to make that connection between the oppression of people.

CLPS: You also talk about the church.

WM: The church is a very important part of the black community, and it's different than a middle-class church, where you go there on Sunday and you're part of the church, but it's not really the heartbeat of the community. It's maybe like the conscience or something behind you whispering, "Don't do that. Don't do that." But the black church in the black community is the heart of your life—everything goes on there. When I went back to Victory Baptist Day School, which I modeled my church after, they showed me an apartment building and said, "This is where all the elderly ladies go for the church wing when they get too old to work and pay their rent." It wasn't like bragging or anything. It was this is what we do for the young people, and this is what we do for the old people. Of course, whenever you have that much emotional weight on an institution, you have some amount of corruption and some problems. So I just wanted to talk about that.

CLPS: There is a dense texture to the social fabric of the novel.

WM: Yes, the book portrays a kind of life that doesn't exist in literature as a rule. Certainly most white people don't know it and therefore can't really write about it. One of the problems when starting to write about black people is that it's very hard for those outside to understand our life because the way the media deals with us: We're drug addicts, we're welfare people. So when I sent out my book, *Gone Fishin'*, which is just like a lot of other black novels—it's not a mystery particularly—publishers were concerned about who would read this book. The book is about two young black men in the deep South following some kind of quest. The publishers weren't interested in this. It wasn't political; it wasn't about women; it didn't really work for an external audience. So what I was able to do in the mystery was to pull people in who are interested in the genre and still talk about the lives of black people.

CLPS: Let's talk about *White Butterfly*.

WM: I think all novels are failures. This is what I honestly believe: that a novel is an impossible art form. It's too large to attain perfection so what it has to do is have an intention and how close it gets to that intention is how good you think the book is, which is one of the reasons that people like crime books, because you can always have a mystery and have the mystery solved. So you get a sense of resolution at the end of the book even though the book itself may not have been completely successful. In *White Butterfly* I was trying to talk about the relations between black men and black women, and then have some kind of reflection on men and women in general and I completely failed, I think. However, in trying to do that, I brought out a lot about the relations between men and women, like Easy's relationship with his wife, Mouse's relationship to women, women's relationships to him, and so on. The whole book is just men and women all over the place dealing with each other on all kinds of different levels. Easy gets older, and as Los Angeles begins to change, he more and more necessarily becomes more involved with the white community through his property investments, his motels. As he gets more involved, he becomes more aware of his limitations.

CLPS: You mean limitations placed on him by the social world.

WM: Right. In *Black Betty*, it's the same thing. Easy is more and more outside of his own world, and also he tries to distance himself from his life. He's just not very happy with what he is doing. Easy likes to do favors for people because he feels responsible, but he wants to be respected and he wants to be aboveboard. He doesn't want to be like Mouse. He doesn't want to even be *with* Mouse. He loves Mouse, because Mouse has saved his life too many times for him not to, but he doesn't identify himself with that world of Mouse and he has to because the world itself won't let him go. So it's not only outside oppression from the world, but inside he is really held back. The same thing happens with him and his wife, Regina. He was raised in a world where you don't tell people what you have. You don't let people know things, and just because she's your wife doesn't mean you've got to open up. She had a hard life, too. Maybe she's going to take away what you got.

CLPS: In *White Butterfly* your opening lines are about a man who is "rage-colored," and I thought about anger and I wondered if you had the recent L.A. riots and Rodney King in the back of your mind.

WM: When people start talking about the riots, it's like this is the first thing that happened. The issue is the violence that happened to Rodney King but it's not particular to Rodney King. It happens every day in every city. You can be sure that there's some black man or not-white man and it may be a white man, too, who has come from poverty, being beat to death in some back alley by some cop who doesn't like him, or by some cop who thinks he's doing the right thing, which is even worse. That's the violence; that's the cost. Someone talks about how the riot costs us a hundred million dollars. Think of the cost of that implosive violence happening every day to people. Think of what happens to that guy who gets the shit kicked out of him in some back alley—sixty to seventy of them every day. That violence has to come back somehow. It's not like it just happens, and it goes away. It's not like you can kick the shit out of somebody and then they just forget it and go back to their lives.

CLPS: Americans measure the cost in terms of property rather than human suffering.

WM: Right. Exactly. There's been no understanding of it. None whatsoever as far as I'm concerned. People talk about Rodney King, but it's Rodney King and the thousands of others like him. Everybody black knows that you're always on the edge of this happening to you. It's the truth and it's frightening and you better not say what you think. In *White Butterfly* Easy always remembers this: "Don't say what you think, don't even let it show, because if you do you're in trouble."

CLPS: So Easy is a reluctant detective who doesn't want to get involved.

WM: Right, he doesn't want to. He's an intelligent man, and he has a philosophical bent and so he realizes in *White Butterfly,* even after he refused to cooperate with the police, that then when a white girl gets killed, he has to become involved. So he recognizes that he, unwillingly, has become part of the racist structure.

CLPS: Except as he says, the one thing he won't do is run down a black man for the law.

WM: Right, as a rule. But he will do it and has done it. It's always that back and forth thing. This is so much more interesting, and, I think, it's so much more of what we need to do in fiction, because I hate setting up heroes that we really can't live by. You know, real people make mistakes, have flaws, do the wrong thing, and you have to be able to deal with that.

CLPS: Why did you have him get married?

WM: Because people get married, that's why. It's so totally the right answer for me. I just sat down and started writing the book, and he was married. The genre has to develop. That *noir* character, who used to be outside of our lives, is now inside of our lives. So instead of looking at him from your armchair, I want you involved. I want Easy to be like everybody else. He's not the smartest guy in the world; Jackson Blue is the smartest guy in that world. He's not the toughest guy in the world; Mouse is the toughest guy in that world. But he's a regular guy, maybe a little better, maybe a little stronger, maybe a little smarter, but he's a regular guy. He has children and he has a wife. That's the way life is. I'm not being critical of Ross MacDonald, Chandler, or Hammett, because they had a different project than mine, but in today's world to write about a guy who doesn't have any responsibility or a woman who doesn't have any responsibility and so therefore can just make her decisions unhampered is a fantasy, and it's a little too light for me. I don't particularly want to read it.

CLPS: President Clinton has been very excited about your books. Any comments or responses?

WM: Well, I'm very happy about Clinton because of what he's done. The way I see Clinton is that he is reaching out for people who have been completely ignored before by the Oval Office, and in his reaching out, I'm really happy he likes my books and I believe he does. But the thing that I'm even happier about is the fact that he would even say it, partially for me, of course, because it's good for my publicity, and partially because black people are out here, writing and doing work and trying really hard and changing the country in so many ways and people just ignore it. So I'm really very happy about what he's doing, and I feel included in a way in the world. He recognizes that here's a black writer in America doing some important work. That's certainly his position in the world, and I'm very pleased, doubly pleased.

CLPS: Let's talk a little bit about *Black Betty*.

WM: *Black Betty* happens in '61. It starts off in a dream and stays in a nightmare. It's a book basically about the violence between black men. The book talks about the dark side of hope. It's 1961 and Kennedy's in office and Martin Luther King is marching down South, and all of a sudden all of that unconscious black anger and rage is concentrated. Easy is sitting there, a part of this world of bright hope, but feeling like he is in the dark, shadowy underside of that hope. He's trying to work his way out of it. There's his belief that, "If I can just save one person's life." The only thing he can do is take somebody's life, but he can't really give life. He comes to all these realizations throughout the book. I'm taking a chance with this book because for me I'm doing a lot of new things like having more than one mystery going on at once. Easy has children, and he lives kind of far away from his basic native community.

CLPS: What about Easy's children?

WM: They live in a house he rents; him and Jesus and Southern. Jesus is going to junior high school, and everybody is happy. It starts off in a dream. In 1956, after *White Butterfly* was over, Mouse got into an altercation. Somebody said something he didn't like, and he killed him. He was captured and sent to prison. So the book starts off with this dream of Easy remembering the death and how senseless it was and how horrible it was. Mouse gets out of jail and he's looking for revenge while Easy is looking for Black Betty. He has to keep Mouse from getting revenge and he has to find Black Betty, and both of them are very difficult.

CLPS: It sounds like Easy is back to juggling.

WM: I remember a long time ago that I read a story about a woman who was on a telephone which had call waiting. She was one of three women who were good friends. One of the other women was on the phone telling her how the third woman was having an affair with her husband, and this woman did not know if she was angrier at her husband or at her friend for this betrayal. On the other line there is this guy from Chile who is being kicked out of the country, but if he went back to Chile, he's going to be killed because of his political beliefs and she was trying to help him. In the meanwhile, she was making dinner and the children are having some kind of discussion, which she is a part of while trying to keep them on the right track and her husband is coming home. So she's doing five things at once. I said, you know, this is really a woman's way of seeing the world, because men are very linear. They go to work, and they start laying bricks. Not all men are like this, but most male work is like that. But women have to deal with all kinds of things all at once, and I started realizing that this is also true for poor people. You're always struggling to survive. If you're doing one thing and you happen to see something else which you *know* is important, you've got to include it. So that's what I was trying to do with Easy with what I call a feminine sensibility. I was thinking about that in writing this book. Everybody's in this book. Easy is trying to weave his path through it in order to get out of the nightmare, but I don't think he's successful. I promise he'll be happier in future books.

CLPS: Your next book was *RL's Dream*, about Robert Johnson.

WM: Yeah, which I'm very excited about. I believe that it's some of the best writing that I've ever done. It's a blues novel and doesn't have anything to do with mystery or anything like that except maybe the mystery of life, as Vachss says. It's a novel in which Robert Johnson is the negative space. How's that? I am very interested in the blues and in Robert Johnson, and I thought it was the thing to do. I think that he is an American genius and really one of the most important artists in this country and even one of the most important art influences in American music and therefore in world music. He was right there at the beginning of jazz, rock and roll, and popular music. He is just a very important American character. To write a novel about him is just one of the things I hoped to do.

CLPS: *Little Yellow Dog* continues the Easy Rawlins series. How does he change in this novel?

WM: I don't know what to say, because I don't think about the books like that. Other people say things about the books, and I'm always very interested in what they have to say. Not that I think that kind of thing is necessarily wrong, I just don't think it has much to do with what I was trying to do in the book. Books get created by the people who read them. For me *Little Yellow Dog* is a story in which I set certain problems up that I realize. It's a funny book, in a way, which I like. It's a sexy book, in a way, which I like. It's also very tragic, because Mouse gets killed, or seemingly gets killed, at the end of the book. It's a story in which the two main bad guys are dead before the book gets started, and the major character is the little yellow dog. So you have the problem of trying to do character development for dead men and for somebody who is not human.

CLPS: You also finally got *Gone Fishin'* published.

WM: Well, it is the first book I ever wrote, and I always thought it was a good book. It got published in that period I call PTM, pre-Terry Macmillan. It's the first book about Easy Rawlins, and I thought people would be interested in knowing where he came from in my head and in his life.

CLPS: Your new book is *Always Outnumbered Always Outgunned.*

WM: It's on the other side of the hard-boiled story. It's not a mystery; it's a series of short stories with a central character. Reading mysteries is kind of like going to a movie. You go and watch it, and afterwards you can go home. In the stories in *Always Outnumbered Always Outgunned* nobody gets to go home. The reader won't be able just to say that was fun. You have to take the kind of thing that happens in these stories seriously. This kind of thing could happen in a mystery, although it probably doesn't, but if it does happen, it doesn't matter. With Socrates this is happening, and it does matter.

CLPS: Tell me about Socrates Fortlaw.

WM: This guy is fifty-eight years old. When he was in his twenties, he was out with his friend and his friend's girl. They were all really very drunk, and the girl comes on to Socrates and he likes that. The friend doesn't, and they get into a fight. Socrates kills his friend and rapes the girl. She starts to fight with him when she realizes he's killed her old man so he kills her, too. He falls asleep, and when he wakes up in the morning, he looks for her not realizing that he has committed a double murder and rape. He goes to prison for twenty-seven years. When he comes out of prison, he's in his fifties. He sees himself as a creature of evil, and he wants to stop being that. He's been living for eight years now in an apartment in Watts and true to his name he is trying to figure out what's right, what's the right thing to do for those who have to break the rules in order to do anything.

CLPS: How does he do this?

WM: In the first story he meets a young boy who has killed a chicken that Socrates knows and loves, and he makes the boy cook the chicken. While he is doing that, he realizes the boy has committed a more serious crime. He makes the boy confess to a murder that he has committed. In the end the boy says, "Hey, what are you going to do?" And Socrates replies, "I'm not going to do nothing, man. You did wrong and all you need to recognize is that you did wrong." The boy asks, "Are you going to turn me in?" He says, "No, but if you ever have any more trouble, you can come here and talk to me." The next story is about a crack dealer. He asks Socrates about whether he would kill a man or turn him in to the police. It is very much a Socratic dialogue. Socrates says, "Listen, it is better to kill a black man than to turn him in to the police." And that goes through the whole series. Those are external stories. Sometimes they are internal. Socrates asks himself if he is going to be in the same situation where he killed his friend and his girl? Or how to get a job looking like he does? It is about a kind of modern-day philosopher who has rolled up his sleeves and sharpened his wits. It's a very hard book to explain. It's more about the dialogue than about moral values.

CLPS: What are you working on now?

WM: What am I working on now? It's a good question. I just fin-ished writing a book of science fiction, and I'm on the second draft.

I'm maybe doing a movie or two. I'm really not sure. I'm writing the next Easy Rawlins. That's what I'm doing.

CLPS: It's plenty to keep you busy for the next several years.

WM: Oh, yeah, it's so much fun to do. I love writing about Easy. I really do think, along with Jerome Charyn, that detective fiction is very important in this contemporary world. It really helps people to think and understand and open up. Crime fiction is very compelling to people; they want to know what happened, they want to know what happens next, they want to know why and they want to feel some sense of resolution.

CLPS: Where would you like to go from here?

WM: I don't know. Certainly, I don't want to stop doing the things I have been doing, but I want to grow. I'm on a path and it's not like I want to get on another path.

Portions of this interview appeared as "The Other Side of These Mean Streets," *The Armchair Detective*, 26:4 (Fall 1993), 8-16.

Margaret Maron

INTERVIEW BY CHARLES L. P. SILET

One of the more significant changes in crime fiction over the past fifty years has been in the increasing number of contemporary crime stories which focus more on characters, their relationships, their families, and the locales in which they live than on puzzles and on puzzle-solvers. Perhaps not surprisingly women crime writers have been largely responsible for promoting this trend, and Margaret Maron has been one of the most prominent.

Maron began as a mystery writer with a series featuring Sigrid Harald, a single, emotionally restricted police lieutenant in the homicide division of the New York Police Department. That original series, now somewhat in abeyance, followed the central character through nine books as she fell in love and blossomed emotionally while solving crimes in the tightly knit art world of the city. One of the major themes of these novels was Harald's search for connections with her own family, a theme which was amplified by her developing personal relationships, and prefigured one of the main subjects Maron is now exploring in her current series starring North Carolina native, Deborah Knott.

Maron conceived of Deborah as self-confident and deeply circumscribed—at times almost suffocatingly so—by her family and its place in a mythical North Carolina county. In short, she was the opposite of Sigrid Harald. The new series emphasizes her interconnections with both family and place, and she uses her power and contacts as a judge for solving *crimes. In writing stories with such connectedness Maron's work now as much resembles that of other mainstream Southern writers as it does the traditions of the crime genre out of which they evolved.*

CLPS: Tell me a little about your background.

MM: I was born in Greensboro, North Carolina, and when I was still a child, we moved back down to the family farm in a community southwest of Raleigh. I grew up riding the schoolbus to a local rural school where all twelve grades were in the same building, thirty-four in my graduating class. I attended the University of North Carolina at Greensboro, transferred to Chapel Hill but married before finishing. He was a naval officer from New York and we went off to live in Italy for three years before returning to Brooklyn where he got his master's and taught art at Brooklyn College.

CLPS: What got you interested in writing?

MM: Who knows where these things start? I was a voracious reader rather early on. My mother had once taught and she had tried to write some fairy tales for her children. One day when I was about nine or ten, I was rummaging in an old trunk, came across these stories, and was almost as thunderstruck as Saul on the road to Damascus. It had never dawned on me that there was a connection between the written word that gave me so much pleasure and ordinary, walking-around people.

What probably confirmed my desire to write was reading Edna St. Vincent Millay's "Renascence" at eleven and learning that she'd written it at nineteen. I thought, "Hey, I can do this." Then I discovered a sad fact of life: It's very easy to write bad poetry—anybody can write stuff that rhymes and scans; but writing good poetry takes a special genius. I grew up reading mysteries. Mother read all the classic, traditional American and British writers and some of the softer-boiled authors like Nero Wolfe, Erle Stanley Gardner and Ellery Queen. I also loved science fiction and history. I'd read anything on any printed page set before me.

CLPS: When did you decide to write crime fiction?

MM: Well, I always knew I wanted to write "someday," but I didn't get serious about it till we were living in Brooklyn. (I was fortunate enough to have a husband who gave me the time and space to develop.) When I decided to find out if I could write salable prose, I actually gave myself a writing course. I brought home all kinds of how-to books from the public library, including John Ciardi's *How Does a Poem Mean?* and the whole *Paris Review* "Writers at Work" series. They helped me understand that mechanics didn't matter as much as perseverance, that old "apply seat of pants to seat of chair" and just write.

I tried my hand at everything: serious New Yorker-type stories, Ogden Nash-type light verse, science fiction, how-to-do stuff articles—but everything I sent out came right back by return mail. Then I hatched a short mystery story (write what you like to read, right?), and when I sent it out, it didn't immediately come bouncing home untouched by human hands. It was actually read by somebody at *Ellery Queen* who wrote on the rejection slip, "Not this time but let us see more." I was just as excited by that rejection slip as if it'd been an acceptance. I tightened and polished the story some more and sent it off to *Alfred Hitchcock* and they bought it in 1968. That was my first mystery acceptance.

CLPS: You published *One Coffee With* in 1982. What did you write between 1968 and 1982?

MM: Short stories. For almost twelve years. I certainly wasn't making a living, but it was enough to claim office expenses on my income tax and I did occasionally sell a non-mystery short story to magazines like *Redbook* or *McCall's*. Don't forget that I started out a poet, and for me poems are short. When I couldn't do poetry, I did stories and most of my short stories are truly short—under 3,000 words. I was scared of the novel; was absolutely sure I could never write one. Robert Louis Stevenson, who was also afraid of the long form, described it as a feat of almost superhuman achievement and I was with him. Then the short story market dried up so badly in the seventies that I backed into writing a novel. *One Coffee With* started out as a short story with a character named Lieutenant Peter Bohr. It grew into a longer story, then a magazine novelette, then a book-length novelette. By the third rewrite, Lieutenant Peter Bohr had morphed into Lieutenant Sigrid Harald. My agent liked the characters, the style, and the story, "But it's too short by half." So I doubled it again by interpolating a subplot about an artist's missing notebooks.

CLPS: Where did the book's art material come from?

MM: While we were living in Brooklyn, my husband taught in the Art Department at Brooklyn College and I substituted as the departmental secretary for nine months. Seeing how poisons and caustics were handled so cavalierly in the workshops made me realize what a perfect setting this was for murder. Too, everybody worried about tenure and that made another good plot device. Although my husband now has white hair and somewhat physically resembles Oscar Nauman, Nauman was actually based on another professor there, as is Vanderlyn College based on B.C. I just leveled a few square blocks on the East River and set it down in lower Manhattan.

CLPS: Tell me something about your central character, Sigrid Harald. What is she like? What makes her tick?

MM: Sigrid Harald took the worst features from two very attractive and gregarious parents. Her mother was a Southern belle who became a respected photojournalist. Her father was a blond Viking who was killed in the line of duty when Sigrid was a toddler. She is quite shy and emotionally blocked. Although she knows she's competent in her work, she's very insecure in her femininity and in social and personal relationships. From the beginning, I had planned this as an interlocking series and I tried to construct a character who could grow emotionally over the life of the series, something that hadn't been done all that much up till then.

Dorothy Sayers and Ngaio Marsh allowed their characters to age and take on grown-up responsibilities, but Hercule Poirot ended almost as he began. Same for Nero Wolfe and Perry Mason. I mean, Mason's boss/secretary flirtation with Della Street never deepened into love or even into good old-fashioned lust, did it? Archie Goodwin stayed a lecherous mid-thirtyish bachelor and Ellery Queen remained the perennial good son and boy wonder. Pam and Jerry North began as a screwball married couple and never got past the cocktail hour. Philip Marlowe, the Continental Op, the list goes on. This is not to fault them. Maybe most readers prefer it that way. But I wanted to do a pivotal year in my character's life, a year in which she becomes involved with a much older man, falls in love, and learns to accept her femininity, to discover that she is desirable and worthy of being loved and that she can enter into a mature relationship as a full and equal partner.

It took me fourteen years to bring her year full cycle from *One Coffee With* to *Fugitive Colors*. In addition to the plots of each book, there's also an uber-plot, so to speak; and each book adds a little more information about the overall story of how her father actually died and what part her mother and her boss played in his death. Although each book stands alone, if the eight are read in sequence, you can better follow the developments. For instance, the officer on her squad who proves to be the rotten apple in *Past Imperfect,* the seventh book, makes a brief revealing slip in the third book.

CLPS: You've now completed eight books in the series, but where do you go now that Oscar Nauman died in the last one?

MM: When I finished *Fugutive Colors,* I thought his death was an accident. Now I wonder if it wasn't murder. If I write another Sigrid Harald book, she'll probably have to go out to California and decide for herself which it was. There are still a lot of unresolved loose ends: the three women in his life before Sigrid, one of whom tried to kill him when he first came to New York. In addition to a large estate, he may also have left an illegitimate child. I don't know. I do know that it sounds affected to speak as if these characters are out there with a life of their own, independent of my devising, but sometimes that's what it feels like. They definitely know things I don't.

In the very first Deborah Knott story, "Deborah's Judgment," Deborah mentions someone named Lev Schuster. I didn't have a clue as to who he was, but she needed to say something about "schmoozing," not a common word in my rural South. So she says in the story that she didn't realize that Lev's vocabulary was still affecting her speech. I thought, "Who the hell is Lev Schuster?" I didn't find out till *Shooting at Loons,* when he turns up and proves to be someone she once lived with. Names will pop out or specific objects, like her late mother's old Zippo lighter, and I'll know there's a story attached, but I won't have the foggiest idea what it is.

To go back to whether or not there'll be another Sigrid book, I honestly don't know. I do have her at a point where I can stop. As I say, if I go back, I'd have to explore Nauman's past. Who knows? It would be interesting, but you can't do everything in one lifetime.

CLPS: You seem to use the art world to comment on the mystery story. You have Buntrock, an art critic, compare Sigrid to a Nauman painting: a seemingly simple surface which conceals unexpected complexities. Is that a description of your own writing?

MM: It's hard for a writer to describe her own writing. I prefer to let others do the sorting and classifying. I do like to write clearly, and it often turns out that after I've finished a book, I can look back and see a theme, but I've never consciously started with one. Like a Nauman abstract, some of the simplest writing can conceal great depths. I've always admired the way Mark Twain's *Huckleberry Finn* seems so clear and artless. Yet when you go back and read it as an adult, you can see so much you missed the first time. I try to write clear and accessible prose, but I also try to put in things which my readers can stumble upon and perhaps be delighted by—not just intellectual ideas, but playful things as well. I am captivated when a writer like Walter Satterthait lets a character at a 1920s house party casually ask, "Is Rebecca de Winter expected?" Not enough to distract, but it does make the scene resonate. In my own case, the Sigrid Harald books have a huge running joke. The only two people who've caught it are my first Canadian editor and M. D. Lake, who writes the Peggy O'Neill series.

CLPS: Are you going to tell me?

MM: Nope.

CLPS: Then tell me why you have Sigrid fascinated by northern European art—Dürer, Cranach, Holbein, and not much interested in Nauman's abstract painting?

MM: "Fascinated" is perhaps too strong. Sigrid grew up going to the great art museums in New York, but I doubt if she'd given art too much thought before she met Nauman. It's the man who fascinates her, not the art; but because he's so forceful, she feels compelled to take a stand in his field. She doesn't understand the abstract. It strikes her as anarchic and anarchy makes her uneasy. She's a total pragmatist and she prefers the concrete and specific, so she takes her stand where her nature is rooted—on the side of the analytical, the detailed, the realistic, her "Gothic" side, if you will. She tries to like Nauman's work, but really can't. He understands this and is so touched by her struggle and her honesty that when he admits to himself that he loves her, he makes a portrait of her in silverpoint (á la Holbein) and gives it to her as a Christmas present. I have on my wall reproductions of a pair of engravings, which come close to reflecting the difference between Sigrid and Oscar Nauman. One is Dürer's *Adam and Eve,* done in 1504. The other is a Raimondi *Adam and Eve,* engraved about the same time. The Dürer is austere, dark, tightly focused—typical late Gothic, while the Italian is all sensuous curves, space, atmosphere and controlled abandon—high Renaissance. To me, one is intellect, the other emotion.

CLPS: *Bloody Kin* has been described as a transition novel between the two series.

MM: It is. *Bloody Kin* was set down here because I wanted to write about my little patch of North Carolina. It's set right here on the family farm although I did invent a fictional county with its own sheriff and deputy sheriff. These felt so right that when I came to write the Deborah Knott series I saw no reason not to keep using them. Besides, I like to pick up old story threads and I recycle endlessly. *Bloody Kin* had two minor characters from *Death in Blue Folders* and one of those two had a tiny cameo in *Bootlegger's Daughter*.

CLPS: But you already had the New York setting and the wonderfully venal art world atmosphere in the Sigrid books. Was it hard to give that up?

MM: I do miss writing about New York, and I wish there were some way to spend more time there. On the other hand, this is home. There's something very satisfying about writing out of current personal experience. In one of the books, Deborah and her father walk out on a moonlit night and Deborah is reminded of a time she and her family walked out like that on a warm June night and heard corn growing. This isn't something I could use in a New York book. A tree may grow in Brooklyn, but not much corn grows in Central Park. I enjoy writing about rural things, and let's face it: I simply don't know the daily rhythms of New York anymore the way I now know the rhythms here.

CLPS: After *Bloody Kin* came out in 1985, when did you realize you wanted to do a second series set in North Carolina?

MM: Bantam had the first series and by the time I'd finished *Past Imperfect*, they'd gotten so backed up in their publishing schedule, that I had time to write something else. Odd. I never considered that before. If those books had been published on schedule, I might never have sat down and created a second series character.

Anyhow, Sara Ann Freed, who was my friend before she became my editor at Mysterious Press, had read *Bloody Kin* and kept bugging me to write another North Carolina book. And I wanted to write about the South, about the attachment to the land, and to family. Sigrid's closest relatives are her mother and her mother's mother. I deliberately gave Deborah a big gregarious family whose members actually like each other. And I wanted to tell stories about how North Carolina is changing right out from under us, going from agrarian to high tech with suburbanization at full tilt. There's much about the state that I didn't know and I thought it'd be fun to make my character a judge and send her out to explore. I wanted her to be of the law so that she wasn't a total amateur sleuth. As a judge, she can command cooperation from those in law enforcement.

CLPS: So who is Deborah Knott? How does she differ from Sigrid Harald?

MM: She was deliberately conceived to be Sigrid's polar opposite. Sigrid was a loner, an only child, uncomfortable with emotions. Deborah likes being a woman, has a wide circle of friends and comes from a large, loving, extended family of brothers, sisters-in-law, nieces and nephews, cousins and aunts, with a bootlegging daddy in the center. One of my readers suggested that Deborah's family feels like the oceans and the mountains, that they're her bedrock. Which they are. They've let her grow up confident and opinionated, secure in her place. On the other hand, a big, nosy family can be claustrophobic, too, the way they hover and advise and criticize and suggest.

There's also the difference between the immediacy of Deborah's first-person voice as opposed to the distancing of third-person narrative in the Sigrid books. First person can be a little constrictive because it doesn't let me tell the reader anything that Deborah doesn't know. She had to see or hear all the propelling action. With third-person, I could have all kinds of things going on that Sigrid never even suspected. In *Fugitive Colors,* she never realizes that the young black woman has been sabotaging the art gallery. Nobody knows except the reader, an old artist, and the girl herself. I can't do that in the Deborah Knott books.

CLPS: You mentioned writing in the Southern tradition. Questions of kinship, a sense of place, the land, the importance of the past, why are these traditional concerns of Southern writers?

MM: Part of it, I think, comes because we lost the war. If you're the victor, you can be magnanimous in your victory and get on with your life. But if you're the loser, you have to explain to yourself why you lost, so you rationalize, you veer between guilt and rage and scalding humiliation, and you keep telling stories to make sense of it. That may be where part of our storytelling tradition comes from. Certainly it helped strengthen whatever tendencies were already there.

CLPS: There are also Biblical overtones in the North Carolina books.

MM: Oh, yes! I love the language of it. I know it drives religious people up the wall to have the Bible thought of as literature and not God's holy word alone, but the King James version is an inspired book. When one of the preachers here tried to preach from a revised text, one of the old timers huffed, "If the King James Bible was good enough for Jesus Christ, it's good enough for me." I'm with him. Was it Flannery O'Connor who said that the South is God-obsessed? I was brought up Southern Baptist, and there's no way you can ever get that voice out of your head. If you grew up reading the Bible—and the Sunday school I went to encouraged us to read it all the way through every two years—that language works its way right down into your bones.

CLPS: A recent Deborah Knott novel is *Up Jumps the Devil.* Tell me a little about that book.

MM: It was written in response to unregulated growth here in central North Carolina. The low rate of unemployment in the Research Triangle has attracted thousands of new residents and they are now spilling out into the countryside. We had an interstate come through here and what ten years ago was nothing but a crossroads in the middle of tobacco and soybean fields is probably going to incorporate within the next year or so. We're becoming one subdivision after another and it just doesn't seem as if anybody's in charge or paying attention to what's happening about ground water, run-off, the loss of wetlands and farms.

At the same time, you have farmers who don't want anybody telling them what to do with their land if it's now more valuable as real estate. Some want to continue to farm as their fathers and grandfathers did and tobacco is still the big cash crop. At one point, I had Deborah's brother Adam, who's left the farm and gone out to California, say, "You people are sitting on seven million dollars." Deborah's floored when she actually multiplies how many acres of land her family owns by how much land is going for because they still think of themselves as relatively poor dirt farmers. In 1970, raw farm land was $350 an acre; now, it's anywhere up to $20,000 an acre. Farmers ask, "Why shouldn't I have a part of that?" I don't know where it's going to end. Which wouldn't upset me if I thought our politicians knew. If we're going to sell our birthright for a mess of pottage, somebody has to question how much that pottage is going to cost us.

CLPS: You've said you don't want to preach in your novels, but crime fiction does seem to deal with social issues almost by necessity.

MM: I think it adds a dimension and richness to them. I'm glad to see social issues in fiction and I'm glad to see more regionalism across the genre so that I can read about people and places and issues unfamiliar to me—Susan Dunlap's Berkeley, Robert Crais's Hollywood, Nevada Barr's wilderness areas. I think it was Carolyn Hart who pointed out that crime novels will probably be a rich source of social history in years to come. You have to spot the anomalies in order to solve the crime, so by their very nature, today's crime novels tend to describe society as it now is.

CLPS: Your latest Deborah Knott book is *Killer Market*.

MM: The title comes from a phrase used in the High Point wholesale furniture market. When retailers place lots of orders, the vendors say, "Boy, it was a killer market!"—a ready-made title. Traditionally, North Carolina has been a big furniture center. They have the International Home Furnishings Market twice a year in High Point, a little town of about seventy thousand people. For nine days in April and again in October, the town doubles in size. Thousands of people come from all over the world. The town has over seven million square feet of showroom space. It's like Paris or Milan in the fashion industry. This is where buyers come to see what's on the cutting edge of fashion.

Just picture the largest furniture mall you can imagine and then cube that: You have wicker cheek by jowl with reproductions of English Chippendale next to California painted furniture next to Mexican tinware. Deborah's in the process of getting her own house, so I thought it would be fun to send her over there with no clue as to how huge the Market is. She can't find a place to stay because hotel rooms book up months in advance. There is absolutely no room at the inn, which leads to some interesting situations. A sales manager is murdered and Deborah becomes an active suspect. There are no real issues here as in other Deborah Knott books. This is probably the purest, most straightforward murder mystery in the series.

CLPS: What is the next one going to be about?

MM: We'll be back in Colleton County, back among her family, and yes, I'm finally going to include a family tree for those who can't keep her brothers straight. There are several things I want to look at in this novel. I want to learn more about the young black ADA who prosecutes in Deborah's court. Why is she so uptight, so rigid with first offenders, so hard on her own race in the courtroom? And I want to look at the conflicted feelings farmers have about growing tobacco. It's still the biggest cash crop, but most farmers know in their heart of hearts that it's addictive and causes cancer. At the same time, it brings in so much money that there's nothing else they can legally raise that will provide that level of return.

CLPS: You often use epigraphs to introduce your chapters. Why?

MM: I like the contrasts and the irony, although the connection to the chapter's action is sometimes very arcane. When you write, you do many things for your own amusement and this is a case of amusing myself as much as anything else. Those quotes from Cennino Cennini in *Fugitive Colors* were wonderful. He's almost like a Julia Child, the way he gives recipes for mixing paints and drawing proportions. Technique then was halfway between alchemy and science—and I enjoyed contrasting the fifteenth-century viewpoint of art as vocation and the twentieth-century reduction of art to commerce.

CLPS: There are often artificial distinctions made between "genre" fiction and "mainstream" fiction. Do you see much difference yourself?

MM: Not really. People love to categorize. We even talk about categories within the genre itself. And there's that whole male/female thing where some feel that women's books aren't as important because a crime novel should be grim and violent to be realistic, while others hold that domestic concerns portray mainstream society more accurately than endless serial killers. Anybody who wants to call a book a mystery has my permission and that goes from the very softest romantic suspense all the way up to post-apocalyptic splatter punk. I'm very egalitarian about this. To me, good writing is good writing whenever it engages the emotions and doesn't insult the intelligence. I've seen some wonderful science fiction that matches anything in mainstream and the same with mysteries. I don't get too hung up on categories. When anybody asks what I write, I say murder mysteries. I've never felt the need to run from that tag.

CLPS: You're a past president of Sisters in Crime. Has that organization been effective in gaining recognition for female crime writers?

MM: Absolutely no question about it. In the past ten years of SinC's existence, women have gotten more recognition, more review space, more shelf space in airports and chain stores, which in turn has brought bigger contracts for female writers and created an atmosphere which welcomes more women into the field. And I credit this directly to the efforts of hardworking SinC committees—our promotional materials, our Books in Print catalog that goes out to thousands of potential buyers, our speakers bureau, our support networks across the country, etc., etc. SinC has more active mystery writers than any other organization so we have a high visibility in the mystery world which we have tried to use to promote the whole field, not just our own members.

CLPS: You've won several of the most prestigious awards for crime writing. What does winning those awards do for a writer?

MM: It can really jump-start any writing career. And not just winning. Even being nominated is an enormous help. Every year at Malice Domestic (and this year at Bouchercon), I moderate a newcomer panel composed of the nominees for Best First Novel. I love welcoming new people into our genre. This year, I had a letter from one nominee who said that she wasn't sure she could continue writing to the detriment of her day job. Then she was nominated. Now her publisher's more interested and she just signed a contract for three more books. Awards do make reviewers notice you more, it would be foolish to pretend otherwise. And publishers and editors are pleased. It's great to be a winner, but editors are happy just to have their authors nominated. I read for the Edgar committee this year and we received around four hundred submissions for Best Novel. To be nominated, to be one of five people out of four hundred? That's a pretty big achievement. You can put that on your books for the rest of your life: "Edgar Nominee," "Agatha Nominee," "Anthony," "Shamus."

CLPS: You had a collection of short fiction.

MM: *Shovelling Smoke.* Douglas Greene at Crippen and Landru has begun publishing limited editions of short stories. He does a print run of about 250 hardbound books which the authors sign, and he also tips in by hand a page of original draft manuscript which the authors provide, complete with crossed-out passages and alternate phrases inked in. Then he does about 1,500 trade paperbacks of the same title. He's providing a real service to those of us who write short stories since most of our publishers don't like to do single-author collections. I have about forty-five stories, so we've selected about twenty for *Shovelling Smoke,* which should be out about now. One of them is a previously unpublished Deborah Knott story.

CLPS: What's the attraction of short fiction?

MM: It's short! If you have an idea that's not book-length or want to explore a new character, you can do it in under 3,000 words. One of my favorites is called "Deadhead Coming Down," about a bored long-haul truck driver who occasionally pulls off the interstate and finds someone to run over. It's a grisly little story—about 1,500 words—and it was fun to do, but it was much too slight to carry a whole book. Stories also keep your name green between books and often they take on a life of their own when they're reprinted in different anthologies. It really tickled me when Bill Pronzini and Jack Adrian selected "Deadhead" for an anthology featuring hard-boiled detectives. Me? Hard-boiled?

This interview originally appeared in *The Armchair Detective,* 30:3 (Summer 1997).

Joy Fielding

INTERVIEW BY CHARLES L. P. SILET

*J*oy Fielding has achieved an international reputation for her page-
turning, best-selling novels of psychological depth and insight into the
lives of women and their struggles for independence and self-recogni-
tion. Since 1981, with the publication of Kiss Mommy Goodbye,
she has written eight highly successful thrillers: The Other Woman
(1983), Life Penalty *(1984),* The Deep End *(1986),* Good Intentions *(1989),* See Jane Run *(1991),* Tell Me No Secrets *(1993),*
Don't Cry Now *(1995), and most recently* Missing Pieces *(1997).*
With each book her reputation, along with her readership, has grown.

*Born, raised, and educated in Toronto, Canada, Joy Fielding spent
the years immediately after university pursuing an acting career, both in
Canada and in Hollywood, where she appeared in theater and on television, including a role on the long-running series* Gunsmoke. *After her return to Toronto she taught herself to write, and eventually sold scripts to
the Canadian Broadcasting Company and three early novels before she hit
her stride as an author of psychological thrillers with* Kiss Mommy
Goodbye.

*Four of her books have appeared as successful television movies both in
North America and in Europe and several more are under option. Her
books have sold well here and abroad, and she is one of the best-selling
novelists in Germany.* See Jane Run *has been a best-seller for three or four
years and is currently number two on the all-time German best-seller list.*

CLPS: Tell me a little about your background. Where you were born, grew up, went to school.

JF: I was born and raised in Toronto, Canada, and I went to school there through university. I got a Bachelor of Arts degree from the University of Toronto, where I majored in English. In those days in Canada—in those days, I mean, it wasn't *that* long ago—we didn't go away to university, like the American system, and I stayed in Toronto. Now things have changed. Now everybody goes away. But I lived at home quite happily.

CLPS: What did you do after you graduated from university?

JF: I always wanted to be a writer, but when I was in university, I got sidetracked into acting which I'd also always loved doing. So once I graduated I decided that I was going to be an actress. I spent a year in Toronto doing a variety of television and stage productions, and then I went off to Hollywood. I never lacked self-confidence so I assumed that Hollywood was waiting for me and would welcome me with open arms. I was fairly naive. I'd come from a very supportive, loving household, and then suddenly there I was in the land where anything goes and nobody cares. I ended up living in this little one-room apartment off the Sunset Strip. The first friends I made were a topless dancer and a hooker. My poor mother.

It was a very strange time for me. Over the next couple of years I found better friends, but it was not what I expected and I ended up working as a teller in a lot of banks. In fact I loved being a bank teller, and I was a good one. It was fun and there was really no pressure. But as an actress I was constantly being told by agents and casting directors and producers that I was very "special." It took me a long time to figure out that it meant they had no idea what to do with me. I didn't really fit the mold. I was not the baby-doll type that was in vogue at the time. So I would go to auditions, but I hardly ever got to open my mouth. I would walk in the door and the producer would look at me and say, "Oh, you are not what we were expecting." So I didn't get to work a whole lot as a actress.

After I'd been there a year I got a part on *Gunsmoke*, and I came close to getting a couple of other parts, but I didn't. After two and half years I thought, "I don't think I want this badly enough, and I am tired going around asking people to like me." I had written my mother a letter telling her that I was generally unhappy but I couldn't put my finger on it exactly why. She wrote back, "You can come home and you can write, that is what you should be doing."

So I went home and actually moved back in with my parents, and I spent the next couple of years getting my self-confidence back and learning how to write.

CLPS: What did you write?

JF: Actually I wrote a couple of scripts which I sold to the CBC, the Canadian Broadcasting Corporation, one of which was produced and the second one was not produced because the show I had written it for got canceled. Then I decided I was going to write a novel. I thought I had nothing to lose. I was living at home. I had room and board and no responsibilities. I had these parents who said, "Be happy and do whatever you want and we're happy to have you here." They were wonderful. I took jobs occasionally to make sure I always had my own money, but I certainly didn't have to worry about living expenses. I set up shop at the kitchen table, and I wrote a novel in longhand in five weeks. I sent it off to five different publishers and two of them accepted it.

CLPS: This was *The Best of Friends*. Tell me about it.

JF: They always tell you write about what you know. So, of course, I did just the opposite. I wrote about a young woman who had been married and divorced and had had an abortion and as a result had a total nervous breakdown and a split personality. All the things I knew about intimately! I wrote this crazy book. I haven't read it in a very long time, but my older daughter read it and she was actually quite shocked by it, so I guess I must have done something right. Other people who read it say that it holds up really fairly well. It wasn't a mystery. It wasn't suspense. It was just this stream-of-consciousness novel about this young woman who was in the middle of having a nervous breakdown.

CLPS: At this time you also wrote *Trance* and *The Transformation*.

JF: Yes, they came after. *The Transformation* was the second book and *Trance* was the third. After the first novel I thought everything was going to be a snap. I planned to take five weeks every year and write a best-seller, but I soon discovered that it wasn't going to be quite so easy. It took me four years to get *The Transformation* published. Helen Barrett, my agent at the time, said to me, "Joy, you know Jacqueline Susann has died, and there is nobody filling her shoes so why don't you try to write about young women in Hollywood. You were there. Do something like that."

She also said, "Suspense sells," and gave me some very basic pointers on how to write suspense: Keep the action moving, thread your plot—put in one plot and just when it starts to get interesting pick up something else, drop it, and start weaving in the threads—always end the chapter where the reader wants to keep going. So I sat down and outlined this story about three girls in Hollywood who were trying to be actresses. The story was organized around a sort of Charles Manson-type killing. I wrote a story that I think was pretty suspenseful, and I was able to draw on some of my own experiences, some of the things I'd been through and had seen when I was living there. For example, the Manson murders took place when I lived in Los Angeles. We ended up selling it to the Playboy Press, a separate division of *Playboy*, which I believe is no longer in existence. It came out as a paperback and sold reasonably well. If I were to write that book now, it would be a completely different book of course, but I was learning how to write suspense and it was an interesting experiment.

In *Trance* I continued to write what I thought other people wanted to read and I wrote much more to a formula. I don't know if that is the right word, but certainly there wasn't anything personal in the approach. This time the book was about a young girl who was kidnapped and programmed to assassinate her father who was a senator. It had overtones of the Patty Hearst kidnapping. So I was relying on some events that were around at the time. I glanced through that book a few months back because somebody asked to see it and some of it is really hokey. But I was young and still learning how to write. Other parts of it are OK. Both those novels taught me how to write page-turners. When I go back and look at them, I find that even if I'm a little embarrassed by the actual quality of the writing, I'm still turning the pages.

CLPS: Did you read much crime or mystery fiction when you were younger?

JF: No, not a lot and I still don't. But I remember when I was in grade three or four, the teacher read us a story called *Leiningen versus the Ants*, which was about these man-eating ants. They later made it into a movie called *The Naked Jungle* which was a much better title. She read to us a little bit every day, and I loved that story. I couldn't wait to get to class to hear the next chapter. I read very little in school until I hit university. But I've always loved suspense. I especially love watching it: horror movies, scary movies, anything suspenseful. In fact, I'm often disappointed by suspense novels. So I find I don't read a lot of them.

CLPS: The first of your current run of suspense novels began with *Kiss Mommy Goodbye*. How did that come about? Did you feel that you had really hit your pace writing it?

JF: It is interesting what happened with that book. I didn't quite know what I wanted to do at the time I wrote it except that I didn't want to write what I'd been writing. At that point in my life I decided to stop worrying about what I thought other people wanted to read and start concentrating on what I wanted to write. I remember an editor suggested that I write a love story. When I thought about it, I realized that you can't just write a love story because that's kind of icky and really who cares? There has to be some conflict. There has to be some reason why the reader is going to want to keep reading. So I figured I'd write a love story but make it more difficult. Let's say we have the story of a rather bad marriage and the woman finds herself involved in an extramarital relationship. But there was still not enough there. Then I read in the paper one morning an article about a divorced couple and the husband had kidnapped the children and disappeared. This was probably in 1979 before spousal kidnapping became common. By the time the book came out it was an epidemic. I thought, "Now that's a great hook." We get this woman, she wants out of this marriage, she meets this guy, she gets her divorce, and her husband disappears with the kids.

I wrote an outline and my agent sent it to a publishing house and the publisher liked it. So we got an advance, and I wrote the book following the outline quite closely. We sent it off to him and the agent called me back a little while later and she said, "He hates it." I just died when I heard that. Even now I just die. I said, "What do you mean 'He hates it?' What doesn't he like?" She said, "He doesn't like any of it." I replied, "But it is exactly what I put in the outline." I wondered what we were going to do. She said, "Well, either you completely rewrite it according to what he wants, or we give him back his money and send it somewhere else." I thought, "We give him back his money?" Unless you're going to fight it out in court, this is what you have to do. I liked the book as it was, and so we sent it to another publishing house. They loved it and they gave me more than double the advance that the other guy did. It turned out to be quite a nice hit.

CLPS: So that book started you on the series of books you have been doing since.

JF: After *Kiss Mommy Goodbye* was when I really decided to write contemporary fiction that was much more reality-based, which dealt with issues that were concerning me. I figured that if these issues were of interest to me that they would probably be of interest to a lot of other women and hopefully men as well.

CLPS: How do you achieve variety in the books so they don't seem the same?

JF: I work very hard to make sure I'm not writing the same book again, because I feel there are a lot of writers out there who do just rewrite the same book over and over. I'm very conscious of not repeating myself. Some of the themes are similar. If I look over all of the works from *Kiss Mommy Goodbye* on, I can see about three different themes that are quite constant: the woman's search for her identity, the mother-daughter relationship, and the search for the mother. The search for the mother figure is interesting to me because my mother died just after my older daughter was born. I guess I'm still searching for my own mother. Those themes seem to be very often what the books are about underneath. They are also perhaps about the invisibility of women in our culture even though they may seem very visible. I like writing about things not being what they seem, about not really knowing other people. I like to take a woman who has a fairly comfortable existence and suddenly introduce something that's out of her control that changes everything.

Given that central theme, I do all sorts of other things to give the books variety. I make sure that the heroines are quite different people. If there has been an evil husband in one book, then I'm going to try to make sure in the next book that he isn't. I change the cities around. I create a whole new cast of characters. I'll also make stylistic changes. I'll maybe write in the present tense, as I did in *The Deep End*, or as in *Missing Pieces*, I'll write in the first person. One time I'll do a book that is more suspense-oriented. Then I'll do something that concentrates more on relationships. I really do try to make sure that the stories are very different.

CLPS: Some writers very deliberately set themselves a task with each book. Do you do that?

JF: I've never thought about it in those terms. You have to be careful not to stray too far from what your audience is expecting, but you really don't want to repeat yourself. I fight against being put in any category or genre. I don't like to be put in a niche. I don't like somebody to say that since you've done that well, do another one. For instance, I don't consider myself a mystery writer. The only book I've written that was a whodunit type was *Don't Cry Now*, and that's because there was somebody killed at the beginning of the book and you didn't know who did it. To me that was the least interesting part of the book. I was much more interested in the characters and their relationships and why they did what they did. I don't think I write mysteries. I write more psychological suspense, and they're all page-turners.

CLPS: You write single books rather than a series. Why is that?

JF: If you have a series then you have books that are basically plot-oriented fiction. I like a strong plot when I'm writing because it grounds me and I find it comforting, but I also like my plot to be character driven. Also, I guess, I've never thought of using the same set of characters as a serial. I think if you do that you either have to have a detective or somebody who is solving some sort of crime or some reason to put this character in a whole bunch of precarious situations, and I'm not really interested in solving crimes. You could do a series of adventures with a particular character but I think I'd rather investigate other types of situations and have the freedom of new people. Besides, I don't always want to know what happens to my characters when I'm finished with them, because like everybody else I kind of hope they will live happily ever after. I would not like to pick up *Kiss Mommy Goodbye* or *See Jane Run* and find out that things didn't work out for these people. Every so often somebody will ask, "Why don't you write a sequel to *The Other Woman?*" That's the one people seem to want a sequel to. Maybe one day I will, but right now everything worked out pretty well, and I don't want to start stirring things up again.

CLPS: A lot of writers can identify their break-out novel. Can you do that?

JF: I think for me it probably was *See Jane Run*, because it did everything I wanted it to. The story was a grabber. It got you from the first line: "One afternoon in late spring, Jane Whittaker went to the store for some milk and some eggs and forgot who she was." And the first chapter ends with Jane frantic because not only doesn't she know who she is but she also discovers that the front of her dress is covered in blood and her pockets are filled with hundred-dollar bills. You have this wonderful situation from the very beginning and a hook that would keep people reading. Then I was able—and I'm not sure entirely how—to keep escalating the tension and upping the ante. Women, especially, identified with the character of Jane to a really phenomenal degree and all over the world have come up to me and said, "You wrote my life story." Well, none of them has ever lost her memory or had blood on her dress or money in her pockets like that, but we've all felt trapped. We've all searched for who we are, and women have had trouble knowing whom to trust. You have the combination of a very interesting story and a character that women identified with at a real gut level. Everything just worked in that book.

CLPS: What is your process of writing?

JF: People always ask where do you get your ideas, and who knows? Once the ideas start coming at me, I start putting them together and I get a theme and a plot developing. Then I sit down and I do an outline of anywhere from ten to twenty-five pages. I have a very clear idea of the beginning, a clear idea of the end, and know several signposts along the way. I flesh those out in the course of the outline. They're not written in stone, everything can change, but that's the blueprint and that's what I go by. I then try to write five pages a day on the computer. Some days I'm flying and I can maybe get seven or eight pages, but that's rare and that's usually toward the end of the book or if there's a lot of dialogue. That usually takes anywhere from three to four hours. I do that five days a week. Because over the years I was a stay-at-home mom, I learned to adjust my schedule to whenever the kids were asleep or at school, so I can pretty much write at any time of the day or even in the evening as long as it is not too late. But I prefer the mornings. Every day I read over what I wrote the day before and rewrite and make changes. I don't do much revising once the book is finished, because generally speaking I have worked it out in the course of writing the book. It is much easier to correct as you are going along than when the book is finished. What often happens is that after the editorial staff sees it, they may say tighten it up or make clear the delineation of the emotions of the characters or clean up the descriptions. The major rewriting part takes a couple of weeks and usually doesn't involve huge structural changes.

CLPS: You mentioned that you don't like labels but one of the ways people might describe your novels is as of the "woman-at-risk" type.

But you also write "children-at-risk" stories. What does working with children allow you to do?

JF: I have a little trouble with that whole women-in-jeopardy idea. What do men write about? Men-in-jeopardy? I find to talk about the books as women-in-jeopardy is a little condescending. I write about people in times of crisis. If there is no risk or jeopardy then generally the story is not very interesting. I'm not sure I can write a novel where nothing really happens and which focuses on an internal examination of a life. In my fiction I like there to be some element of risk. With children you have to be careful, I think. You don't want to exploit a child's suffering, and I'm always very careful, if children are involved, that I'm not exploiting them. I feel uncomfortable with that. I'm really writing more about women and the effect on them of either the child being in danger or of losing a child. Every mother's worst fear is something happening to her children. There are certain books I've stopped reading because they've put a child in such a precarious situation that I'm reading about the child's actual suffering. I don't want to read that, and I certainly don't want to write it.

CLPS: Why don't you write "straight" fiction rather than suspense thrillers?

JF: Actually that's what I think I do. I would just like to write whatever I feel like, and I would always hope that the fact that my books are page-turners would be an element. When people say to me, "What do you write?" I say that I write contemporary fiction. Certainly with *Missing Pieces,* that's what I tried to do. There is a thriller element to the story, but it is really about this woman, a therapist, who is having trouble controlling her own rather dysfunctional family. I wanted the irony of that whole situation. This woman has a neatly ordered life, and then suddenly it all changes: Her mother is in the beginning stages of Alzheimer's; her daughters are very rebellious and growing away from her; and an old boyfriend enters the picture to shake things up further. On top of everything her loony half-sister announces that she is going to marry a man who is on trial for the murder of thirteen women.

The interesting part of the story is how this woman's neatly ordered existence is absolutely falling apart and how little control she has. Kate is a middle-aged woman, which you almost never see in fiction, dealing with menopause, with an elderly infirm parent, and with rebellious teenagers. She's a typical member of the sandwich generation. Everything just keeps happening to her. That's what I want to explore. *Missing Pieces* is much more into mainstream fiction than it is a thriller. It is sold as a thriller, but I'm not sure if that's a good approach to take or not.

CLPS: Are there differences between the thriller and the mainstream novel?

JF: I do think there are differences. There are novels you can categorize as thrillers, because they are either about murders or somebody in real physical danger and the plot all turns on their life being in jeopardy. Maybe the story had horror aspects or maybe a lot of violence or the threat of violence. So I do think there are some books that fall quite neatly into the category of thriller. Even though there are elements of that in *Missing Pieces*, I still think my books are not quite so easy to categorize. Certainly *Kiss Mommy Goodbye* is not, strictly speaking, a thriller, and *The Other Woman* and *Good Intentions* aren't at all.

CLPS: As a writer what do you think you do best?

JF: I write very real dialogue. People always say, "Did you have a tape recorder on in my living room?" I have a very good ear for the way people say things so my dialogue never sounds stilted. Also I understand women very well because I have a firm understanding of myself. I don't think women are very well represented in fiction, and I really do get across the female point of view and the female perspective in a way that most male writers miss entirely. For a lot of female writers, especially commercial fiction writers, it also doesn't seem to be a high priority.

CLPS: What are you working on at the moment?

JF: I'm not altogether sure. I submitted a new outline to my publishers but they didn't like it. I think it was too much of a departure. They want another *See Jane Run*. We'll have to see.

CLPS: Your books strike me as eminently filmable.

JF: Hollywood is very much an old boys' network, so if I were to write a book about men it would have a much better chance of making it onto the big screen. Television seems to be the place that the powers-that-be in Hollywood feel anything by women for women belongs. I've had a number of TV movies made of my books. *See Jane*

Run was, I believe, the most popular TV movie of the year when it was on a couple of years ago. *Tell Me No Secrets* was also a TV movie and did quite well. The same producer has both *Don't Cry Now* and *Missing Pieces* on option. German TV did *Life Penalty* and *The Deep End*. They also have *Good Intentions* under option.

CLPS: Do you sell well abroad?

JF: I sell amazingly well abroad, and I really don't understand it. I'm very flattered and very surprised by it all because I always felt I was writing books for a very specific, North American kind of audience. Lo and behold these books are popular all over the world. In Germany I'm a phenomenal success. At one point I had three books simultaneously on the best-seller list. *See Jane Run* has been on the best-seller list for three or four years, and it was number two or three on their all time German best-seller list. It's sold millions of copies there. I don't understand why, but I'm very grateful for it.

CLPS: It must say something about a universal appeal of your fiction.

JF: The more particular you make something, the more generalizations people can extract from it. I'm writing very specific stories about very particular women and the more real I make them, the more particular I make them, the more real it is for women all over the world or readers all over the world. They identify with the characters and situations in the books. Obviously the feeling of being trapped, of being unsure of who you are, and the loss of control are all issues that are very common concerns, especially for women. When I was in the Czech Republic recently, I would go to a bookstore signing and I'd say to my husband, "God, I hope somebody shows up." We'd get to the bookstore and people would be lined up around the block. I'd be signing books for hours. And they would bring me presents. One woman approached me with tears in her eyes and she said, "Thank you for your books, and thank you that you exist." Of course, I burst into tears and I looked at my husband and I said, "When was the last time somebody thanked you just for existing?" It is very moving to really touch people's lives in that way and to know that you are writing something that has such meaning for them.

Barbara Parker

INTERVIEW BY RICK KOSTER

Barbara Parker uses the Day-glo vistas of South Florida as a back-drop for her best-selling novels—the popular Suspicion series (Sus-picion of Innocence, Suspicion of Guilt, Suspicion of Deceit) and stand-alone titles, Blood Relations and Criminal Justice. A former prosecutor with Miami-Dade state attorney's office, Parker writes with assurance about where she has lived and worked for more than twenty years. Ms. Parker's next novel, Suspicion of Betrayal, is due for release in April 1999.

RK: You were already an attorney when you decided to start writing. Was being an author an ambition you'd secretly harbored all along?

BP: Well, no. I got C's in college English. And then I became a lawyer, and *then*, when I decided I wanted to write, I went to Florida International University and got my M.F.A. in Creative Writing. So I studied it, you know? I guess maybe there was some talent there to begin with, but it certainly helps to figure out what you're doing.

RK: You've rapidly made a mark in writing legal suspense. When you started, had the whole Scott Turow/Richard North Patterson/John Grisham phenomenon happened?

BP: Actually, no. I didn't know what I wanted to do when I started. I remember Turow's *Presumed Innocent;* I'm not sure when it came out, but I think I probably read it in '88. As for writing *Suspicion of Innocence,* I did that because I'm a lawyer and I figured I'd better do the proverbial "write about what you know." And I don't know if Scott Turow was an actual influence. I can tell you that John Grisham was *not* happening yet, by which I mean I simply hadn't heard of him when I started. I do think that Scott Turow is wonderful, and that *Burden of Proof* is one of the best books I've ever read.

RK: So many attorneys have become writers of legal thrillers. The movement has become enormous.

BP: To that end, Grisham made the legal thriller accessible, and, more importantly, popular. And once someone enjoys Grisham, they naturally start looking at other writers of a similar style or genre. Grisham may be a one-man industry, and he may have his detractors, but he certainly made it easier for the rest of us.

RK: On that note, do you think that it's reached the point where the legal thriller is a must-have for every publishing house?

BP: Well, they're just very popular right now. And if they sell, the publishing houses are going to try to do it. In fact, I've just recently gotten manuscripts from two Florida writers of legal thrillers who want me to blurb their manuscripts, and they're both lawyers. Is there a bandwagon aspect? Sure, but that's commercial fiction for you. A lot of the books are derivative, but, generally, if they're good, they'll sell. And I have no problem with that.

RK: When you made the decision to write, did you start off with short stories, or even think about mystery fiction?

BP: Not short stories, because I don't have the voice for them and because when you're hitting forty, you don't have time to hang out in coffee houses and write poetry and short stories and drink and smoke cigarettes and have affairs. That's behind you, if you ever did it, so it's time to get serious. So I asked, what's selling? What gives me the best chance of making a living? I thought, well, it's got to be a novel. OK, fine. What *kind* of novels are selling, and of them, what are the common elements that make them marketable and successful? From there, it wasn't too difficult to figure out.

RK: No, as evidenced by your first two books, *Suspicion of Innocence* and *Suspicion of Guilt,* thrillers which featured a recurring protagonist, Gail Connor, who happened to be a female attorney.

BP: Right. I don't know, for example, how James Lee Burke constructs his novels, or how anybody else does it. But I knew I wanted to write a book with a lawyer in it. As a fairly beginning writer, I knew I'd have a better chance if the protagonist were a female. Therefore: *female lawyer!* I knew she was going to live in Miami because I'm from South Florida—not because I found South Florida intrinsically interesting but because I happen to *live* down here; it's part of my experience. And the next step was to ask, well, what's the worst thing that can happen to this woman? Hmm, what if she was charged with the murder of her sister? And I was off.

RK: Once you had the manuscript for *Suspicion of Innocence,* was it difficult to get an agent?

BP: Not very, actually. I think, really, if you've got a product that's marketable, you won't have much of a problem. [laughs] That's what my agent tells me, anyway.

RK: After two Gail Connor books, you decided to move away from the series concept and wrote *Blood Relations.* While it's still a legal thriller, it has a new, male hero, a Miami prosecutor named Sam Hagen. Why did you shift gears?

BP: I write what I feel I have to write, and I write about what's going on in my life and in the world. Plus, I had said at the time everything I wanted to say about Gail and Anthony [the quasi-love interest who defended Gail in a murder trial in *Suspicion of Innocence* and became a recurring character]. Other things were interesting to me. I didn't want to get in a rut with [Gail and Anthony]; I don't know if Sue Grafton ever feels she's in a rut after so many mysteries, but I wonder sometimes if she wishes she would get to the letter Z a little more quickly so she could get on with something else. On the other hand, after doing two books unrelated to Gail Connor and Anthony Quintana, you might be surprised that I went back to them with my next two novels, *Suspicion of Deceit* and *Suspicion of Betrayal.*

RK: The hero of *Criminal Justice* is another male attorney, Dan Galindo. Like Sam Hagen, Galindo is a compelling protagonist, but they're pretty different characters.

BP: Yes, Dan Galindo is not a real macho guy, though he's certainly not weak. Hagen was very tough, a Vietnam vet. And the reason I went to him was because I'd done a female protagonist in the first two books. So I thought it was time to try a male protagonist and I went from Gail to a real tough guy. And then I was able to pull back in *Criminal Justice* with Dan Galindo.

RK: All of your heroes have been attorneys, though they've run the gamut from high-dollar corporate types to hard-nosed prosecutors to a disgraced former U.S. attorney scraping out a tattered existence in a threadbare defense firm. Another consistency in your work is the South Florida setting. Do you think of your books as literary valentines to South Florida?

BP: I was born in South Carolina and raised in western North Carolina and didn't actually get to South Florida until 1974. So, having not spent my childhood down here, it took me a long time to feel that this place was home—which is complicated by the fact that South Florida is changing so fast that I'm surprised anyone could call it home. Dade County is now more than half-Latin, and early on I began learning to speak the language. I've always felt that things were changing right out from under me, even as I tried to get my bearings. I think that is particularly true of South Florida. I am *finally* beginning to feel at home here. My books have been an attempt to find a sense of belonging and to place Miami in the context of the United States. I've found that here on the frontier the American ideals of independence and striving are as strong as they are anywhere else in the country—maybe more so.

RK: Are the changes in Miami disillusioning?

BP: Not at all. But Miami, being at the far end of the farthest appendage in the continental U.S., is very much its own world. And the change is enormous. It's like trying to step in the same river twice; you know that old saying? It's a philosophic question which means things are changing so quickly that there's no stability to anything. And then, six years ago, I moved north of Miami so I could find a school for my son that wasn't filled with graffiti, trash, and metal detectors. But he's in college now, and I'm back in Miami where I belong.

RK: So the suburban setting in *Criminal Justice* is a reflection of the time you've lived away from Miami? In the book, Dan Galindo's ex-wife lives very much that out-of-the-city, "planned community" existence.

BP: Definitely. Some of the primary issues in *Criminal Justice* are, one, the clash of culture, and, second, my attempt to find Home, which I think springs from my own *lack* of home. But I wouldn't have written *Criminal Justice* . . . I couldn't have written it if it had not been part of my experience. When I first moved up here I heard the drag lines chewing into the Everglades twenty-four hours a day—all night, all day, clank-clank-clank-crunch—and I *had* to put the drag line in the book; it's all metaphor. I hated it from the moment I moved there, but there wasn't much I could do about it at the time. To be sure, it's very pretty, and the kids can ride their bikes and play in the streets, but my main complaint about gated communities is that they tend to make us forget what's going on in the city; we can ignore it, but the cities really are the fountains and engines of our strength, our economy, and our identity as people. No one says, "I'm from a certain area of suburbia." When we move there, we put up our barricades and we live safely in green and quiet places and we forget the city and the people who live in them. I have no solutions, but I find myself continually pondering the problem.

RK: Do you work from outlines?

BP: I try to have an outline, and I pretty much know where a book's going when I start. I used to outline a lot more than I do now. When I'm under deadline, I have to have *some* plan because otherwise I get lost. It's tempting to go down all these different routes, but I have to stick to the point. Invariably, the books tend to be headstrong and take off in their own directions, and all I can do is follow along. It's like having a kid, you know: you tell it where to go but you've got to follow it around a little bit, too.

RK: Not only are you renowned for your plot twists, but it's refreshing that the line of delineation between the bad guys and good guys is frequently blurred. Vince, the DEA undercover agent in *Criminal Justice,* is one of those characters who might go either way.

BP: A lot of that comes in the writing, and very often I'm surprised, myself. As far as plotting goes, in *Criminal Justice* I got to an absolute dead end. I just wanted to throw up my hands and say, "I don't know what to do next." But if you sit in a chair several hours a day, weeks at a time, eventually something comes to you. And, as for characters like Vince Hooper . . . [laughs]. Well . . . he's just overzealous. I feel very uncomfortable with totally evil characters, because I don't think they exist in real life. There's nothing we can learn from them.

RK: Another character in *Criminal Justice*, Miguel Salazar, might be thought of as pure evil.

BP: Well, you have to consider his background. He just wanted to come to the States and make a success of himself. You've gotta come down to South Florida. Miguel Salazar, Klaus Ruffini in *Blood Relations* . . . these people are *common* down here. I don't know why that is but, like I said, Miami hasn't been here very long and it's a frontier. People come here on the make; they're greedy and ambitious for life and for other things like power and money. The sands are always shifting out from under you, so you've got to run real fast. And you might step on a few people.

RK: Miami certainly has its share of characters, though there's an entire generation whose views of Miami were probably shaped by the film *Scarface*.

BP: Oh, that was *way* overdone. But it's an icon, absolutely. Remember Al Pacino's sidekick, played by Steven Bauer? Well, guess what? They made a TV movie out of *Suspicion of Innocence* and Steven Bauer played Anthony. He's really Cuban-American, too.

RK: Did you get to go to Los Angeles for any of the filming or get to meet any of the actors?

BP: I wish. My agent tried to figure out where they were filming and what they're doing. But once you sell the rights, it's over. You're just the writer [mock stern voice]. They don't care about you.

RK: Did you write the teleplay?

BP: No, I didn't even get to do that. It would've been nice if they'd let me see it at least. But this was my first one, and it's been, gosh, almost three years ago now. I was just grateful to get anything at that point. Maybe next time I'll at least have them let me look at the script first.

RK: Did you read voraciously as a child?

BP: [laughs] Nancy Drew. And I don't think she ever did kiss Ned Nickerson. Well, times have changed.

RK: Indeed. There is a bit of erotica going on in your books.

BP: As in *Blood Relations*? Well, I pulled back a little bit for the next one, *Criminal Justice.* But . . . all the books are different from each other in sexual content.

RK: Is that easy to do?

JF: It just happens. I'm a different person each time I write a book. That's why it's difficult to do a series. At least for me. I don't know about other people, but I write about what's happening at the moment. When I return to Gail Connor in subsequent books, she's guaranteed to be a different woman, because I will have changed. I won't know how she'll be different, but she will be. I can't help it; I can't *not* do it.

Edna Buchanan

INTERVIEW BY CAROL SORET COPE

CSC: Edna, you've spent all your professional life writing about crime, both real and fictional—all the horrible things that people do to each other. How did you get yourself into this?

EB: I suppose it goes back to my childhood. When I was four years old, I taught myself to read using the metropolitan New York dailies. The most fascinating stories were about Willie Sutton, the Babe Ruth of bank robbers; George Metesky, the mad bomber; and mobster Lucky Luciano—all the dark princes of my childhood. I was fascinated by lawlessness and evil and what makes it flourish. Evil was very alive to me then.

CSC: And now?

EB: Evil is still very much alive. That's why justice is so important, and so rare, even more rare today than when I was a child.

CSC: You grew up in Paterson, New Jersey, and your childhood was tough, wasn't it?

EB: My father abandoned us when I was seven years old and I never saw him again. My mother and I lived in a tenement, and she worked two or three jobs to support us. I worked from the time I was twelve, always had a job. I worked in a coat factory after school and during the summer, and then in a candle factory. And I was underage. It was a major event when I turned sixteen and got my official working papers. I could make more money then.

CSC: What were the bright spots in your childhood?

EB: Reading was always important to me from a very early age. My parents belonged to a book club, and I read absolutely everything— from Ellery Queen to *Forever Amber*. And I read lots of animal stories. I loved animals, especially horses and dogs. I loved *Black Beauty* and *Lad of Sunnybrook Farm*.

CSC: What else?

EB: Movies. I sat through double features twice, every chance I got. Pure escapism. My favorite was *Sinbad the Sailor* with Douglas Fairbanks, Jr., and Maureen O'Hara. My world was so bleak, all gritty shades of black, white and gray. And there on the screen was this gorgeous Technicolor world—brilliant blue skies, turquoise seas. And Sinbad, fighting evil monsters and surviving marvelous adventures. Sinbad searched the seven seas for the mystical island of Dariabar, the home of his father. I absolutely loved it. Many years later, after I moved to Miami, I saw the movie again and was struck by my obvious identification with Sinbad—the missing father, the search for home. Because I never really felt at home in my life in New Jersey. I was a misfit, a displaced person.

CSC: And then you came to Miami?

EB: When I came to Miami on vacation, it was like coming home. I knew where I belonged at last, even though I'd never been here before. It was like stepping out of a black-and-white newsreel into Technicolor. The brilliant sea—the sky—the vivid sunsets. I went back to New Jersey, packed up and moved to Miami. It's been a love affair ever since.

CSC: You never looked back?

EB: Never. Many people never find their place in the world, and I'm so lucky to have found mine. From the first moment, I've felt such a passion for Miami, such a strong connection. It's where I belong. It's home.

CSC: You won a Pulitzer Prize for your crime reporting at the *Miami Herald*. Yet you never studied journalism. Never went to college. In fact, you dropped out of high school. How can this be?

EB: Yes, I dropped out in the tenth grade. Never went to college or studied journalism. And yet I did win a Pulitzer and taught a journalism class at Florida International University. Ironic, isn't it? The truth is, I absolutely loathed school. I suppose it was a result of feeling awkward and out of place. I had trouble with teachers, except for one who believed in me. Edna Mae Tunis. She was the one bright spot, my seventh grade English teacher. She asked me the question that changed my entire life, forever. "Will you promise to dedicate a book to me someday?" She thought I could write. She made me believe I could.

Through tough times since—dealing with editors, agents, and publishers, even negotiating with Hollywood producers—so many times I was in over my head and thought that I simply could not do this. Then I'd think, Mrs. Tunis thought I could, she *said* I could do it. So I would. Her words were my mantra. She died when I was in the eighth grade. But she will always be alive to me. And, of course, *The Corpse Had a Familiar Face* is dedicated to Edna Mae Tunis.

It's fascinating how we weave each other into the fabric of our lives. Encouragement is so important, especially with children.

CSC: You taught journalism at Florida International University, right?

EB: A wonderful experience. I knew it would take a great deal of time and commitment, so I agreed to do it once, just once. One class, one semester, only. I loved it. Since I'd never been to college or attended a journalism class (except to lecture), I didn't know how it "should" be done. So I planned each class as an event for the students. Once I staged a "crime" in the classroom. The students reacted, all thought it was the real thing, until I ordered them to "Freeze!" and write a quick news story describing what they had just seen. Their versions differed wildly. My point was to show them firsthand how unreliable "eye witness" testimony can be. And yet it is so beloved by juries.

Another time we took a field trip to the morgue, for more than three hours, and nobody left. They were just fascinated. Students finally began bringing in friends, boyfriends, their mothers—people who'd heard about the class and wanted to take part.

CSC: Did you stick to your vow to make it a one-time-only class?

EB: Oh, yes. That was my only adventure in teaching. I enjoyed it so much. We had our class picture taken surrounded by police crime scene tape. I've kept in touch with many of my students. I go to their weddings, write them references. Some have gone on to promising careers in journalism. I'm so proud of them.

CSC: Maybe you were Edna Mae Tunis to one of them.

EB: I hope so! Journalism has been so good to me. I needed to give something back, to encourage others. And they knew they would be my only class. We had a blast!

CSC: Has anyone ever told you that you made a difference in his or her life?

EB: Several people, actually. Young journalists. The families of crime victims, readers who felt that something I wrote changed them or the quality of their lives. It's quite satisfying.

CSC: Let's go back to the beginning of your career. How did you get started at the *Miami Herald*?

EB: I decided to try for a reporting job at the *Herald,* the biggest and the best newspaper in the South. But the woman in the personnel department was quite blunt. "Unless you have a degree in journalism or five years experience at a daily newspaper, don't bother," she told me. So I went to a small local, the *Miami Beach Daily Sun.* When the pale, chubby editor, Ted Crail asked me if I had studied journalism, my heart sank. I had not. "Good," he said happily, "you won't have to unlearn anything."

Finally, I was a real reporter, hired to cover the hard news and ferret out the truth. It scared the heck out of me, but I did it. I was a general-assignment reporter and I learned to take news photos. But I never forgot what I'd been told at the *Miami Herald.* After I'd been at the *Sun* for five years, during which the paper's ownership changed five times, it was time to move on. I wrote to the *Herald*'s executive editor George Beebe, whose name I'd found on the masthead. Now I have five years experience at a daily newspaper, the *Miami Beach*

Daily Sun, I wrote. How about it? Weeks after a daylong battery of interviews and tests, I'd heard nothing, so I wrote Steve Rogers, the city editor, a one word letter. "Obits?" Editors love brevity. He called the next day to ask when I could start. My heart pounded as I told him, then said goodbye. "Wait, haven't you forgotten something?" he said. I had no idea. "Salary," he said. "You haven't asked me the salary."

CSC: How did you wind up on the police beat?

EB: As a general-assignment reporter at the *Herald,* then covering criminal court for a year, I could see that something was lacking in our coverage. Miami's crime rate was soaring, but we still "covered the cops" with any general-assignment reporter who happened to be free when the shooting started. It seemed a catch-as-catch-can method. I had caught a number of good stories in court that we had overlooked at the time of the crime. So I casually suggested to my editor that a reporter pay daily visits to the major police departments, read the reports, rap with the troops, and then drop by the morgue and the jail to check the overnight arrivals. "Sounds good," the editor said. "Why don't you do it?" I stood frozen in panic. It was only a suggestion. I did not intend to volunteer, but somehow I had. That is how I came to cover the police beat.

CSC: Do you ever wonder how your career—and your life—might have been different if you'd had the opportunity to go to college? To study journalism?

EB: Sure. Perhaps it would have stifled my creativity! Maybe I would have won more Pulitzers sooner. Who knows? College was never an option for me, never even discussed. My mother was quite relieved when I quit high school and went to work full-time. It meant more income. If I'd been happy in Paterson, New Jersey, and successful in high school, perhaps I would have just graduated, married and settled down there. Perhaps I'd have been a housewife and raised a family. I doubt it, but who knows?

CSC: That would have been such a loss for the rest of us! How did you make the switch from journalism to writing crime fiction?

EB: I always read novels rather than nonfiction. And when Mrs. Tunis said I'd write books someday, I always envisioned writing novels, stories I imagined. But my first two books were nonfiction. *The*

Corpse Had a Familiar Face was autobiographical. But I resisted my publisher's urging to do another nonfiction book, even though *Corpse* did well.

I really wanted to write fiction, to create the story, and the ending. I wanted the good guys to win and the bad guys to get what they deserved. I wanted justice, which is so rare in real life. I was determined to write fiction. It wasn't easy at first. I kept looking to my left for my notebook, the notes I'd depended on as a reporter. And there were no notes, I was on my own, and it was terrifying, yet exhilarating, especially when my characters sprang to life and began committing outrageous and unexpected acts that shocked even me! Fascinated, I wanted to spend all my time with them. They became my closest companions.

CSC: Any stumbling blocks in your writing?

EB: Intruders! I hate them. When you are in your characters' world, on a roll, in an action scene, and the doorbell rings. I am filled with rage, ready to run to the door and plunge a knife into the heart of the intruder, whether it be the Fuller Brush man, the Avon lady, or my mother. I always worry that I won't be able to get back into that other world in the same place, into the scene, at the same pace. I want to barricade the door when I'm working, to keep the outside world away, to prevent them from dragging me back into the mundane, everyday world of reality. I want to be there, in the adventurous, romantic lives of my characters. I don't want to miss anything.

CSC: You have written ten books, five in the popular Britt Montero mystery series. What's coming out next?

EB: Avon will publish my new novel, *Pulse,* in May 1998. It's a stand-alone suspense novel, not a Britt Montero book. Avon will also publish the next Britt Montero book, called *Garden of Evil,* which I'm working on now. Both are set in Miami, as always. Miami is always a major character in my books.

The hero in *Pulse* is a wealthy middle-aged businessman who collapses while out jogging. Diagnosed with terminal cardiomyopathy, he becomes the recipient of a new heart, a heart transplant. That's when the fun begins. He wants to make things up to his family, pay more attention to them—a figurative change of heart as well as a literal one. But strange and ominous events intervene. He eventually realizes that his "donor" is not dead, and is a killer, now stalking him. Of course, no one believes him!

CSC: What else are you working on?

EB: A possible TV series, which I would write and appear in, and short stories. I've written four since last summer. I love them! Again, this goes back to childhood when I read short fiction in *The Saturday Evening Post*. That's where I first read John D. MacDonald. Even newspapers used to publish short stories. I miss that. But it may be coming back. *U.S.A. Weekend* now publishes a summer fiction series. In July they used my short story called "The English Tourist." Another, "The Widow's Secret," appeared in *Orlando Magazine*.

CSC: Why do you like writing short stories?

EB: Because they're short! You don't have to worry as much about interruptions, and if I keep on, I'll eventually have enough for an anthology.

CSC: "The English Tourist" and "The Widow's Secret." What else?

EB: Last summer the *Mary Higgins Clark Mystery Magazine* published "Foolproof," for which I resurrected Dan Flood, the dying detective from *Miami, It's Murder*. That story is also included in an anthology called *The Plot Thickens*, a charity project for literacy. Next year, a story I called "The Red Shoes" will be published in an anthology about obsession. The hero suffers from a foot fetish and first appeared as a minor character in *Margin of Error*.

CSC: What wisdom and/or advice do you have for aspiring writers?

EB: Do it. Don't wait for inspiration. Just do it. Sit your bottom on the chair and get to work.

CSC: Anything else?

EB: Life is short and editors are treacherous.

Robert Crais

INTERVIEW BY JAN GRAPE

T here's no one in the world I'd rather dance with than Bob "Fred As-
taire" Crais. He's my all-time favorite Texas two-stepper. When
everyone stops laughing I'll tell you why I've made such a rash statement. Long long ago in a galaxy far far away (or maybe it was only
eight or ten years ago at Bouchercon in Philly), a group of us were at an
establishment across the street from the convention hotel listening to a
local band and tossing back a few Perrier's with a twist. After a few sips
of sparkly water I decided I wanted to dance and as Bob was the only
male from our group not on the dance floor I asked him to dance. Now I
should preface this by saying I barely knew Bob, but then I'm not shy. He
surprised the heck out of me when he said, "I don't dance."

I couldn't believe it. In Texas you grow up learning how to dance before you can do much of anything else so I said, "Honey, if you can walk
you can dance."

Well, several folks in the group thought that was funny—of course
you had to have been there, but needless to say Bob and I did not dance.
He wasn't lying. He didn't dance. But it became a joke between the two
of us and a couple of years ago when he finally learned how he asked
everyone except me to dance. (You still owe me a turn around the floor,
Bob.)

Mysteries written by Robert Crais featuring Elvis Cole are one of the hottest private eye series today. Crais won the Shamus Award for the Best Private Eye Novel of 1997 for the sixth book in the series, titled Sunset Express. The Shamus awards, given by the Private Eye Writers of America (both the award and organization were created by Robert J. Randisi), are selected by committees of published private eye writers. For the first in the series, The Monkey's Raincoat, (1987) he won the Anthony, awarded by the Bouchercon World Mystery Convention, and MacCavity, selected by readers of the Mystery Readers Journal of Mystery Readers International for Best Paperback Original, and also received nominations for that book for both the Edgar, given by the Mystery Writers of America, and the Shamus.

All told, he has been nominated for two Edgars, two Anthonys and four Shamus awards and an Emmy for his work on Hill Street Blues. Other TV shows include: Cagney & Lacey, Miami Vice, and L.A. Law.

Crais says, "I grew up in Louisiana and my mother was a hard-core Elvis fan. We had one of those ugly black velvet paintings in our house. There was the crucifix and there was Elvis."

We shall put the rumor to rest that he ran away to join the circus. It was actually a carnival and it was a summer job and his parents were glad to see him gainfully employed.

He now lives in Southern California with his wife, Pat, and daughter, Lauren. He may be seen at various mystery conventions or on tour promoting whichever book happens to be hot off the press. He admits to liking the "road tour," which makes him a minority among fellow writers. Crais recently told Paul Bishop in an interview that he gets to hang around a bookstore all day, then in the evening sits with a big stack of books which he signs while talking to the nice people who are buying them.

The most recent Elvis book as I write this is Indigo Slam and many people are curious about its title. The term refers to the color of ink used in the printing (slamming) of counterfeit foreign money. It was, in my opinion, even better than Sunset, but as readers and fans that's exactly what we hope a writer does—improve with each book.

Crais and I talked a little about his writing career, his likes and dislikes and about the new Elvis book which sounds bigger and bolder and one I'm definitely looking forward to reading sometime in 1998.

JG: Many writers began writing at an early age or at least knew deep inside that writing was what they wanted as a life career. When did you write your first story, article or book?

RC: Well, you've got to understand, I was raised to be an engineer or a cop, like everyone else in my family. I'm from a real blue-collar, working-class town in Louisiana, and that's what my family did . . . you know, you either worked for Exxon or you busted heads. But here I was, this Martian with a burning interest in movies and TV and books. I didn't know that I wanted to *write* until, oh, I guess late high school, but as far back as junior high I knew I wanted to tell stories, and I didn't much care the medium—comic books, TV, movies, books. I loved all that stuff. Only I had to keep it secret. Such dreams just weren't allowed.

JG: Must have been tough keeping all that inside. Which authors influenced you early in your writing and reading?

RC: Specific to the genre, I'd have to say Chandler and Stout and MacDonald, all of whom I discovered in a second-hand bookstore down in Baton Rouge. Really torn up, ratty paperbacks. But as to what I'm most moved by, I'd have to say, get this, Stan Lee, the comic book genius who created Spider-Man and the Fantastic Four and the Incredible Hulk. Stan was a genius because all of his stories were about the *human being* trapped within the superhero. He wrote about being human. I think I do that in the Elvis Cole novels. Then, later, my tastes became more sophisticated and I inhaled writers as diverse as Hemingway and Bradbury and Harlan Ellison, all the while being influenced by filmmakers such as Sergio Leone.

JG: And what led you to the private eye story?

RC: Well, I'd always read the stuff, and knew it to be a very personal form of expression. After all, it's how Chandler commented on life in Los Angeles, and gave vent to his bitterness. Anyway, I'd been trying to write books while making my living writing television . . . I had written two *really* bad, formless monster manuscripts—I'm talking mutant versions of the Great American Novel—when my father died. His death led to my learning some things about my mother—about who she was as a human being, as a person, here in this modern age, unable to do many things which most women took for granted, like writing a check, and what their marriage had been like—and I just had to write about it. That's the way I do—I use the writing as a form of therapy to work through things going on in my life, or as a way to make sense of the world around me. Anyway, my dad died and I had to take up the slack, and I wanted to write about it in a way that would let me save my mom, as it were, so I transmogrified her—I like to say I was issued a Calvin & Hobbes transmogrifier at birth—into this character named Ellen Lang and me into this character named Elvis Cole, and I was able to use my fiction to work through my feelings about her dependence on my father. Freud could probably get really sick with this stuff, but you have to understand that once it's fiction, it's fiction. I am not Elvis Cole. But he grew from me, and my needs.

JG: I really liked Ellen Lang and how she grew as a person. She really made a transformation. What's the easiest thing about writing fiction?

RC: I get to set my own hours.

JG: And what's the hardest thing?

RC: I have to be my own boss. That means I can't cut myself any slack. If I tell myself I can't get into work because my car battery went dead, I know that's bullshit. You see?

JG: And you can't call in sick.

RC: No way.

JG: What's your writing day like? Is it a typical nine-to-five job?

RC: I'm a very structured person, so yes, it's like working for Exxon! Ha, my dad would love that! I'm not a "muse" type person. I hear writers talking about the muse, I want to puke. I'm there every day. Not kidding, *every* day, seven days. I rise very early, like 4:30 in the morning, I'm in the gym by 6:00, home by 7:15, and straight to the Mac. During the early part of a book, I tend to burn out by about 3:00 P.M. or 4:00 P.M., but when I get into Deadline Madness—what some people call Deadline Hell—I start pumping twelve, fourteen hours a day, sometimes more. This is a period when it is *not* fun being a writer. Better to sell BMWs.

JG: Is your office at home?

RC: Yeah. When *Indigo Slam* made the *LA Times* best-seller list, friends called and said, "Well, we guess you'll take the limo from your bedroom down the hall to your office, now." I love working at home. I never have to leave the house, which I hate to do because this is Los Angeles and there are millions of people clogging the streets.

JG: And you don't want to add to the pollution. Will you describe the office for us?

RC: I work in this big, high-ceilinged room with a glass wall overlooking our front courtyard. That way I get to see who's coming and going, and shoot them if I have to. The inner walls are lined with books and posters and framed things that mean something to me, like my dad's old combat unit photograph from World War II, or Elvis Cole's Silver Star, which was given to him by the man who earned it, Kregg Jorgenson. Like that.

JG: Can you compare yourself to Elvis?

RC: Elvis Cole and I share the same attitudes, the same sense of humor, the same interests. I cook, he cooks. I'm quite a good cook. I like Disney icons and Kenneth Tobey movies; so does Elvis Cole. We both do yoga and try to keep ourselves in shape. For all the reasons that I wrote *The Monkey's Raincoat*, which was the first book, it was important to me that Elvis Cole be as personal an expression of myself as possible. I'm aging more quickly, though. When I started all this, Elvis was a year older than me. Now, ten years later, he's a little younger than me. Funny how that works.

JG: Some people might compare Elvis and Pike to Parker's characters, Spenser and Hawk. What do you think are their similarities? What are their differences?

RC: Well, the differences are generational, I think. In the attitudes and definitions that are embodied in Elvis and Joe, versus Spenser and Hawk, and in who they are within the larger world. Elvis Cole seems a more flexible character to me, a more flexible man, who is willing to expand his world, whereas Spenser seems far more rigid. Hawk is a criminal. I see him as far closer to Walter Mosley's character, Mouse, than to Joe Pike. Where Hawk is a criminal, like Mouse, Joe Pike is a law-abiding man who is only willing to step outside the law when he feels the law is indefensible, as it sometimes is. Now, Joe Pike is a dangerous man, because he is willing to use violent means to accomplish his ends, and he is very good at violence, but his ends are dictated by what he views as "good." Joe is also a thoughtful man, and might tell you that he believes laws are necessary to maintain public order, but he would also tell you that laws are artificial—created by society to maintain society—and should serve some larger "good." Clearly, Spenser and Hawk and Elvis and Joe are both in the long tradition of the "buddy" concept—Nero Wolfe and Archie Goodwin, Nick and Nora Charles, Holmes and Watson, Batman and Robin. Robert B. Parker, by the way, is going to go into the books as the fourth of the American Big Four. There were three: Hammett, Chandler, and MacDonald. But Parker will be linked with them in the development of detective fiction, as he should be. He twisted the paradigm, and writers like me and Mosley and Harlan Coben and Dennis Lehane and Janet Evanovich and, Christ, a whole generation, have been affected.

JG: Which of your books is your favorite? And why?

RC: The latest is always the favorite for me. I know that sounds bogus, but it's true. You're always closest to the one that's most recent. It's the one that's the most alive to you. So, now, as you interview me, the most recent is the one I'm writing, which I think will be the Elvis Cole break-out novel. I'm trying new things, writing a bigger book—this mother's fifty percent longer than the others—and I think people are going to flip when they read the Joe Pike sections detailing his years on the police force and what happens between Lucy and Elvis . . .

JG: Okay, you're hooking me. Which book was the hardest for you to write and why?

RC: Oh, I'd have to say *Voodoo River* because of the adoption angle. All my books are personal, drawn in some way from my own life, but that book—wow, that book was a bear to write. I had to dig really deep, and confront things I'd never confronted before as an adopted child. There were scenes in that book that, literally, took days and days to write. I was sitting at the Mac, tears streaming down my face. Just a brute to write, but I'm very proud of that book. I think it's a good one.

JG: I know you've written a number of TV scripts for series and movies and I wonder if it is easier or harder to write for TV?

RC: Much easier. Much. Listen, to write well for any medium is hard, but your basic one-hour TV script is so much shorter. Think about that. You only have to be good for fifty-five pages, as opposed to five hundred, which is what this new book will be. I can write an hour script in a couple of weeks. A book takes eight, ten months. That's a lot of pain. So the difference is like, which is easier, to hold your hand in the flame for two weeks or ten months?

JG: Do you see Elvis Cole on the big screen? If so, who would you like to star as Elvis? Pike?

RC: First, I've turned down eighteen offers from film and TV companies for these characters. So far, I haven't been interested. I keep count because people find this odd. I have no wish to option these things or see them made into movies. I'm an odd guy. We all have to accept that. Now, having said that, I'll tell you. I saw this movie called *Grosse Pointe Blank* with John Cusack. I think he'd make a great Elvis Cole. Just great . . .

JG: If Elvis ever is a TV series or movie would you want to write the script?

RC: Wouldn't happen.

JG: Do you research extensively before starting a new book or just do it as you go along and need it?

RC: I research as little as possible, except for going out with the cops. I go out on ride-alongs and stuff a lot. Go to LAPD's Police Academy. Go to the rifle range or the pistol range. Hang with people who are real private investigators. Hell, I'd do that for fun anyway, and just call it research. When I wrote *Indigo Slam* I got to spend a lot of time with Treasury Department counterfeiting experts, and this guy who was a government spook counterfeiting Vietnamese currency during the war, things like that. But when it comes to looking things up in the library, that's not my style. Hate that. Do as little as possible, though I will do it.

JG: Are you toying with another book—something other than Elvis?

RC: I'm writing the eighth Elvis Cole novel as we speak. In the life of the series, I've never considered writing anything else because I've been able to say what I want to say how I want to say it through Elvis Cole . . . he's been my perfect mouthpiece . . . but the type of story I'm telling now is so much larger, so much more complicated, that I'm beginning to see possibilities other than Elvis Cole. I'm not saying that I'm going to write a non-Elvis Cole book, but this Elvis Cole novel is a multi-character, multi-view-point book, and I'm having such a good time writing it that it's made me think that I might have fun writing a stand-alone, non-Elvis Cole novel. This is new to me, so I'll just have to see if a story presents itself.

JG: Who critiques your work? Agent? Editor? Friend?

RC: Pat Crais is my first reader and always has been. She reads the book first, and tells me whether or not I'm on track. After that, both my agent, Aaron Priest, and my editor, Leslie Wells, take over. Aaron has only been representing me since *Indigo Slam,* so we're still learning how to work together, but Leslie's been my editor since I've been with Hyperion, and she's brilliant, absolutely terrific. I consider very closely everything she says. But that's it. I don't show the books to friends, or workshop them, or any of that. I know writers who do, and that's fine for them, but not for me.

JG: Which comes first for you—plot, character, setting?

RC: Character comes first, always. I have this little sign I made for my office. It's what I believe. "The only thing worth writing about is the human heart." End of story. I absolutely, one hundred percent believe that, and live by it. That philosophy drives everything I've ever written, every teleplay, every short story, and every novel. I start with a character, a human being with a problem. In *The Monkey's Raincoat* I had Ellen Lang. In *Indigo Slam* I had Teri Hewitt, the lit-tle girl who has to be an adult because there are no responsible adults in her life. Always, a character first. The story grows out of the characters, and how Elvis Cole must solve their problems.

JG: Do you know the ending before you start a book?

RC: Yeah. I'm an outliner. I can't do it any other way, so I'll spend three months or more just figuring out what's going to happen and why and all of that. This way, I can make sure the book is "balanced" and better tailor the pacing, I think. I have friends who make it up as they go along, people like Tony Hillerman and Tami Hoag and Janet Evanovich, and I'm just awed by that. That they can have some general idea and just start typing and out comes this incredible story. If I wrote like that, I'd end up with a big mess. I have written like that, and it was just horrible . . .

JG: *Sunset Express* just won a Shamus Award. Was that a big surprise?

RC: A huge surprise. I had no idea I would win, didn't expect to, didn't even think it was possible. I mean, we're talking a strong field this year, and, on top of that, I've gotten this "bridesmaid" mentality. I've been nominated for things a lot, and not won. Nominated for a couple of Edgars, nominated for, I think, maybe three Shamuses before this one. So I kinda figured it was my place in the world to always get aced out. When S.J. Rosan called my name I looked at my wife and said, "Did she say me?" I couldn't believe it.

JG: As good as I think *Sunset* is, I personally think *Indigo Slam* is even better. The children are wonderfully drawn and Elvis always relates to children in a very real way. Is he childlike or just treats them as adults?

RC: Well, he certainly treats children respectfully, and I think he also treats them as human beings. Elvis Cole is a man who has worked very hard at holding onto his innocence and wonder, he's a guy who sees great value in these things. He might tell you, if you asked him, that he equates one's ability to love and enjoy life with one's ability to see the world with fresh eyes, i.e., as a child sees the world. Elvis volunteered for Vietnam when he was very young—he was a Ranger, you know, and saw quite a bit of combat there at the end of the war, in the early seventies—and he saw other young men age very quickly. He knew that this could happen to him, too; that at the age of twenty he might become a very old man, and he has worked against it ever since. Something in you recognizes that there is a fork in the road. You can let yourself die, or you can strive to live, and Elvis Cole decided to live, and children are life. Elvis Cole recognizes that and values it, and I think he sees himself—his purpose—as a protector of that. He protects and nurtures the child in all of us.

JG: To do this interview I reread *The Monkey's Raincoat,* the first in the Elvis series which was nominated for an Edgar and a Shamus and won the Anthony and MacCavity. Elvis has really grown up, hasn't he?

RC: Well, I've grown up! Sure, Elvis has evolved, but because I've evolved. I wrote *The Monkey's Raincoat* eleven years ago. I'm eleven years older, with more life experience, hopefully wiser. If I had never written any of these books, and sat down today to write *The Monkey's Raincoat,* I am sure it would be a very different book than the one you read. I'm just a different guy. So the Elvis Cole today reflects the man I am today, and the Elvis Cole in *The Monkey's Raincoat* reflects who I was then.

JG: If Elvis gets married and becomes a father to Lucy Chenier's son, will that change the series too much?

RC: Why should it? People evolve. I'm evolving, you're evolving, why shouldn't Elvis Cole or Kinsey Milhone or whoever? I know that there's this holdover paradigm of the private eye as "loner," and I respect that, but I don't feel obligated to it. We're in the nineties now. I look around me at all my single friends—I mean, I've been married for over twenty years, so I'm an old married guy—but I look at my single friends, and AIDS has killed the singles scene, that whole eighties thing of one-night stands is over. People want romance. People want to be in love, and in monogamous relationships. Why shouldn't Elvis Cole? Now, I'm not telling you that Elvis Cole and Lucy Chenier are going to get married, or move in together, but they might. The task for me is to explore how to tell involving, interesting stories either way. If Elvis Cole gets married, okay, how does that impact upon the novels? It wouldn't be my intention to turn the Elvis Cole novels into soap operas, but you never know . . . those romance novels sell a lot of copies! And I have plans. We just have to see how it works out. . . . Heh-heh.

JG: Any words of wisdom for writers?

RC: Don't follow the herd or the marketplace. It's like the stock market. Once you read in *Money* magazine that you should buy

Intel, all the big money has already been made. Write what's in your heart. And write every day.

JG: Okay let's have some fun now. What's your favorite food?

RC: Well, this is the toughest question you've asked! You know, I'm a serious cook . . .

JG: Really?

RC: . . . and I cook many things—general American, Thai, Mexican, Chinese, Italian, whatever. I've taken classes with Hugh Carpenter and Mary Sue Milliken and Susan Feniger. I'm talking serious, here. But I'd have to say that, first, I like spicy. I'm from Louisiana, and I grew up in a household where my mom put Tabasco sauce on our scrambled eggs! So for me, my comfort food is cajun/South Louisiana cooking. Red beans and rice. Jambalaya. Gumbo. I cook it, and I like to eat it.

JG: Me, too. What's your favorite color?

RC: Red.

JG: What's your favorite TV show?

RC: *Buffy the Vampire Slayer.* Used to be *Beverly Hills 90210,* but this year it's Buffy. (Sorry, Jennie.)

JG: What music do you listen to?

RC: I'm pretty eclectic. Everything from Filter and Sneaker Pimps to Bobby Darin and Jerry Vale to Jann Arden and Shawn Colvin to soundtrack CDs from *Grosse Pointe Blank* and *Riverdance.* Depends on my mood and what I want to think about. Right now I'm in love with Jann Arden. She blows me away. I'm listening to a lot of the chick singers right now—and don't beat me up for "chick" because that's how they bill themselves. Alanis, Garbage, No Doubt. Tracy Chapman, though Tracy probably doesn't bill herself as a "chick," though I don't know that. I'll listen to classical, though not as much as I used to. Doesn't have to be cutting edge or in-the-moment, but would it surprise you if I said that I think Ice-T is brilliant, absolutely brilliant? Listen to his rhymes and cinch down your jump harness—he's the best poet/songwriter since Paul Simon!

JG: Besides your lovely lifemate, Pat, what famous person would you like to be stranded with on a desert island? Let's say dead or alive?

RC: So I get two categories. Okay, with the dead people, I'd like to be hooked up with either Ernest Hemingway or Mary Shelley. Ernie could fish for us, and I hear Mary was pretty bizarre. We might make a good couple. With living people, it's tougher . . . I'd have to say the entire female cast of Cirque du Soleil. They're pretty flexible . . .

JG: If you could choose to live anywhere in the world where would it be?

RC: Los Angeles. No doubt about it. But I'd also have a ranch in Colorado or Montana.

JG: What does your best pal say about you?

RC: That he trusts me.

JG: What do you consider your greatest success?

RC: My daughter, Lauren. "A" student, great writer, and better than all that, good person. I love her, but I also like her a lot.

JG: Tell us a secret about Bob Crais?

RC: Everyone thinks I'm a nice guy. Well, I am, but if you mess with my home or my family, I will put you down. People don't see that side of me. There's this great Japanese fable about the forty-seven ronin who go to work for the guy who kills their boss, and, twenty years later or something like that, they finally get their revenge. That's me. You mess me over and I will get you if it takes twenty years, and you will never see it coming. Remember, Joe and Elvis are reflections of me. There's a reason for that. You will never see it coming.

JG: What do you wish an interviewer would ask you and pretend I just asked it and answer that question?

RC: No.

JG: Well, then that's it, folks. Thanks for your time, Bob, and I'll see you on the dance floor?

A Robert Crais–Elvis Cole Checklist:
The Monkey's Raincoat (1987)
The Stalking Angel (1989)
Lullaby Town (1992)
Free Fall (1993)
Voodoo River (1995)
Sunset Express (1996)
Indigo Slam (1997)

Julian Rathbone

INTERVIEW BY JANE WILLIAMS

JW: American crime fiction is a vast field. Which bits are you familiar with?

JR: I'm a very eclectic reader and I don't read all that much crime fiction anyway. In 1988 I went to this crime week that was held in Gijon in the north of Spain. It's called the *Semana Negra* (Black Week) and I met a lot of American writers there. That really put me in touch with American crime writing and I subsequently started reading it. Up till then I doubt if I had read much since Dashiell Hammett and Chandler. To begin with I started reading people whom I'd met at the conference, and of course I was very impressed. I found it generally more exciting and stimulating than the British crime fiction that was around at the time although I do think the scene here has changed a lot in the last five years.

JW: Why were you so impressed?

JR: To begin with the Americans were more realistic. They had their feet in the streets and wrote about real problems—alcoholism for instance. One of the first I read was Lawrence Block's *When the Sacred Gin Mill Closes*. Subsequently another of his books that impressed me very much was *Eight Million Ways to Die*. It deals to some extent with the reformed alcoholic who, faced with temptation, slips again and it's also about prostitution in a fairly realistic, streetwise way. I like the general grittiness of these people. They write about characters whom you feel that you could meet on the train or see on the bus rather than the usual English sort of thing. Others I picked up at the time and liked a lot included Joe Gores, and even at the more cozy level, the Canadian writer Eric Wright. His books are closer to the conventional English mystery with a bit of police procedural thrown in. Again, there's a development and a depth that he puts into the relationship between the policeman and his wife. I thought that was very impressive and very much more the sort of thing that you expect in a novel than you do in a thriller.

JW: Who would you place at the top of your list?

JR: The one whom I fell for both as a person and as a writer when I met him in Gijon and afterwards was Ross Thomas, who died in 1996.

JW: Why as a person first of all?

JR: He was very charming . . . it's the wrong word really, but he was a very generous person. Generous with his time, generous with his ideas. He had an endless stream of anecdotes both from the writing world and from the political world that he knew so well.

JW: And as a writer?

JR: I hadn't read any of his books when I met him but not long after I read *The Seersucker Whipsaw,* which is about a group of Americans doing the sort of job that Ross Thomas did, that is, managing people's political campaigns. The book is set in a country which I imagine is based on somewhere like Nigeria and it builds up a very, very well-drawn picture of the hero and the girl in the party. They both come across as genuinely nice people and their relationship develops in an extraordinarily generous way. Then, blow me, they get killed at the end, which is appalling. There again is the ability to take on a possibility which most British writers would shy away from, or their editors would tell them, "You can't do this." Of course, I may be maligning British writers when I say this happens more in America than it does in Britain. Then I read *Missionary Stew,* and when I met Thomas again I said, "This is Graham Greene written by Mickey Spillane." I'm not sure I liked his series books about the three guys—

there's a stream of buddiness in them which doesn't appeal to me personally. He describes places so well, such varied places from the Philippines to Mexico to Africa. Washington is always brilliant, and then there was *The Briarpatch*, set in Hollywood and all about Californian politics. I was very sorry when he died. In fact I'd just started reading his last book published which was *Ah, Treachery!* and he was so much on the top of his form that it was very sad to be reading it.

JW: What have you been reading more recently?

JR: I'll put in a word for Ed Gorman! I enjoyed *The Marilyn Tapes* very much indeed. I felt the description of the kidnapping of the small girl and her near-murder were done with a particular intensity that was very exciting, even though I faintly suspect that the ultimate happy ending was a cop-out, possibly directed at Hollywood. There again, Gorman handled the relationship between the parents skillfully; in not allowing them to get back together he showed a readiness to face up to the reality of life. Then there was a serial killer story called *Prayer for the Dead* by David Wilse. I've never heard of him before or since but I thought this was a far better book than *The Silence of the Lambs*. It was decidedly gruesome in places but it felt as though he was approaching the whole business with a proper awareness that you don't often get in British crime writing.

JW: What about the American hard-boiled practitioners?

JR: I don't get on too well with Walter Mosley or James Ellroy. I've met them both and like them but I find Ellroy a bit heavy going. I can see virtues and I've only read Mosley's first two books so probably the later ones are much better. Recently there's Joe Lansdale's *Mucho Mojo*. I got a little bogged down with it a third of the way through and stopped reading and then went back and thought the last two-thirds were terrific. We actually share the same publisher, Gollancz. I also got into James Crumley a bit and liked the first two books very much but I felt *The Mexican Tree Duck* in particular was a bit over the top, especially toward the end—the battle and the whole business of a supermarket of weapons being deployed was too much—but I like his writing and I like the presentation of Montana very much. I recently read Elmore Leonard's *Get Shorty* and when, as a writer I read books, I say to myself 'I could do that or better.' Here I said, 'I couldn't do that, it's a terrific book!'

JW: Apart from the realism what else do you admire?

JR: One thing that the Americans do so well is a sense of place, which seems to me extraordinary in that whenever you see American cities in films, Philadelphia looks exactly the same as St. Louis, and I get the impression that one city is much like another. Yet these writers somehow dispel that feeling and make you feel that these places are different from each other and have their own ambience. I think that a lot of British writing is now picking up on this; there's John Harvey's Nottingham and Val McDermid's Manchester and Ian Rankin's Edinburgh, and it's also beginning to catch onto the gritty reality which Americans have and this is exciting. I liked Minette Walters's *The Sculptress* very much, but I was a bit disappointed in *The Scold's Bridle* which seemed to me to be reverting to the mystery story. I feel sure that people like her are under a lot of pressure to be the next P.D. James or whatever and I think it's a mistake of the publishers to put writers under that sort of pressure.

JW: The two writers that you have referred to as the great exponents of the spy thriller were both British . . .

JR: Yes. Eric Ambler and Graham Greene were both British but they were both expatriates and hardly ever wrote about Britain. It's the Jane Austen syndrome, carving the piece of ivory, miniaturization of detail and subtle feelings minutely done that still dominates British writing even at the level of somebody like Martin Amis—it's terribly introspective and I find it boring after a bit.

JW: Your own books are rarely set in Britain . . .

JR: I found it very difficult for a long time, I still do, to set books in England. It's partly an inability to see the wood for the trees. As soon as I start writing about England I get bogged down in detail. London is too big to cope with and somewhere like Burley, where I live, is too small which is why some of these provincial writers writing about smaller towns do achieve something. If you live in France or Spain, as I have done, you get a broader picture.

JW: In your books you are very much concerned with a worldview, something larger than what happens to the individual . . .

JR: Yes, I like to see the individual in a wider context where other big things impinge on them—they may be specific things like the environment or big business. One is constantly shocked at corporations and what they have been up to—the Shell business in Nigeria for instance—and I begin to wonder if I wasn't right all along!

JW: Have you become cynical over the years?

JR: No, I don't think I have at all; in fact in some ways I've become less so. I am cynical about most institutions, although I don't think all of them are all totally bad. There are lots of good policemen in my books.

JW: You had a short story in *London Noir* which a review called "one of the most nightmare-inducing pieces a reader is ever likely to encounter." Can you say something about it?

JR: Really? I think the reviewer probably muddled me with one of the other writers! You are sure it wasn't Ian Rankin's which was nightmarish?

JW: Do you enjoy the short story form?

JR: I've done very little of it until recently. It really started because I had this idea which popped up at the Gijon conference of doing a modern Sherlock Holmes pastiche, with the Holmes character as a very thin woman and Watson as an extremely fat sociologist. I wrote three stories and the first one was published by a German friend in an anthology. Then, Maxim Jakubowski got hold of them and published two, and the second one actually won the Crime Writers Association short story prize, so that was quite encouraging. I've written a fourth which is about 20,000 words, not quite a novella. I really do quite like doing them and I'm hoping to get a different publisher to commission three more so that there is a book there.

JW: Can you make any comparisons between short story and novel writing?

JR: I find it quite difficult to be serious in a short story. Mine tend to have, albeit black, humor in them. I feel this replaces the sort of themes that you can explore in a novel. As far as the ordinary short story market is concerned mine still come out too long, usually between 8–10,000 words and magazine editors look for 5,000 or even 2,000 words and I find it very difficult to do anything worthwhile in 2,000 words. It's odd because twice in the last year I have been asked to adjudicate short story competitions and I've seen some very good work from amateur writers. It is so difficult to get short stories published and it's a shame that the form isn't more popular but I suppose it's gone into television writing—half hour soap operas.

JW: I noticed that you didn't get a mention in Julian Symons's book *Bloody Murder*.

JR: In the first place I met him at Gijon as well and one of the first things he said to me was that he was surprised that I was there at all because although he had reviewed some of my books quite nicely he always thought of me as a novelist not as a crime writer. So perhaps he was making his excuses. He was very much a genre writer and an expert in his field. I don't like the idea of genre writing myself. On a personal level we got on very well but on a theoretical level we didn't get on at all well. In fact there were quite exciting debates at Gijon. The Americans, Latin Americans, Spaniards, French were generally all for taking crime fiction seriously and thinking that it should be approached by the writer as dealing with serious matters: death, dying, killing people are all quite serious matters, whereas Julian was getting very angry on the other side. "It's entertainment, it must be entertainment, it can't be anything other than entertainment, we should be as entertaining as we can be." I certainly wasn't as extreme on the serious side as some of the Americans or particularly the Latin Americans. There were half of us there who occupied a sort of middle ground; Ross Thomas does really and Eric Wright.

JW: You mentioned genre writing. Do you think publishers are responsible for this insistence on genres?

JR: Yes they are entirely—how can we sell this? I come across it all the time, even now with Victor Gollancz. I'm doing non-crime novels, straight "literary" novels with them and I offered them the Sherlock Holmes stories. Mike Petty, their crime editor, liked them a lot but Gollancz had a meeting about it and said, "We can't sell Rathbone as two different things. We can't have him as a writer of Holmesian pastiches on the same list as a writer of serious art fiction type novels."

JW: Is that why you have two different publishers, Gollancz and Serpent's Tail?

JR: Yes, even then they're so tight that Serpent's Tail isn't interested in the Holmes stuff because they want me to write environmental/

political thrillers of the sort that I used to write more of than I do now.

JW: Do you feel you are written out in that area?

JR: Well I'm finding it more difficult. I think I've always found it difficult to break out into a "super reality," not exactly fantasy but looking more at bizarre and garish ways of writing and themes to tackle and in some ways the novels I'm doing for Gollancz have more of that in them. My most recent book isn't a thriller; it deals with a man on holiday with his family who suddenly realizes that by the end of the holiday he will have lived longer than his father and this makes him wonder whether he ought to or not. Then he explores his relationship with his father and his children. I want to write a sort of sequel to it taking the son who is fourteen years old in the first book and putting him and his mother and sister into 2035 and using all the prophecies of doom that are around now and realizing them. Even then Gollancz is having problems with that because it's set in the future and they say, "This should be on our science fiction list."

JW: What are you trying to do in your writing?

JR: One thing that interests me in writing and that I like in other people's books for that matter, is a sense of history, a sense of the past creating the present and that things don't happen in a contemporary vacuum. Very often my books have gone back over a long period of time, like *A Spy of the Old School* which goes right back to the thirties.

JW: Which of your books do you like the best?

JR: My favorite is the Perón one, *Lying in State*. It was a very difficult book to write. It started off absolutely based in fact. Perón really did record a whole lot of tapes which revealed a lot of scandalous things about the CIA, about American interference in Argentinian politics, as well as a lot of sexual scandal. Perón gave them to this actress when he went back to Argentina and she put them up for sale. My then-agent was part of a consortium who tried to buy them. In fact they were bought by Planeta, publishers of a literary Spanish magazine and were finally published in an extremely expurgated, harmless version. My agent told me the story and I started writing the book. He got sight of an early draft and he said, "Oh no, this is too close. We'll all get sued rotten or machine-gunned in the street."

But I'd invested so much in it that I reinvented the whole thing; it became the story of a man creating pseudo tapes.

JW: Did you do a lot of research for the book?

JR: I was fairly well-grounded in the Spanish part. I was in Spain in 1973–74, the year before Franco died and then again just after he died. The Perón bit I did have to research but I found a very good biography which was immensely useful. I sent a copy of the book to Graham Greene, saying that a lot of any of what was good in any of my books was due to him and he wrote back from Antibes and the date on the letter was the date of my birthday, and he said he thought it was a very good book but at his age he found the plot a bit complicated!

JW: What would you say is your main contribution to the spy thriller?

JR: In some ways I've consciously tried to subvert it. *A Spy of the Old School* was very consciously done like that and it was interesting because it did get reviewed as if it was written by somebody who was trying to write like John le Carre, which to a certain point I was. At the same time I was enjoying standing the whole thing completely on its head. On the first page you know who the spy is and then I was trying to present sympathetically the motivations of somebody like Anthony Blunt, who got caught up in these things. I think there are two sides to the story which I tried to present.

JW: Do you know any spies?

JR: Spies don't tend to tell you they're spies. I think I lost my best friend because he was a spy and I wrote a book about him. He was in the navy, was taught Russian intensively and was at a listening post on the border with East Germany. He disappeared for about two or three years; he definitely went through Turkey and the Middle East and I was in Turkey at about that time and much later I wrote a book called *Hand Out* in which he was the spy Adrian Hand—sympathetically drawn, a good adventure story. I didn't hear from him for ages then about three years after this book came out he wrote to me saying, "I think you've put me in a book," and he wasn't pleased at all. I wondered if my fantasy about him had got a bit nearer the truth than I'd thought. He then became a schoolteacher.

JW: Do you devote all your time to writing?

JR: No, no. I don't devote enough time to writing, certainly not enough for my bank manager. My wife runs a translation agency from our home and the result is that I spend far too much time in Sainsbury's (supermarket) and fetching the children to and from school. There's also the drama club that I act in, I do a mean dame, and this summer I'm directing *An Inspector Calls* [JB Priestley].

Paul Doherty

INTERVIEW BY MICHAEL STOTTER

MS: Although your name is quite well known amongst the history mystery fraternity, little is known of your background. Perhaps you could begin by telling us something about yourself?

PD: Quite a conventional path at first. I studied for two to three years for Catholic priesthood. In my other life I am now a headmaster at a Catholic school. My earlier training gave me a very firm grounding—a rather strange preparation for murder. One of the things it does is give you an insight to the medieval mind—the theology, the philosophy, the Latin, the Greek, the culture of the Middle Ages. So, although I didn't know it at the time, I was really being prepared for writing history mysteries. I love history, always did, and so I left there and went to Liverpool University, where to their surprise (and mine) I won a first class honors degree and a scholarship to Oxford.

MS: What was your opinion of Oxford?

PD: It's a great place, a bit like Shangri-La. A place lost in time. Some of the people I really liked—the scholars, the real scholars. Some I didn't; just because you've written the definitive study of Roman toilets in eastern Northampton that doesn't make you an authority on everything—I couldn't stand that! I also liked teaching. I've always wanted to be a teacher. So I finished my doctorate and went into teaching.

MS: What was your doctorate on?

PD: Queen Isabella, wife of Edward II—Marlowe's Edward II, and she was a first class madam. Anyone who studies equal opportunities in the twentieth century should study Queen Isabella—she rode in armor; her husband was bisexual and his lover was de Spencer, ancestor of Diana, Princess of Wales. Isabella went abroad, met fourteenth century "Medallion Man," Roger Mortimer, who escaped from the Tower and swam the Thames to a waiting ship. They hired some hit men to go into England to kill de Spencer but were arrested and executed. So Isabella and her lover, Mortimer, landed in Essex. They deposed Edward II and put him in Berkeley Castle. De Spencer was taken to Hereford and, while Isabella was having breakfast they hanged, drawn, and quartered him. She then arranged for four assassins to enter Edward's cell at Berkeley, where they thrust a red-hot poker up his backside. According to medieval medicine this was one way of killing a man without leaving a mark on his body! (You could tell from the expression on his face that there was something wrong.) A big state funeral followed and still, today at Gloucester Cathedral, Edward II supposedly lies buried under a beautiful purbeck marble tomb.

MS: So in fact, you were already accumulating background research for your mysteries?

PD: One of the things about studying history, once you get off the beaten track, you find a real undergrowth. Legitimate historians don't want to wander there. The evidence is nebulous; you get these shadowy figures who were basically hit men, secret agents, and confidential civil servants. One of these went to Berkeley Castle after the king's death and, in a letter, let slip that the king actually escaped. Isabella and Mortimer were later overthrown by young Edward III. They were caught in bed together in Nottingham Castle. Mortimer was the first man hanged at Tyburn. Isabella was put in a convent where she was wheeled out for State occasions but basically told by her son to shut up. That was in 1330 and about five or six years later the young king gets a letter from a high-ranking French priest saying, "I've got some good news and some bad news. The good news is that your dad's still alive. The bad news is that he's disappeared again." At a place in northern Italy called Butrio, there is a tomb to an English king called Edward. Now, I thought blimey, how did they get away with a public funeral? Now, as you know, in the Middle Ages whenever a king or a great general was killed in battle, they always exposed his body. Richard III's body, for example, was displayed in a horse trough in Leicester for about four or five days. Of course, what they did with Edward II was shave his face, put a sort of wimple around his head. If you had a look-alike you could pass it off. I wrote a novel called *Death of a King* on the mystery of Edward II's death. It did very well in this country but even better in the States. I thought, "Now I'm going to use all my research." It is fascinating that people think that complex murder is a marvel of the twentieth century. It isn't. Once you get away from the conventional history books you do enter this mysterious world of murderers, special agents who arranged accidents, and political assassinations. There's even one assassin I came across who actually turned up in an Italian court and had a table of charges for killing a duke to a priest—and people hired him. The same thing was going on in other places. Louis XVI's court for example, you get a black magic circle that was broken up by a police inspector. Most of his notes are gone but we know that they were involved in some very naughty business. You get the so-called political accidents that happened to people like Rufus being killed in the New Forest. Or Richard II "dying" in Pontefract. So I thought "Fine, I'll create plots with a medieval feel." In the Middle Ages the only people that could read and write properly were monks (Brother Cadfael) or clerks. Some of the nobility were educated but others depended very much on these men. They had tremendous power and whenever there was a *coup d'etat* you killed the generals, you killed the family, but you never killed the clerks. Clerks who served Richard III on the 18th August 1485 can be found quite happily a month later serving Henry Tudor. The kings would not kill well-educated, intelligent clerks because they were in short supply. I thought that this is the sort of forte, métier I want to write in. Of course, in the Middle Ages you get this marvelous combination of religion and violence. I think the nearest thing you get to the Middle Ages is the American Wild West.

MS: Your novels depict the duality of that social structure, don't they?

PD: It was a very violent time; if I took you back to fourteenth-century London, you had to be armed. On the other hand, you get this marvelous spirituality represented by Brother Cadfael, the monastery, the abbey, the beautiful cathedrals, all the chanting. Then you get these violent switches. For example, the Crusaders—they weren't being hypocrites, they really believed they had to go out and fight and die for Christ, and the Church was a very holy thing. You also have a time of superstitions, the fear of the dark, the fear of black magic, the fear of warlocks and wizards. This is the same age that can produce a beautiful Gothic cathedral like Canterbury, which even now we can't equal in aesthetics or beauty. So the medieval period was a time of contrast and it's marvelous. When you look at the great modern writers like Chandler, I notice how he also plays this combination of contrasts: the private eye who can't survive on what he earns but he's hired by the very rich and the very powerful; he enters their beautiful homes with swimming pools and so you get these marvelous conflicts. In the medieval period it is even more so. There is nothing better than these areas which are supposed to be morally upright, law-abiding, and God-fearing which were just the opposite. Of course, the monasteries are the best example of that. The abbot, for example, is supposed to be a man of God, a man of prayer, yet he might be indulging in murder, even a bit of lechering or black magic. For a writer it provides a marvelous platform to write a story, and that's what I've basically done.

MS: These earlier novels, like *Death of a King*, were published by Robert Hale and were one-offs that concentrated on a mystery, rather than crime, concerning a key figure in history; tell us more of the others.

PD: Yes, I did *Man in the Iron Mask, Joan of Arc*, and the death of Richard II, plus the *Princes in the Tower*. These were one-offs: real mysteries which attracted me. It wasn't just crime, you're right, Mike; it was the genuine mysteries I always found fascinating. Like the *Princes in the Tower;* there's a well-known manuscript where Elizabeth I, years afterwards, showed a Frenchman visiting England a secret place in the Tower which contained the two skeletons of two boys. So they knew they were there. *The Man in the Iron Mask:* There's an entry in Charles II's secret accounts of agents being paid to take a man from England and deliver him to French secret agents at Dieppe. This man, I and others think, by following the trail is the Man in the Iron Mask. So he came from England. God knows who he was or what he was doing here. Apparently the French paid a hell of a lot of money, and the English sold him. This sort of thing fascinates me. For *Joan of Arc* it was the same. You know that DeGaulle always maintained that he was a descendant of Joan of Arc? I thought, how could he? She was a virgin when she was executed.

Then you get this marvelous story about a fiddle being carried out, a switch being done, of someone being burned for Joan. No one really saw her face, Joan was supposed to be released by Cardinal Beaufort. She went to Lorraine, married this handsome young man, settled down. They had a family and, of course, DeGaulle is their descendant.

MS: After these novels you were drawn into series characters, those of Roger Shallot, Hugh Corbett, and Brother Athelstan. Why the switch?

PD: A good question that. I don't know.

MS: A nice book contract with Headline?

PD: That was a factor. The other thing was that you can create a character and you find it easier to deliver. You begin to identify with them. I suppose you're always copying from other people.

MS: With that in mind, what was your source?

PD: I love Conan Doyle and Colin Dexter. The quiet, introspective man you find in Morse, you can also find in Corbett. Clerks were very good but they didn't know their way around the streets, so you get this second character Ranulfatte Newgate. He is a felon, a poacher turned gamekeeper, and that allows you to play. However, Corbett is the true medieval figure; he cares about the law and bringing people to trial but Ranulf, he doesn't see the point. If someone has broken the law—kill 'em. That allows you a certain richness, to write a novel and create a plot and a mystery. You're really dealing with one character which is divided into two people. The medieval people loved the law, they thought the law was marvelous; on the other hand you've got this absolute contempt for it by the outlaws/wolfsheads. Others of my characters develop this theme. Men like Cranston (who's a typical medieval civic official). Cranston has a love of the law but he lives life to the full—he goes to church, he loves his wife, and gets pissed as a newt when he can. (Medieval people ate and drank a lot; they would drink us two under the table like that!)

He's a soldier, a cynic but he also needs a clerk. And Athelstan, a Dominican friar, serves this purpose. The Dominicans were always involved with people; whenever there was an uprising in England it was always the Dominicans who were arrested because, like in South

America, the priests were very powerful with the people. My research can take me into the London court records to seek people like Watkin the dung collector and Pike the ditcher. When Wat Tyler's rebellion was put down you get these characters there. They were really crude democrats. They knew there was something wrong, they knew they should have a vote, but they're not too clear how to articulate this. So the best way to do it is to kill the rich. Tyler planned to kill all the bishops, all the priests, all the nobles. Not the King—he was a good guy. It's not very different from the Khmer Rouge politics to kill everybody and start again. You get these incredible thought patterns, sometimes very modern but suddenly you've gone back hundreds of years. There's the legal principle: "What affects all Must be approved by all" (that's fourteenth century, that's modern democracy). At the same time, you get these medieval ideas which certainly don't make sense today.

MS: It's clear that Athelstan is derived from a rich source.

PD: I've always loved Chaucer. I think his character sketches are brilliant. He is a brilliant writer. The Prioress was supposed to be a woman of God, dedicated to a life of religion, but she had her pet lap dog, her little handsome priest, her nice little palfry, and you think, "I've seen that hypocrisy myself." The Yeoman is really the "Medallion Man" of the fourteenth century; he's got his bracelet on his wrist, and a dagger on his belt, and his bow and arrows; he's almost macho man. The Knight who was really a quiet and gentle man, courteous and in a couple of lines Chaucer gives it a twist—he likes killing people. These sort of characters are asking for novels to be written about them.

MS: Medieval legal documents must provide you with a wealth of information. Do you depend on them?

PD: When you look at the legal records you get these very sophisticated murders. Even in the seventeenth century you get this scheme to kill Cromwell on the steps of St. Paul's by a crossbow on a timeswitch. It was all set up, and we know it went wrong. Then you get this love of poisons. For example, in Venice, if you and I were found guilty of murder, and they didn't have enough proof, they'd give us the Abrin seed to chew. If you were innocent, Mike, that's all right, you'd survive. If you were guilty, you'd die. What's the catch here? Apparently, with this seed, if you swallow it like you'd swallow tea or coffee you're fine but, as you know, most poisons begin in the mouth; if you chew it you're dead. So in other words if the authorities say, "We want this fellow let off," they'd give him the seed and say, "For God's sake don't chew it." What a marvelous use of toxins!

MS: Mmm, sounds very reminiscent of *The Name of the Rose* when the poison was in the text ink.

PD: Catherine de Medici did the same thing; she was the queen of poisons. She sent a nobleman apples and gloves. The poor nobleman thought the apples were poisoned so he chucked them. He thought the gloves were poisoned outside, he checked them—they weren't. What he didn't check out was when he put his hand inside the poison was there. She even smeared poison on door handles and you think, crickey, these people could really show these modern criminals something. Then you get the spies: Walsingham in Elizabeth I's time was a spy master and I think he said that he wasn't sure who his own spies were working for. There were people being triple agents, spying for the Catholics, spying for the Protestant monarchy, and spying for France. Basically spying for anyone who paid the highest. They wouldn't shift camp, they'd take the money from me, you, and anyone else and delivered for everyone! What marvelous people they are, and this was what made me start the Shallot series. Shallot, I based on these Elizabethan spies and my hatred of Henry VIII—I can't stand him!

MS: When I mentioned to a few people that I was coming to interview you they said, "I hate these history mystery series, they're never right." But you've already defended these well-researched books. But their argument was first off, there were no detectives. Secondly, today's psychology wasn't around in those days, and thirdly, life was so cheap that they bumped each other off without investigating murders.

PD: With the psychology, Mike, people haven't changed. Bumping people off isn't a twentieth-century invention. The really great massacres in Europe occurred then. As to detectives, they were there, and they investigated.

MS: You've written books that have only appeared in the States as C. L. Grace; tell us a little bit about them.

PD: One of the things I came across was that up until 1520 women were allowed to be doctors. And I love Canterbury and basically I wrote this series of a woman doctor in Canterbury in the 1470s. It did quite well. I've written three or four and I don't know if I'll continue because I got one or two things on my mind. Oh, then there's the time-travel series written as Ann Dukthas, where I've returned to the historical mysteries and I've done one on the death of Darnley, Mary Stuart's husband, and another based on the Mayerling deaths entitled *Time of Murder at Mayerling* (St. Martin's Press). The problem is I just can't stop telling stories. But I think there's only so much the market can take. I try and make each line different—hence the different names. I really do try to work at it.

MS: With the passing of Ellis Peters, her crown is up for grabs by a handful of history writers. Would you consider yourself a contender?

PD: Ellis Peters, in my view, presented a perspective of medieval life which was genuine. I think she was a great author. I actually thought her previous novels were really historical: *The Bloody Field by Shrewsbury* as Edith Pargeter was excellent. The problem is to "catch the period." The same applies to historical films: Umberto Eco's *Name of the Rose* I thought transferred accurately, and the *Hour of the Pig* was brilliant. I want to make sure that my novels are medieval and not costume dramas and that's the great danger. There are a lot of novels that are supposedly historical yet they bring the whole lot into disrepute, hence the previous criticisms. But Ellis Peters, Umberto Eco, Rosemary Sutcliffe are brilliant. Lindsay Davis's about ancient Rome are equally good; she knows her stuff and that's obvious.

MS: You have this wealth of background information, you've got good sources, so this must suggest storylines to you. For instance, perhaps a line or two in a legal document or parish record tells of John the privy cleaner, friend to the king, who was found dead in mysterious circumstances. Could this suggest one thread of a plot?

PD: I get storylines from many, many places. For example, from modern films I transfer it back. You can get it from a medieval chronicle. I can't actually say they come from one source, they just occur and you follow it through. Like for example *The House of Crows*, which is an Athelstan novel. I was watching the news about corruption in our modern day parliament. I thought, "What about the medieval House of Commons? They were corrupt as well. What about someone bumping MPs off?" Someone with a grudge against them?

Then you're away; all you've got to do then is: What was the grudge? Who are the characters? What is the great secret? What time period do you put it in?

MS: Then does that suggest your main characters, whether it is going to be Shallot or Corbett or Athelstan?

PD: Oh yes. I came across an entry about the Guild of Hangmen in the sixteenth century. I thought, "What a marvelous idea, what if there was a murderer killing the hangmen?" So you got *The Gallows Murder*. You throw in the historical mystery of the Princes in the Tower as well because it's based in the Tower and you've got the genesis of a novel and you develop it from there.

MS: Is there a disadvantage of series writing?

PD: Yes, you've got to be careful you don't get clichéd. That you don't start repeating yourself and cheat on your reading public. I try to give each of my novels my best shot. But the danger there is that you shouldn't get blasé or complaisant just because it's another Corbett novel. I don't think you've got to get too involved with your characters. Once you get their personal private life overtaking the plot, it's time to kiss them good-bye.

MS: So you're very plot-driven for the core of the novel?

PD: Yes, otherwise you can get the same novel time and time again. I watch everything on TV I can about crime. Remember the *Kojak* series? That series took a dive as soon as Kojak's private life began to intrude. Same happened to *Miami Vice*—it was a brilliant series.

MS: So what's next?

PD: There's one of each series out now: *The Devil's Hunt* (Corbett), *Assassin's Riddle* (Athelstan), *The Demonic Murders* (Shallot), which I enjoyed very much, and *Ghostly Murders*, the fourth in the Canterbury series. A big novel called *The Rose Demon*, which is a mystery novel based on the medieval idea of the incubus (a powerful demon who could move from body to body, and very much part of the medieval period). I finished *The Mayerling* last week. . . .

MS: Where do you find the time? Headmaster by day and writer by night?

PD: With great difficulty. But one of the great things about doing research when I was younger gives you this great discipline in your approach. So each day I always spend an hour and a half writing. If I have to get up at two in the morning, then I'll get up and write.

MS: That's dedication. What would you say is your main aspiration as a writer? What's driving you on?

PD: I don't know. I've always wanted to be an author. I love the medieval period and I love telling stories. I love teaching. I give history mystery lectures. I just enjoy it and I hope that people who read my books enjoy it. If someone says, "I think your books are crap," then I'm sad and disappointed but I reply that I didn't intend to be that. You're also writing for a restricted market. One of the great barriers the history mystery novels have got to break, as I mentioned earlier, is the costume barrier. Your Athelstan is not a twentieth-century man. Nor is Cranston, or Corbett, or Ranulf, or Shallot.

MS: Have you ever thought of changing styles? You do change from third to first person, but possibly by making them hard-boiled? Approach it from a different angle?

PD: I'll try it. I think you've got to be diverse. Like in *The Devil's Hunt,* people like Corbett were threatened. If a medieval clerk went to do a dangerous task they sometimes met with a nasty accident. So in the next Corbett novel, something happens to Corbett and his entourage—I won't let on too much. I'd like to make them grimmer and grittier.

MS: How would you approach that?

PD: By ending certain series. Life expectancy was short.

MS: That's the good thing about your novels; they don't romanticize the period.

PD: No, it wasn't a romantic period. Thomas Cromwell was created Earl of Essex at the beginning of May; six weeks later he was in the Tower facing charges of high treason—he lost his head. Out of favor. Out of life. If you lost in medieval politics, you lost, you went down. Read about the career of William Catsby; he fought for Richard III at Bosworth; they caught him riding away from the battle. They took him into a tavern, got a priest to hear his confession, got a clerk to take his dictated will, and hanged him on the nearest tree. Richard III began the Battle of Bosworth as King of England; twenty-four hours later his hanged body was thrown in a horse trough in Leicester. Walter Raleigh was supposed to inscribe on a window seat at Greenwich Palace: "Feign would I rise but I fear the fall." And Elizabeth was said to write underneath, "If you're frightened, don't climb at all." When you fell in the Middle Ages, you fell fast like Lucifer and you didn't rise. This violent, grittier side I'd like to bring out more.

Laurie King

INTERVIEW BY DEAN JAMES

Winning an Edgar for Best First Novel from the Mystery Writers of America happens to a select few writers, and in 1994 it happened to Laurie R. King, a third-generation Californian who published her first novel, A Grave Talent, with St. Martin's Press. A Grave Talent introduced a compelling main character, a San Francisco homicide detective named Kate Martinelli, with a secret to hide. Trying hard to keep her personal life from interfering with her job, Kate walks that fine line like many contemporary women. In addition to winning the Edgar, King also captured the John Creasey Award for Best First Novel from the Crime Writers Association of Great Britain. King's third novel, To Play the Fool (St. Martin's), records a further case for Kate Martinelli. It was followed by With Child (St. Martin's), which was nominated for the Edgar for Best Novel, as well as for the Orange Award. This latter is a literary award for women writers in the United Kingdom.

Not content, however, with creating one distinctive series character, King also published The Beekeeper's Apprentice (also St. Martin's) in 1995, which introduced to the world the extraordinary young Mary Russell, who literally stumbles across Sherlock Holmes in a Sussex field in 1915. This book was nominated for an Agatha Award for Best Novel by the members of Malice Domestic, the mystery convention devoted to celebration of the traditional mystery. The second Mary Rus-

sell novel, A Monstrous Regiment of Women *(St. Martin's), received the Nero Wolfe Award for Best Novel. The third in the series,* A Letter of Mary, *was published to excellent reviews in January 1997, followed by* The Moor *in 1998. King's works are presently available in fifteen languages, and in addition to her literary achievements, King has received an honorary doctorate from her graduate school, The Church Divinity School of the Pacific.*

The following interview was conducted in two parts, about two years apart. Section One was originally published in Mystery Scene *magazine (issue #48, July/August 1995).*

SECTION ONE (1995)

DJ: Why did you choose to write mysteries, rather than some other type of fiction?

LK: If by "choose" you mean a deliberate, conscious choice, I never did *choose* to write mysteries. The first piece of fiction I wrote was a futuristic sort of novel, where I kill off nearly all the men (nothing personal, Dean) and leave a decimated population of women. Oddly enough, the title I eventually gave it was *Daughters of Men,* and as P. D. James has since then published her *Children of Men,* which also presents a future of limited fertility and a decimated population, mine may not be published for a very long time. At any rate, a year or so later I was visited by Mary Russell, and the choice of genres was decided for me. I continue to write mysteries because I feel at home with the basic structure, the skeleton on which a writer may hang so many and varied bodies— like the sonnet, I suppose, or the haiku, as compared to the free verse of mainstream fiction. There's also the freedom to create, in effect, a story thousands of pages long, by working in a series.

DJ: What is your conception of the mystery novel? Do you consider any writers to have been of significant influence upon your view of what a mystery novel is (or can be)?

LK: I don't write whodunits, and I rarely read them. (Similarly, I can't stand crossword puzzles, word games, or logic conundra, and the only time I do a jigsaw puzzle is on Christmas or Thanksgiving, when I become compulsive and ill-tempered until it is complete.) To me the point of the mystery novel is not the solution of the crime, but how the crime affects the people around it, how the protagonist wrestles with restoring order to the universe, and how the lives of the main characters and the solution of the mystery interweave. As for influences (assuming that admiration creates an influence), I would have to say Dorothy L. Sayers, for the elegance of her language, Josephine Tey for her slyness in twisting the genre to her purposes, and Peter Dickinson, for his sheer bloody brilliance.

DJ: You have a master's degree in theology. How does this background inform your conception of the moral dimension of mystery fiction?

LK: I'm not quite sure how to answer this. Obviously morality is an unstated assumption in both "god-talk" and in the mystery genre, but I don't know that an academic degree in theology has a whole lot to do with morality. Perhaps it would be safe to say that I have always been interested in humankind's relationship with the divine, in both the abstract and the day-to-day expressions, and whereas with the M.A. I was looking at the development and history of that relationship, the broad spectrum as it were; in writing mystery novels I can delve into the specifics of how an immoral act (although that seems an awfully weak description of murder) affects us all. Applied theology, perhaps, or even practical morality.

On the other hand, my background in theology certainly has influenced the topics in the stories, which range from the Trickster archetype I wrote about for my Bachelor's thesis (used in *To Play the Fool*) to the investigation of the feminine aspects of God that was the topic of my Master's thesis (used in the second Mary Russell story, *A Monstrous Regiment of Women*, due out this summer) and the question of women in the leadership of the early Church (using a purported letter from Mary Magdalene in which she calls herself an apostle, a third Mary Russell story to be published in 1996).

DJ: Your first published novel, *A Grave Talent*, won the Edgar for Best First Novel. Has the award made a significant difference in your career thus far?

LK: Of course. People return my phone calls after the third or fourth time now, instead of after five or six tries.

DJ: The main character in *A Grave Talent* is a lesbian. Was that a deliberate choice on your part?

LK: As you may have guessed by now, there are few deliberate choices on my part in the development of a novel. Looking back I can see the various threads that led to a character being one thing or another—

Mary Russell, for example, had to have an American element in her background in order to excuse the occasional slips in vocabulary and attitude, but when she introduced herself, she simply *was*. Similarly, Kate Martinelli was to have a close relationship with an older man, her partner Al Hawkin, but without the dimension of sexual attraction, and although it is very possible to have simple friendship between the sexes, making her unequivocally a lesbian made the limits clear from the start. Or nearly the start, because I took some time getting around to describing her home life. However, this is all hindsight; in the process of writing, she simply (*ahem*) came out that way.

DJ: In police work, as in many spheres of life, women are often treated as outsiders. As a lesbian, Kate Martinelli has a double mark, in a way, against her, even in San Francisco. How do you think this perspective affects your work? Or does it?

LK: Although the San Francisco Police Department is less encumbered with homophobia than other departments, as you say, it's still there, and before you ask: No, last time I asked, there were no women homicide inspectors. So of course this is one source of pressure for Kate, and I am finding it coming heavily into the third in the series, which I am now in the process of writing.

DJ: I read in another interview that, even with the second book in the series, *To Play the Fool,* you have begun to tire of Kate Martinelli and her partner, Alonzo Hawkin. Is this true? If so, why? What about these characters no longer challenges you as a writer?

LK: I was fed up with them after *A Grave Talent,* much less five years later when I wrote *To Play the Fool.* Every time I finish a book I'm sick and tired of the characters I've just spent several months following around the page. I wouldn't say there is no challenge left in them, and in fact future books continue to take shape in the back of my mind. Kate is, however, a more limited person than, say, Mary Russell, simply because she's more real, and the situations in which she finds herself have to be more firmly rooted in humdrum daily life of the late twentieth century. In a sense, she is more of a challenge, because I have to work at the Martinelli books, whereas the Russell & Holmes books tend to write themselves.

DJ: In *To Play the Fool,* you make reference to another case, the "Raven Morningstar" murder, which sounds fascinating. Is this anything we're likely ever to see in print?

LK: I don't think so. It was put in as a means of tying *Fool* in to *Grave Talent*, the Morningstar case being the means by which Al Hawkin pulls Kate back onto the job at the end of *Grave Talent*. However, it's obviously a depressing and distressing case, with a disastrous ending, and is hardly the thing, if I were to write it up, that most people would want to read. Too *noir* for me, so I will probably just leave it a tantalizing but unknown episode. However, anything is possible.

DJ: With your two main characters, Kate Martinelli and Mary Russell, you have unusual women with strikingly different points of view. How does each of them represent your ideas of the roles of women in their respective worlds?

LK: Mary Russell is the embodiment of the New Woman of the early twentieth century, when women had run England during World War I and, with the vote, anything seemed possible. Kate Martinelli is the practical outcome of that great new beginning, at the far end of the century when the revolution has revolved, ending up in just hard work and variations of the same problems there were to begin with. Ironically, Kate is much more vulnerable to male oppression than Mary Russell is, because Mary is so immensely self-contained, and because Mary is, after all, in a country that has a tradition of such remarkable individuals such as Gertrude Bell and Mary Kingsley, coddled Victorian women who found themselves wandering the Arabian desert or the West African tropics, unaccompanied except by hired native men. The American continent has produced its share of eccentric women, but not I think such striking examples.

DJ: Where did Mary Russell come from? Was the notion to match her with the "great" Sherlock Holmes there from the start?

LK: God only knows. Again, using hindsight, I think she had her beginnings in an upsurge of feminist sentiments, triggered by a television production of one of the Holmes stories, the feeling that really, this much-vaunted man was only using skills possessed by any woman who has a child over the age of two, and many women who were not mothers at all. Call it common sense or feminine intuition, when it is found in a male it is considered extraordinary. And yes, she needs Holmes as her counterpart: He represents the height of Victorian, masculine thought, whereas she is the embodiment of modern feminism. Equal brains, different settings, different times.

DJ: The relationship between Mary and Sherlock in *The Beekeeper's Apprentice* is quite warm, and many readers have already suspected that the relationship is destined to bring them even closer. Does the "M. R. H." with which Mary ends her "Author's Note" mean what all we readers think?

LK: We shall have to wait until I decipher future manuscripts to be sure, but I doubt it means what you think. I really can't imagine that Sherlock Holmes would go so far as to adopt her, do you?

DJ: St. Martin's told me that Mary's next adventure, *A Monstrous Regiment of Women*, is due out late this summer. Would you care to give your fans any more tidbits about further exploits of Mary Russell and Kate Martinelli?

LK: A bit of gossip? Very well. *A Monstrous Regiment of Women* is based on a treatise by the long-suffering John Knox, the full title of which was "The First Blast of the Trumpet against the Monstrous Regiment of Women," in which he rails against women rulers in general and his own disapproving queen in particular. My own *Monstrous Regiment* involves a charismatic woman religious leader in the early twenties, a time just after the First World War when so many young men had been killed or disabled and the women they might normally have married were called, in the press, "surplus women." So flattering. Mary Russell gets involved with this woman's community, tutoring her in the feminine aspects of God that can be found in the Bible, and finding her more appealing than the continually ill-tempered and irritating Holmes. There is a murder, and a kidnapping, and a lot of fog.

The next Kate Martinelli book I am now trying to write, not an easy thing when I'm supposed to be traveling the country and talking about *To Play the Fool*. Nonetheless, a page at a time I am putting together a story about Kate and particularly about Jules Cameron, the young girl who appears in the end of *Grave Talent* and whose mother is involved with Al Hawkin. The name at this point is *With Child*, and it's due out, assuming I finish it, next February. And yes, Lee is in it too. And Lee's mad Aunt Agatha. And a homeless boy named Dio. And a racoon named Gideon . . .

SECTION TWO (OCTOBER 1997)

DJ: Looking back at the above interview, is there any question that you would give a different answer than you did in 1995?

LK: Yes, my response to the question of the Edgar's effect on my life was far too flip. The award, along with *Grave Talent*'s Creasey award from Britain's CWA and then the Best Novel nomination for *With Child* in 1996, were tremendous honors, and the more I look back at them, the more amazed and humbled I am. In fact, I'd like to re-read *Grave Talent* one of these days (I haven't looked at it since I worked through the galleys in 1992) to see if I agree with the judges.

DJ: What is the first piece of fiction you wrote? What happened to it?

LK: In the summer of 1984, on a trip to England to celebrate the completion of my M.A. degree, I started to fiddle with the idea of fiction. This was eventually to become what I called *Daughters of Men*, mentioned above, and it taught me a lot about how not to write. I did eventually finish the thing, after I had written two or three mysteries, but it needs to be severely rewritten before it can be submitted again. I will say that parts of it are not bad (which is about as enthusiastic as I get about my own prose) and although it still remains unpublished, I think some day it will find a home.

DJ: Do you work a set number of hours every day? How long do you typically spend in writing a novel?

LK: Writing is my second job; I am first and foremost a mom, with all the myriad demands and chaos that entails. So I have to say that, no, there are days when I have too many other things to do, even if I am working against a deadline. On the other hand there are some days when I spend twelve hours working. When actively writing I try to do at least five pages a day, about 2,000 words, though I have done as many as 10,000 when I'm on a roll.

Preparation time for a book varies hugely, depending on the amount of research required and how clear the story was when it came to me. The actual writing time works out to about three or four months, after which I like to leave it to go cold for some time before I pick it up again for the rewrite. Say seven months altogether before I give it to the editor.

DJ: If/when you're feeling blocked, or something isn't coming just right, what do you do?

LK: You know, I have found that when writer's block hits while I'm working on a book, it is usually a sign that something is going wrong in the story. It feels different from sheer laziness, or the state of just plain confusion I get into when I don't know what is going to happen next—for those the solution is to sit and push the pen across the paper (literally—I write with a fountain pen). Writer's block for me is much more a nervous affliction, a restlessness and a deep urge to go and clean the oven or clear out every closet in the house. And often that's what I do while I wait for the back of my mind to come up with the location of the problem and thus its solution, because if I push it then, if I force the pen to produce the words, I will soon find that I have trapped myself into some problem plot line that has been developing without my being aware of it. I try to remind myself that writer's block is my friend, even when I burn myself on oven cleaner, lose track of everything the closets used to contain, and know that I will never be able to write again.

DJ: How important is the writer/editor relationship to you?

LK: Absolutely vital. I have been blessed with having first Ruth Cavin at St. Martin's, and now Kate Miciak at Bantam. Both women are true editors with an eye for problems and solutions yet who trust their writers to know what they are doing. I can't imagine how writers manage at the many houses where editors are mere acquirers of manuscripts, and have no time actually to edit their authors' books. Maybe other writers have a clearer sense of plot than I do, and don't get into the sticky places I do, but I can't imagine turning one of my raw and unedited manuscripts loose on an unsuspecting public.

DJ: What is the best piece of writing advice someone ever gave you?

LK: To tell you the truth, I can't recall anyone giving me any early advice, though I'm sure it must have happened. I was one of those writers who had three books written before anyone outside my family even knew I was dabbling in it. After I was published, the only advice I got was of the sort I couldn't take such as, "You must outline!" or, "You have to have a New York agent." I don't, either.

DJ: What is the most difficult part of the process for you? What do you worry about the most?

LK: I worry that the whole thing is a fluke, that with whatever book I'm working on at the moment, it will emerge that I don't really have any skill at writing. I fret that this book will be the one that dribbles off unfinished. I invariably worry, with each and every book, that as

I reach about page 180 I will only have about forty pages of story left to me, and wonder how on earth I can turn in a 220-page novella. That's one of the reasons why I started keeping a writing journal, to remind myself that the exact same doubts crop up each time.

So the most difficult part is faith. Trusting that the words spilling out of my pen aren't really as deadly dull as I think they are, believing that the whole miraculous process of giving birth to a story will happen again this time, telling myself that the few feeble sparks of light I see in the morass will be sufficient to illuminate the whole.

DJ: Do you ever think about taking a break from the two series and writing something different? If you did, what would it be?

LK: Funny you should mention it. The book I'm working on now is a non-series novel called *A Darker Place*. It involves a woman, two children, an FBI agent, and a religious movement, and the difficult thing about it is, it's not a mystery, so I don't have all those nice tidy guidelines about body and clues and suspects and investigator. It's a novel, period, although I think Bantam, my new publisher, will be calling it a thriller (whatever that means). I don't see it as a third series, but a stand-alone book (although I admit that *A Grave Talent* began as a singleton, too). The two series I'm involved with will keep me going for a while, unless I can figure out a way to write three books a year.

DJ: Fifty years ago, most writers could stay at home and write, concentrating on their art. Nowadays, they have to get out and travel—promote, promote, promote. How does this affect you and your writing? How does this much contact with your reading public affect you as a writer?

LK: Even fifty years ago, a number of writers went on lecture tours. Arthur Conan Doyle, for example, traveled the world to promote his ideas—and his books—on spiritualism. These days, the mania for promotion, and particularly for self-promotion, has reached a ridiculous state. Why break your back, your bank account, and your self-respect by climbing into your car and driving across the country to promote your new book to groups of three or ten people who have nothing better to do on a rainy night? Very few first novels benefit by it. Local signings, sure, but isn't the writer better off staying at home and polishing the second novel? My first tour was for the third book, by which time a decent handful of people in each city had heard of me and were willing to come and hear me speak.

There's no doubt that travel trashes a person's writing schedule: Five weeks on the road eats up ten weeks of life, as it takes that long to catch up on all the thousand jobs that have accumulated while you were on the road. It's hard on you, hell on the family, and although you do feel that by God you're doing all you can to make this book a success, dollar for hour I am not convinced that it is worth it.

It is, I admit, terribly good for a person's ego. This in itself may be bad for a writer, since we all know that the only reason any of us write is that we feel inadequate in real life, and to have a hundred people patting and stroking us and laughing at our tired old jokes makes us begin to believe that we just may be hot stuff, and why should we work on improving our writing if everybody loves it so much as it is? When this temptation strikes, I strongly recommend finding some kids, even if you have to borrow them. There's nothing like disgruntled kids with unwashed laundry and five weeks' worth of unfinished school projects to get a person back in line, fast.

DJ: With *A Letter of Mary*, you gave a rather audacious "twist" to the Holmes legend by having Sherlock and Mary married. Have readers written and asked, "How dare you?" How do you respond, if at all?

LK: It is interesting, but most of the "How dare you!" responses have been told me indirectly, as in "My husband the Sherlockian won't read your books," or "I refuse to review someone who writes such and so." More often, the letters or comments I receive are along the lines of "I hate Holmes pastiches but I was forced to read one of your stories and now I love them."

I think that the *idea* of Holmes married may be more troubling than the actuality within the Russell books. The potential for soppiness and actions that do violence to Holmes's character is considerable, but the books are written as if by a dignified older woman (i.e., Mary Russell) setting down her memoirs, so that many things, personal things, are left unsaid. The Holmes and Russell marriage is by and large an extension of their professional partnership, a fulfillment of it.

Incidentally, it has recently come to my attention that there is a sub-genre (sub-sub-genre?) of Sherlockian erotica, which I have to say is one of the most nauseating ideas I have encountered in a long time. If I found myself writing anything that might be mistaken for that, I think I would burn the rest of the manuscripts.

DJ: The fourth Mary Russell novel, *The Moor* (St. Martin's, 1998), takes Mary and Holmes back to Devon and the area of Conan

Doyle's *The Hound of the Baskervilles*. How closely related is the story of *The Moor* to Conan Doyle's classic?

LK: It is closely intertwined with the *Hound* story, obviously—otherwise what would be the fun of it? However, it is by no means a rewrite of the Conan Doyle story—the hound in *The Moor* belongs to another Devonshire legend, that of Lady Howard, and the residents of Baskerville Hall aren't the Baskervilles. There are, in addition to Holmes and Russell, two main characters in the book. One is the Reverend Sabine Baring-Gould, a fascinating (and true-life) Victorian squire/parson/novelist/hymnist/theologian/antiquarian. A genuine Enthusiast, and very like Holmes in many ways. (Strangely enough, Baring-Gould's grandson, William S. Baring-Gould, was an eminent Sherlockian who wrote a "biography" of Holmes—filling in the missing details with stories of his grandfather's childhood.) The other central character is Dartmoor itself, in all its peculiar beauty.

DJ: Is there a new Kate Martinelli book in the works? When might we expect to see a follow-up to *With Child*?

LK: After I finish *A Darker Place* I'm going to try to do another Martinelli novel, aiming for publication in February 2000. There are a couple of story lines I'm playing with in my head, so there will probably be at least two or three more Martinellis before that well runs dry.

DJ: After *The Moor*, where will Mary and Holmes venture next?

LK: In *The Beekeeper's Apprentice*, there is a chapter where Holmes and Russell leave England for several weeks and end up in what was then called Palestine. One of the reasons I had that chapter in the book, in addition to the needs of the story, was that I very much wanted to write a book about that land and that time. The country is a small gem, the history compelling, the peoples fascinating, and the problems, even then, immense. That book is tentatively called *O Jerusalem*, is set in January and February of 1919, and will I hope be out in August 1999. Then another Holmes and Russell will follow, picking up Ali and Mahmoud Hazr, the two guides who lead the pair around Palestine, but in England this time, and set in 1924, immediately following the action of *The Moor*.

Which takes me to the year 2001, and beyond that I cannot think.

Loren D. Estleman

INTERVIEW BY DALE L. WALKER

I n 1976, when he was two years out of Eastern Michigan University
(B.A. in English lit. and journalism) and a police beat reporter with
the Ypsilanti Press, Loren D. Estleman, age twenty-four, published
his first novel, a gritty gangster story written during his senior year in
college, titled The Oklahoma Punk. In 1978, his first Western, The
Hider, appeared, as well as a novel-length pastiche, Sherlock Holmes
Versus Dracula, or the Adventure of the Sanguinary Count. In 1980,
his Motor City Blue was published, introducing his Detroit private eye,
Amos Walker. His "Detroit Series" of novels—Whiskey River, Motown,
King of the Corner, Edsel, Stress—was sandwiched between the Walk-
ers and Westerns.

In the twenty-one years since his professional debut as novelist, the
Collected Estleman consists of forty novels, one nonfiction book (The
Wister Trace, an analysis of classic Western fiction, published in 1987),
two collections of short stories, and a vast number of reviews, essays and
articles in major periodicals.

He has earned three Spur Awards from Western Writers of America,
Inc., the American Mystery Award, three Shamus Awards from Private
Eye Writers of America, the Michigan Arts Foundation Award for Liter-
ature, and has been nominated for many others, including the Pulitzer
Prize.

His most recent books are Journey of the Dead, a Western novel, and

The Witchfinder, *an Amos Walker mystery. He lives in Whitmore Lake, Michigan, with his wife, Debi, who writes under the name Deborah Morgan.*

Marilyn Stasio, writing in the New York Times Book Review *said, "Mr. Estleman writes like a man in the know and what he knows is guns and cars and dirty politics. He also knows people, all kinds of people."*

And, as the following interview demonstrates, he knows noir.

DW: You wrote a story in *Alfred Hitchcock's Mystery Magazine* a few years ago titled "The Man Who Loved *Noir*," and you've said it was autobiographical. *Noir* seems to defy definition. As a man who loves it, please take a shot at defining it.

LE: That story provided the plotline for *Never Street*. The title is autobiographical, as I do love that movement. The French word means, simply, "black." The connotations of that color—or rather the lack of color—are emotional, and go back to early man, for whom the night was filled with saber-toothed cats and mortal enemies, doubly dangerous because they were unseen. Consider the fear quotient in such phrases as "Darkest Africa," "Heart of Darkness," and "blacking out," and you've arrived at a definition of *noir* that defies Webster.

DW: What do you love about it?

LE: With danger comes a corresponding tingle, like the breathless anticipation of a ride on a roller-coaster and the euphoria that sets in at the end, making you want to go back and experience it again. *Noir* in fiction enables me to recapture that sensation vicariously, without the threat of physical danger. I love the icons connected with classic *noir:* wide-brimmed fedoras, rumpled trenchcoats, sinister shadows, coils of cigarette smoke, guns, speeding automobiles, long-legged women, brutish thugs, cityscapes lit by stuttering neon signs. You can't explain the effect of such images from an intellectual standpoint. It's entirely visceral.

DW: In detective fiction, are "hard-boiled" and *noir* synonymous? Are there hard-boiled detective stories that are *not noir*ish?

LE: *Noir* is necessarily hard-boiled, but hard-boiled is not necessarily *noir*. Mickey Spillane's hard-boiled Mike Hammer novels are too direct for *noir*, yet *Kiss Me Deadly*, one of the greatest film *noirs*, is based on a Mike Hammer novel. Director Robert Aldrich had to introduce the atomic bomb to Spillane's story to make Hammer sufficiently vulnerable. On paper, the character is too indestructible for the reader to fear for his life; and the imminence of death around every corner is the essence of *noir*.

DW: Is it possible for a *noir* film to take place in daylight?

LE: Yes. No nocturnal scene ever filmed can disturb more deeply than the spectacle of Cary Grant fleeing for his life from a machine-gunning airplane through a Kansas cornfield at high noon in *North by Northwest*.

DW: Then, there is such a thing as cinema *noir* in color?

LE: There *are* color film *noirs: Party Girl* led the way in 1958, daring not to mute the colors but to make them even more garish, after the fashion of a detective pulp magazine cover. The use of red is especially sinister here. Hitchcock's *Rope* and *Vertigo* managed to make effective *noir* statements without reverting to black-and-white photography. *Body Heat, Blood Simple, Seven, Fargo,* and *The Usual Suspects* have extended the canon through muted shades and ever-darkening subject matter.

DW: Let me throw some unordered names at you and you tell me if they are *noir* or not. Feel free to elaborate. Spenser?

LE: Not. Like Hammer, he's too armor-plated and full of himself to experience the mind-numbing fear required. Also the Spensers aren't mysteries. *Noir* raises disturbing, lingering questions, and Spenser tends to answer all questions on the spot with his fists (or buddy Hawk's guns).

DW: Matt Scudder?

LE: Scudder can be *noir* all by himself, without a case or an enemy to put him in jeopardy. *Noir* follows him like the dark cloud over the head of some comic strip characters.

DW: Shell Scott?

LE: Too lighthearted, although many of Richard Prather's titles, such as *Gat Heat, Slab Happy,* and *Take a Murder, Darling,* are deliciously *noir*.

DW: Sharon McCone?

LE: Yes. The murky moral complexities of the world Marcia Muller has created for this first and best of the new breed of female fictional private eyes are very much in the tradition.

DW: Travis McGee?

LE: He is. Read *Nightmare in Pink*.

DW: Nero Wolfe?

LE: Not, although Archie Goodwin's description of Milo Zeck suggests that Stout understood the world of *noir*.

DW: Poirot?

LE: Too self-possessed in too orderly a society.

DW: Nameless?

LE: Is. Hey, the guy's so paranoid he won't even introduce himself.

DW: The 87th Precinct?

LE: The 87th Precinct showed *noir* promise until the Deaf Man arrived. The character belongs in a James Bond movie, not a realistic depiction of the urban underworld.

DW: James Ellroy?

DW: He is showily, self-consciously, cloyingly *noir;* Jim Thompson at his most overcooked.

DW: Andrew Vachss?

LE: Too morally indignant; although it helps to obscure the fact that he's a wretchedly bad writer.

DW: Eric Ambler?

LE: Is. Not many Brits are. The short list includes Gerald Kersh and Graham Greene.

DW: Sherlock Holmes?

LE: Holmes is *noir* in "The Man With the Twisted Lip" and "The Adventures of Charles Augustus Milverton"; in "The Adventure of the Red-Headed League" and "The Solitary Cyclist" he is not.

DW: Thomas Harris?

LE: Decidedly. His serial killers are less frightening than the prospect of his heroes climbing inside the killers' minds, then having trouble climbing back out. The result is a bone-chilling, claustrophobic panic.

DW: Dick Tracy?

LE: The essence of *noir*. Chester Gould came up with him in 1934, when it looked as if conventional forces of law and order were fighting a losing battle against bootleggers and bank robbers. Tracy is the textbook case of the honest loner turning down those mean streets. I count the first film, *Dick Tracy*, as *noir*, with Mike Mazurky as Splitface. Anything with Mazurky is *noir*; even his guest shot on *The Beverly Hillbillies*.

DW: Amos Walker?

LE: He is, but unlike the others on your list, he's aware of it. The situation compares with that of a sleeper who realizes he's having a nightmare and attempts to exercise some control over it.

DW: Is the hard-boiled detective mostly a male creation? Who are the women detective-mystery writers you admire? Do any write hard-boiled stories?

LE: It's a male invention, but this particular sub-genre has always been known for its tough, often dominant female characters, so it was only a matter of time before women writers embraced the form. Sara Paretsky and Sue Grafton are fashionable and, I think, viable members of the hard-boiled community, but long before they came along, P. D. James was dealing matter-of-factly with subjects that would raise the hairs on Agatha Christie's neck. Sharon McGrath writes the most hard-boiled *titles* in the business.

DW: "Hard-boiled" annoys me for some reason. Who came up with it? What does it mean? Isn't there a better term for this kind of story?

LE: Etymology stands forever on quicksand, and the development of slang is even less stable. Who invented it? I vote for Joseph "Cap" Shaw, who when he took over as editor of *Black Mask* recast that greatest of all detective pulps in the image of Dashiell Hammett's Continental Op stories. Another possible candidate is Carroll John Daly, who predated Hammett and invented the fictional private eye. His work is often denigrated today, mainly by writers less skilled than he. The term itself seems appropriate: a brittle shell on top of a re-silient membrane tempered by heat.

DW: In hard-boiled detective fiction, Philip Marlowe, Sam Spade, The Continental Op and Lew Archer seem to be the prototypes. Were these, or others, inspirational in the creation of Amos Walker?

LE: I proclaim the Chandler influence proudly, as should we all; al-though, curiously, I was experimenting with similes and metaphors—his hallmarks—before I was aware of his work. He's still the best, for the combination of cynical humor, idealism carefully banked with defensive bravado, and withering social commentary. Few writers have managed to blend those elements so smoothly. Ross Macdon-ald was the most successful at taking his inspiration into other areas. Chandler once said he saw no objection to writers traveling on bor-rowed gas so long as they traveled farther than the writers they bor-rowed from. In my own case, there is more of Chandler in the Amos Walker novels than in the Amos Walker short stories; for these I em-ploy the surgical economy of Hammett.

DW: Who are some of your other writer mentors?

LE: There is a good deal more of *me* in all my work than any one of my many unwary mentors: Leo Tolstoy, Ernest Hemingway, Jack London, Edith Wharton, Edgar Allan Poe, Somerset Maugham, H.G. Wells, and a host of far more obscure writers who entered my consciousness the day the bookmobile first visited my hometown. Style is something that happens whether you work on it or not; but it happens quicker when you don't.

DW: Back to Holmes a moment. You've written a couple of excellent Holmes pastiche novels—*Dr. Jekyll and Mr. Holmes* and *Sherlock Holmes vs. Dracula*—and are a student of the Sacred Writings. Aren't the Holmes stories—so many of them grim, night-borne tales—*noir*? What of the Basil Rathbone-Nigel Bruce movies?

LE: The roots of *noir* go deep in the Holmes stories. You must remember that Arthur Conan Doyle was influenced by Poe, and if we're going to discuss who invented *noir* we need to go no further than that troubled, brilliant artist, haunted by the death of everyone closest to him and by the very real fear of premature burial. Holmes once shuddered when Watson mentioned the pastoral beauty of the country, maintaining instead that the very remoteness of the life there made unspeakable crimes possible. That's a *noir* statement if ever there was one. In the Rathbone films, I would single out *Terror by Night* and *Sherlock Holmes and the Spider Woman* for definite inclusion in the classic *noir* cycle; but that quality disappears from the series in inverse ratio to the increasing stupidity of Nigel Bruce's Watson.

DW: Given the fifty or sixty years separating the Chandler-Hammett era from Amos Walker's, how does he differ, aside from his Detroit milieu, and how do other modern hard-boiled P.I.'s differ from these classic creations?

LE: Walker, like Marlowe and Sam Spade and the Continental Op, is both an anachronism and a product of his time. The post-Watergate, post-Vietnam era offers many of the same doubts and anxieties presented by the era of Prohibition, Depression and world war. Add to those the complex issues of electronic automation and unprincipled science, and the field is fertile for the crime writer. Apart from that, Amos Walker has developed, as I have, both as a writer and as a human being. The prospect of a relentlessly honest hero-for-hire in the Arthurian tradition placed against the backdrop of an amoral world yields results as rich as ever. But unlike his predecessors, Walker lives in a desegregated world, in which minorities aren't just props but dynamic players, and the tough cop who threatens his license may as likely be facing maternity leave as early retirement. It's the same game, but with twice as many pieces.

DW: Your *Never Street* is a novel *about noir*. Amos Walker is hired to locate a missing businessman named Neil Catalin who spends his free time watching *noir* movies in his private home theater. His wife is convinced he disappeared into a film he was watching—*Pitfall* with Dick Powell, Lizabeth Scott and Raymond Burr. Catalin sounds a lot like Loren Estleman. You have a home theater, a collection of *noir* films . . . you disappear into them at times?

LE: Often. But thanks to my wife, my family, my friends, my work, and a certain amount of common sense pounded into me by my parents and their example, I always come back out.

DW: In a *Mystery Scene* article about writing *Never Street,* you describe cinema *noir* as "Dark films with warped gangsters and neurotic heroes and dangerous women. Shiny wet streets and big black cars with their headlights on . . . dirty money, poisonous women, demented villains . . . self-devouring angst." Is this a particular *type* of cinema *noir* you like best?

LE: Yes. I prefer my heroes flawed, my villains psychotic, and my *femmes* fatal—in the movies. Nothing brings a grin to my face quicker in a dark room lit by the silver screen than an unexpected plot twist or a glimpse into yet another side of the naked id. If you can work in a firefight in a room full of mirrors or a vehicular homicide in a dark alley, I'm in paradise.

DW: Let me name a few examples of cinema *noir* and ask you to comment on each. Start with *Nosferatu,* the original *Frankenstein, Dracula* and *The Wolf Man.*

LE: The German Expressionism director F.W. Murnau used in *Nosferatu* gave birth to the distinctive "look" of cinema *noir,* and the religious and moral issues, nocturnal creepy-crawlies, and schizo tendencies of the great Universal horror films prepared audiences for the full-frontal onslaught of *noir* that came after World War II.

DW: *Public Enemy* and *White Heat.*

LE: *Public Enemy* helped define the gangster as a kind of perverted Horatio Alger American Dream hero, while *White Heat* brought that character to its logical extreme, beset by insanity and a hint of incest. How appropriate that James Cagney was cast both times, making it easy for even the least observant viewer to witness the deterioration.

DW: *Kiss Me Deadly.*

LE: In much the same way, Ralph Meeker's sadistic Mike Hammer in that film represents the moral degeneration of the cynical private eyes portrayed by Humphrey Bogart in *The Maltese Falcon* and *The Big Sleep;* suggesting that a sardonic attitude can be sustained only for so long before the character himself becomes corrupted.

DW: *Double Indemnity* and *The Postman Always Rings Twice.*

LE: Pure *noir*, in that there is no redemption for the hero, and as the forces of law and society close in on him, they are closing in on us as well, for we've been persuaded to identify with him.

DW: *Detour.*

LE: It just misses pure *noir* because I, for one, have trouble putting myself in the position of a protagonist who is so consistently stupid. The poor sap blames all his troubles on a pernicious Fate, when in fact it's his uncanny ability to do the exact wrong thing required in every situation that's got him in Dutch. This kind of film belongs to a category I call Dumbass *Noir*.

DW: *Cape Fear.*

LE: The original—not the heavy-handed remake—more closely represents the idea of a dire situation brought on not through the fault of the hero, but because he did the *right* thing, and because the law is powerless to step in until he does the desperate thing—at which time the law turns against him.

DW: *Nightmare Alley.*

LE: It manages to make us identify with a scoundrel, and to feel as betrayed as he when a far more subtle and dangerous scoundrel gets the best of him. It's also one of the more disturbing films in the cycle, representing, with *Kiss Me Deadly* and *D.O.A.*—both versions—its darkest inner ring.

DW: I saw the 1945 *Dillenger* on TCM recently. It seemed to me to have some classic *noir* features: scroungy hotel room with peeling, stained wallpaper; sleazy offices; cigarette smoke; dark streets, a lot of rat-tat-tat dialogue; a slinky woman (Ann Jeffries); some wonderful spear-carriers like Eduardo Cianelli, Marc Lawrence and Elisha Cook, Jr. Was I watching *noir*?

LE: That original *Dillinger* is *noir* almost entirely because of its star. Lawrence Tierney was the best and most charismatically menacing of B-movie heavies—and still is, although he's almost physically unrecognizable as the head of the underworld gang in *Reservoir Dogs.* Barry Gifford, in *The Devil Thumbs a Ride,* writes that "there is no sunshine" in Tierney's face. That was true in 1945 and it's true now. One of the truly great little-known icons of *noir*. And any movie whose cast includes Eduardo Cianelli, Marc Lawrence and Elisha Cook, Jr., couldn't avoid being *noir* if it tried.

DW: Peter Haining, in a collection of hard-boiled stories titled *Pulp Fictions*, writes of reading the stories for "cracks"—the wiseacre remarks made by the hero-narrator. Parker's Spenser is famous for them but nobody makes cracks like Walker. The funniest one in *Never Street* is "She wore trim-fitting brown stirrup pants with the champagne-colored blouse, and she hadn't anything in the pockets." But I also like the moment when Amos, searching for the missing Neil Catalin, goes through Catalin's file cabinet: "It was a standard bar lock, as old as the chastity belt. I had it open with my pocket knife in two seconds. Inside I found files. Not a one of them was labeled *Where I Went*." These are better than anything Chandler or Hammett ever wrote. Is a sense of humor necessary to write the hard-boiled P.I. story?

LE: It's probably not necessary, but it never hurts. In my case the humor boils up unexpectedly, but it's mainly a defense mechanism. Walker uses it both to distance himself from the downbeat life his calling has forced him to lead and to keep his enemies off-guard long enough for him to come up with a plan of survival. A lot of writers who try to ape Chandler slather on the wisecracks for their own sake, using them by the cupful when a pinch will do. The best humor, like the best horror, comes out of an objective presentation of outrageous circumstances. If you lean too heavily on what's funny or frightening, you achieve the opposite result.

DW: I laughed out loud when Amos, listening to Latin music and watching the silver-haired dancers at the Castanet Lounge, says, "I felt like Jane Goodall, crouched in the bush with binoculars. Time clicked past on flamenco heels." And there is the guy who "tugged back one of his lacy cuffs to consult his Casio," and "a table the size of a cornplaster," and "Well-dressed white children pounded basketballs off the concrete pads in front of the garages in the daytime, looking to fight their way out of the upper middle class with nothing but their trust funds and a dream." Is Amos's streak of cynicism wider than yours?

LE: I'd say we're neck-and-neck. Cynicism being idealism gone brown around the edges.

DW: Jeff Siegel, in *The American Detective: An Illustrated History*, says that Robert B. Parker's Spenser was one of the best hard-boiled sleuths since Lew Archer but that somewhere Parker made Spenser a sort of couth Mike Hammer with a "Vengeance is Mine" attitude. Aren't violence and vengeance common fare for hard-boiled heroes?

LE: Not really. Hammer, Spenser, and their clones often take the role of avenging angel, but as a rule the private eye of lore is a defender of those who cannot defend themselves. The bad guys tend to get their comeuppance, but only in the course of rescuing the innocent. Imagining that one can right what's wrong by destroying one aspect of a great evil calls for a naivete that the soul-weary knight-errant set aside long ago. He knows he can't save the world, but he hopes to be able to clean up a tiny piece of it, if only for today.

DW: This has become among the most famous and quoted of opening sentences in any modern western novel: "He was dying faster than usual that morning, striping the sides of the dry sink with bloody sputum and shreds of shattered lung. His ears rang and his head felt hollow." This is Doc Holliday in your *Bloody Season* and that novel is definitely *noir*, right? Are there *noir*ish qualities in your other Westerns?

LE: I've been credited with inventing Western *noir*, but others deserve that honor, and I never really set out with that in mind. The historic West was at times far grimmer than it's been presented in fiction, as well as richer and more fascinating. Death—from violence, hardship, and disease—was a daily reality, even when the prospect of a live birth was a challenge, and the elements themselves conspired against human habitation. Insanity was a common danger. The success stories are exalting, but the stories of failure are chilling. Any attempt to paint an accurate picture of life is bound to employ techniques commonly associated with *noir*.

DW: Bill Pronzini, in that marvelous collection of Westerns written by crime writers, *The Fatal Frontier*, says the crossover between the two genres by you, Ed Gorman, Bob Randisi, Joe Gores, Marcia Muller, and others is a natural thing since the crime story and traditional western are fundamentally allied—in their violence, principally. Do you see it that way?

LE: A great deal more than violence ties the Western to the story of crime and detection. Both are American inventions; authentic, home-grown art forms with an outlaw history, like jazz. Both have to do with our native fascination with rebels and bandits, with our faith in the lone outsider stepping in to retrieve justice. Both pit that outsider against a wilderness, natural or urban. Finally, the two forms are allied by geography. It's no coincidence that Edgar Allan Poe invented the detective story amid surroundings familiar to James Fenimore Cooper, or that Hammett and Chandler rescued the genre from the British by setting their hard-boiled stories in San Francisco and Los Angeles, locales known to Wyatt Earp and Jack London. When Sergio Leone set out to film the quintessential Western, he based his screenplay for *A Fistful of Dollars* on Hammett's *Red Harvest*.

DW: Your Detroit saga novels are classically hard-boiled and since Amos Walker is, and many of your Westerns are or contain elements of *noir*, would it be fair to say that *noir* is the best single word to describe your oeuvre—and also your body of work?

LE: It's as good as any, in-so-far as any writer's career can be summed up by one word.

DW: What new can be done with *noir*?

LE: It's being done every day. We have *noir* science fiction—*Blade Runner, Alien, Invasion of the Body Snatchers;* spy *noir*—*Six Days of the Condor, The Falcon and the Snowman;* children's *noir*—*Willie Wonka and the Chocolate Factory, Matilda;* even gay *noir*—*Bound.* No subject is taboo. As the world becomes more mechanized and mobile, exposing its population to greater dangers, the *noir* landscape has become global. But no matter its scope, *noir* will always concern itself with the narrow confines of the human mind. If *Never Street* has a message, it's that as dark, complex, and frightening as film *noir* is, it's nowhere near as dark, complex, or frightening as the world in which we live.

Michael Connelly

INTERVIEW BY JERRY SYKES

Michael Connelly arrived on the crime writing scene in 1992 with the Edgar award–winning The Black Echo, which introduced one of the most intriguing and fascinatingly-named cops of recent years— Hieronymus Bosch. At once the archetypal loner, he was also very much a man of the times—in the first book, Bosch is living in a plush pad in the Hollywood Hills, paid for by selling to the movies the story of his involvement in the hunt for a serial killer.

As well as being riveting mystery stories, the books also provide the reader with an insider's view of Los Angeles and the LAPD—for many years Connelly was a reporter on the LA Times. In the aftermath of recent scandals and natural disasters, it is a place where nothing is what it appears to be and no one can be trusted and Connelly exploits this to the fullest.

In 1995 Connelly followed four Harry Bosch novels with his take on the serial killer novel. The Poet begins with Jack McEvoy, a reporter, being told of the suicide of his brother, a Denver cop. In order to overcome his grief, McEvoy begins researching a story on cop suicides, only to discover that lines from the poetry of Edgar Allan Poe keep appearing in the cops' suicide notes with disturbing regularity. So begins the cross-country search for the killer, with McEvoy riding shotgun on the FBI's investigation.

In Connelly's latest novel, Trunk Music, Harry Bosch returns after a *period of suspension for assaulting a superior officer. His first case back, in-vestigating the murder of a Hollywood producer found in the trunk of his car, soon finds him embroiled in the political mind games and slugfests that characterize Connelly's view of law enforcement in the City of Angels.*

JS: Before turning to fiction you were a crime reporter for many years on the *LA Times*. What kind of stories did you cover?

MC: At the *Times* I was primarily a front line police reporter, mean-ing that I wrote about the daily occurrence of crime as opposed to writing about the police department as an institution or about the so-cioeconomic reasons behind crime and crime rates. It was my job to write about the day's murder or other unusual crime. In a city like Los Angeles, a crime usually had to be a murder or something out of the ordinary to find space in the paper. It was unfortunate that deci-sions were made like this but that's the news business. As the lead character, a reporter, says in *The Poet*, there are big murders and there are little murders. When I was at the *Times*, I was always looking for the big murder.

JS: Was it your experience in this field that led to you becoming a novelist, or was that something that you'd always planned on doing?

MC: I always hoped to become a crime novelist. I devoured crime novels in high school and when I discovered Raymond Chandler's work a few years later, I knew that was what I'd like to do. But I knew I had to make a living so I decided on a career in journalism because I knew it would help me learn the craft of writing while putting me in the vicinity of cops and criminals. I was a reporter for several dif-ferent papers over the years and didn't try writing fiction until I was about thirty.

JS: Was there any particular case that triggered *The Black Echo*, your first novel?

MC: Two things from real life inspired or triggered the story in *The Black Echo*. The bank heist using the stormwater tunnels beneath Los Angeles is based in exacting detail on a real heist that happened in 1987 in Los Angeles and remains unsolved today. As a reporter I was given access to the detectives on the case and knew exactly how the burglars did it. I used those details in *Echo* because I thought it was a fascinating and well-planned caper. The second part that inspired the book was my fascination with the tunnel rats in Vietnam. I just missed going to Vietnam. I was in the last draft but the summer I registered, the war ended and I escaped it. But through high school I had anticipated that the war would drag on and I would end up in it. Therefore, I paid a lot of attention to it. A man who worked for my father had come back from the war and he had been a tunnel rat. It was not something that he would talk about, which made it all the more fascinating to me. Then a book called *The Tunnels of Cu Chi* was published and it was one of the scariest books I ever read. It stayed with me. And so many years later when I was thinking about writing a fictional account of this bank heist, I decided to bring in the tunnel rats.

JS: Is Harry Bosch based on anyone, a cop, that you know from your time as a journalist?

MC: Harry Bosch is not based on any singular cop but I think he has attributes that I observed in many cops. He also has a world view that I think is similar to mine. But in other ways I intentionally made him the opposite of me because I thought it would be more fun and challenging to write about someone who is different. For example, he smokes and I don't. He's an orphan who is a loner. I come from a big family and have been married twelve years. It's fun if you're not writing about yourself all the time.

JS: Why did you choose the name Hieronymus Bosch for your character? For me it immediately conjures up images of hell. Is this how you saw him, a character adrift in the hell that is Los Angeles?

MC: I picked the name Hieronymus Bosch because I think the fifteenth-century artist's paintings are fascinating and highly detailed. I wanted or hoped my character would be the same. I was also looking for the metaphor. If the reader knew about the original or real Bosch, then maybe they would make the connection of this fictional Bosch being, as you say, adrift in the hellish landscape of Los Angeles. This is not to say that Bosch or I look at Los Angeles as pure hell. It sure can be hellish at times and a lot of people here don't do much to improve it, but for all its bad things there are many good things. Deep down, Harry loves his city. So do I.

JS: One theme that ran through the first four Bosch novels was that of Harry continually facing up to events from his past, and with *The*

Last Coyote that seemed to bring things to a conclusion. Did you find it difficult going back to him?

MC: I have always been fascinated by the idea that the past informs the present, and it is a theme I wanted to explore in the Bosch novels. But you are right, there was a sense of conclusion with *The Last Coyote* and that is why I went on to write a non-series book, *The Poet*. But he continued to fascinate me and I think there are many more stories I could do with him. He's back in the new book, *Trunk Music*, which to a large degree is a straightforward murder case. But I had to dig up the past a bit so in this one Harry comes across Eleanor Wish, the woman he had a short but intense affair with in the first book.

JS: Your last book, *The Poet*, was a tautly plotted novel that followed the hunt for a serial killer of cops. Do you plan ahead, or just set out from the main character's perspective and see where it takes you?

MC: I plan ahead but not a whole lot. Generally I don't start writing until I have what I call A and B. A is the starting conflict, the murder, and B is the ultimate resolution of who did it. Between A and B I do a lot of riffing, meaning I kind of go where the story takes me, always keeping in mind that I've got to eventually steer this thing toward B.

JS: There was a lot of detail about how the FBI conducts such an investigation. Did they help you much in your research?

MC: They didn't help a whole lot. I had to rely on FBI documents revealing how investigations were done. I was always free to call Quantico to ask questions but they turned down my request to physically visit the Behavioral Sciences Section. Luckily, there was a huge amount of documentation and books about the unit to help me.

JS: Serial killers are often portrayed as highly intelligent people playing games with their hunters, keen to pit their wits against an intellectual equal. In your experience, both as a journalist and as a novelist, do you think that is realistic or is it just a fictional device?

MC: The skill and intellect of serial killers is probably exaggerated in books and movies. But you have to remember that the examples we have in real life are only those who get caught. I know from being a journalist that there are many out there who don't get caught. And there are some that get caught for one case and are suspected of many other slayings but the cops can't find the evidence. There was one such case in Los Angeles where the cops had a case against a guy for one murder but couldn't get the necessary evidence to convict him of others they were sure he was responsible for. This became a cat-and-mouse game, with the killer taunting the cops; he even used to call me at the paper and gloat. Luckily, he was convicted of the one murder—but someday he'll get out. But this guy was as cunning and creepy as any fictional killer I've come across. There are others. Ted Bundy comes to mind. Also, the Nightstalker out here in LA played a lot of mind games with the cops. But in fiction, the ultimate goal is to entertain and that is why you see so many masterful serial killers. In fiction, they have to be entertainers as well as killers.

JS: You seem to have an ambivalent attitude towards journalists: Compare Jack McEvoy to the guy who scoops him on the Poet story, or the journalist who features in the first three Bosch novels. Is this the voice of experience, the story is everything?

MC: I think I do have a cynical view of journalism. It shows up in extreme in some books like *The Concrete Blonde.* I think this comes from the loss of idealism. People go into journalism because they think it's a job where they might be able to have an impact on society, maybe make some changes, expose some wrongs, right some wrongs, explain things to the public. But it was my experience that while some of that is certainly done, competition soon becomes all important and you are looking for the big story simply to have something that no other paper or news program has. The altruistic part of it evaporates.

JS: All the journalists in your books see the writing of true crime books based on cases they have covered as high points in their careers, or at least lucrative earners. Do you think that such books help us to understand, and therefore prevent, psychopathic behavior, or just pander to people's voyeuristic tendencies?

MC: I don't really think true crime books prevent anything, but the good ones can explain why things happen more thoroughly than a newspaper or magazine story. Yes, they pander to voyeuristic tendencies, but in explaining why things happen they can also serve as warnings about what is happening in our society. I think it's been in the last ten years that true crime books have descended to lower intellectual levels. They are put together quickly and without much thought or investigation into root causes of the evils they depict. There is still a minority of true crime writers who do excellent work. But it's too bad there hasn't been anything like *In Cold Blood* in recent years. When I was a journalist I always thought I would write a true crime book. I thought that was my way into the bookstores. In fact, if the cops had solved that 1987 bank heist with an arrest, I may have written a nonfiction account of it instead of *The Black Echo*. Obviously, I'm now very thankful those guys got away with it.

JS: Your new book, *Trunk Music,* brings back Harry Bosch after his suspension. A lot has happened in LA in the meantime, not least the OJ trial. Have these events influenced the new book?

MC: As you know, the LAPD has been through some difficult and interesting times in the last few years. I try to get a reflection of that in all my books about Harry Bosch. The public disdain and dissatisfaction of the police department has increased with the acquittal of O.J. Simpson and the revelation of detective Mark Fuhrman's racist attitudes. All of this, I believe, is to my benefit as a writer. It only makes the LAPD more interesting to write about. So in *Trunk Music,* my first post-O.J. book, I do try to be reflective of the current environment. I have Bosch double-thinking at times when he is at the crime scene, knowing what a Dream Team of defense attorneys can do with the smallest of mistakes. I have several incidents where elements of racism within the department are exposed. And in one spot I have used a racial invective for the first time in one of my books. This was not done without a lot of thought. It is used in the book by a person as a calculated means of distracting another person, catching him off guard—which I think in a small way is analogous to how race has been injected into recent events in Los Angeles, as a distraction meant to inflame rather than something to objectively talk about and maybe learn from.

I think the problems of the current LAPD are useful as a counterpoint to the character of Harry Bosch. I think all good crime novels are so because of character. Character is illustrated through conflict. Having Harry Bosch in place in a troubled organization like the LAPD is an opportunity to build and show his character. The LAPD is in effect a conflict that he must cut through or overcome. He is a good man in a bad organization. He tries to rise above it. To me that is a good dramatic setting to have as a background to the larger conflict, a murder investigation.

Lawrence Block

INTERVIEW BY HARLAN COBEN

HC: What haven't you ever been asked before?

LB: Gee I don't know.

HC: [Pause] Okay, Larry, thanks for taking the time.

LB: After you do this awhile, you begin to welcome the familiar question because then you don't have to think about it. You push the button and off it goes and you can think about something else for a while.

HC: So maybe you're writing a book as we speak.

LB: No. I'm eating my dinner. Ask a question.

HC: What is your favorite part of writing? At what moments during the process do you feel your most euphoric?

LB: Any time one is in that zone. This might sound strange, but after all this time, writing is as enjoyable as it's ever been—maybe even more. I've been having great fun lately. I just finished the next Burglar book. *The Burglar in the Library*, and the next novel I'm going to do is a Scudder that I'm going to write in Ireland.

HC: I know that you and Lynne love to travel, but I thought you never wrote when you went on your distant sojourns.

LB: Sojourns. Good word.

HC: I've been taking night classes. But back to the question. Do you write when you travel with Lynne?

LB: The answer used to be, never. But we were in Scandinavia in September and I had a yellow pad along and we were on a cruise ship in Norwegian coastal waters and the third day out of port I woke up and decided to try to write a short story. So I took the yellow pad to the ship's library, just for an hour and a half. When I stopped, I had a thousand words written. So I went back every day like that and by the end of the week I had a 7,500-word short story.

HC: And you never wrote before on a trip?

LB: On a vacation like this, never. But what was a real revelation for me was the idea of handwriting a story. Since I learned to type my assignments in tenth grade, I haven't handwritten anything longer than a laundry list. So now I plan on handwriting the new Tanner book when I'm in Ireland.

HC: So even after fifty-plus novels, you still stumble across change.

LB: Most definitely. With locations, too.

HC: What do you mean?

LB: I find that I use a place up in terms of work. If I have an office, for example, I hate working there after a while. People often wonder if they'll be able to work in certain places. I know that for me if it's new, the answer is yes. I'll be able to work there just fine.

HC: Can you give us some specifics of places where you've written?

LB: I go to writer's colonies frequently, for one thing. I wrote a story not long ago while sitting in the lobby of a Vienna hotel. Since I've been back in New York, I've been going mornings to coffeehouses like the standard Greenwich Village dweller pretending to be a writer. It works great. I enjoy it. As long as the place is new.

HC: You also said that you find writing perhaps even more enjoyable now than ever. I'm surprised and encouraged by the answer. Could you explain why?

LB: I don't know.

HC: That's your second "I don't know."

LB: One thing is, I suppose, that I don't write anything unless I like it. I've been able to do that for a while now. It's very important.

HC: Are you a better writer now than you were, say, five years or ten years ago? Will you keep getting better?

LB: I suppose there is a point where you start getting worse. But if you maintain good relationships over the years, no one will tell you and then you won't have to know about it.

HC: Good one. Is writing easier, harder or the same?

LB: A lot of things get easier—you know how to get your characters from one room to another, for example, or you know what to cut, what to leave in or out, that kind of thing. There are a lot of things one knows that one didn't know and as a result it makes things easier. But the writing itself does not get easier. I don't think it should. If it does, it probably means that you're phoning it in.

HC: What else has changed for you in terms of your writing process?

LB: One problem over the past couple of years—and it took me a while to realize exactly what it was—was that I came to hate the work while I was writing it. Not that I hated doing it. But I came to believe that the manuscript itself was terrible. It took a few books in a row like this for me to realize that this was a pattern that had absolutely nothing to do with the merits of the book. In each case, the book came out and it was well-received and I was the only person who had felt that way about it—and in fact, I liked it by the time it came out.

HC: I always figured that this self-doubt was something for beginners, that it mostly played on young writers' insecurities.

LB: I never had it when I was young. And quite often back then it would have been probably justified. Some of my stuff was awful. But I didn't have a clue.

HC: How do you combat this new self-doubt?

LB: I tell my mind, thanks for sharing but leave me alone. What else can you do? You push through it.

HC: If all goes well, how long does it take you to write a novel?

LB: If everything goes well—and that's a fairly big if—less than two months. But very often something slows me down or I decide to start over.

HC: Under two months? The idea that you produce, say, a Matt Scudder novel in that short of time boggles the mind. Are you a madman during those two months? Do you become obsessed?

LB: I prefer to be, which is why I like to go away and be by myself. At home it's harder to ignore the phone, the fax, the email, whatever. All of that is just sort of in the way, and when I go off by myself I don't have to contend with it. That doesn't mean I'm putting in twenty-hour days. The mind gets tired after a certain point. But it's important that I establish some sort of pattern or other. It's a little different each book. When I used to type, it would be so many pages per day. Now with the computer, I use a word count. I'm not sure what I'll do with the handwritten work. But there's a certain amount I try to get done each day. If it works quickly I stop early, if it goes slowly I stay on it longer.

A thing that I find interesting, too, is that afterward I can look at a book and there will be sections that just felt as though they were writing themselves and others that I really labored over—and you can't tell the difference. Also, what's going on in the writer's personal life doesn't matter too much.

HC: Can you give us an example? A time of turmoil that you wrote through or something?

LB: The third book in the Tanner series I started, I think, in 1966. I wrote the first fourth of it and then my entire life turned inside out. I left my wife. I had this very public, high-drama affair with the wife of my then-best friend. Turmoil all over the place. So I said to hell with this and I went over to Ireland, found a little bed-and-breakfast over there, rented a typewriter, and finished it. To this day, I can't find the seam. I have no idea exactly how much I wrote before all the turmoil began.

HC: So when someone sees something happening to Bernie or Matt and they think, well, this must have been happening to Lawrence Block at the time, they're wrong?

LB: It could be true, but more likely it's not.

HC: Was it cathartic for you—writing during this time of turmoil? Was it therapy? Did it help you get through it?

LB: Well, I had to do something. But you know, I continue to be fairly crazy so if it's therapy, I'm not sure how effective it is.

HC: Is Lawrence Block different personality-wise or work-wise when you are writing, for example, a Matt Scudder novel versus a Burglar?

LB: No, I don't think so. As different as the books are, the process of writing them is similar. Simply put, writing in and of itself is not amusing. Essentially you are trying to figure out what has to happen next and how to make it happen. That doesn't change whether the book is light or dark. The Burglar books are a little more demanding in terms of plot. The Scudder books are a little more demanding in terms of mood and subtext. [Pause. We eat.] On the other hand, I can imagine now one difference. I've thought about writing a book on an extended cruise sometime and I can see doing that with a Burglar book more easily than a Scudder. I could do that with a Scudder if I were alone, but if I were with a companion or sightseeing I don't think a Scudder would work as well. So I guess a Scudder does involve a more total immersion.

HC: The Scudder book you're going to write in Ireland—does it take place over there?

LB: No. Matt is still in New York.

HC: I would have thought it would be easier to write a Scudder when you are here in New York. The city plays such a key role.

LB: No, it's no easier. The city is important to Burglar books as well, albeit differently. I carry the city around with me—I don't have to be right there. Of the Scudders, the ones I've written elsewhere include *Out on the Cutting Edge, Ticket to the Boneyard, Dance at the Slaughterhouse,* and *A Walk among the Tombstones*—all four of those were written at colonies away from Manhattan.

HC: Okay, here is one I've asked you about in private conversations and you always waffle. No waffling now. Scudder or Burglar—if you could only be remembered for one, which would it be?

LB: [Long pause] I think the Scudder books are playing in a tougher league and maybe have more claim to artistic merit. That's not to say that they are more likely to last. It may very well be that Bernie wears better. Also, in any possible scenario as to what the afterlife amounts to that I can come up with, I have not yet figured out one where the surviving soul gives much of a rat's ass what anybody back here thinks.

HC: Are there books of yours that you don't like? Do you ever look back at old work and cringe a bit at how much better you are now?

LB: I find it very difficult to read most things that I wrote much more than, oh, ten or fifteen years ago because . . . I don't think it's the writing . . . I think it's that I don't really want to look at the person who wrote it. I think, "Oh that stupid kid, what the fuck did he know about anything?"

HC: Do you have any favorite books? Ones you hold dear to your heart?

LB: I usually like the most recent.

HC: Unless you're writing it.

LB: That's right, very true. But I think it may simply be that a newer book is a more immediate reflection of one's self. That said, I guess that *When the Sacred Gin Mill Closes* is one that I will always stay fond of, and it is the height of altruism to say that because it is currently the one that is out of print.

HC: One of the most amazing things about both series is how you've been able to keep them fresh. You and I once talked about the fact that you did not originally conceive *A Long Line of Dead Men* as a Scudder book—

HC: No, I always planned it as a Scudder book.

HC: Then again maybe I wasn't listening very closely.

LB: In fact, when I got the idea, I was in agony riding a fucking Bactrian camel across the Takla Makan desert.

HC: A *what* kind of camel?

LB: Bactrian. It means two humps instead of one. And I say that merely in the interest of accuracy.

HC: It's appreciated. Go on.

LB: Lynne and I were in this godforsaken desert and I really just wanted to think about anything but what we were doing. So I got the idea and I thought about it some. At first, I did think that it would work very well alone—as more a stand-alone, multiple-viewpoint thriller than a mystery—but then I thought about it a little further and it came to me that thematically the book would work well as a Scudder and I wanted to do it that way.

HC: So in this case, you did not say to yourself, "I need to come up with an idea for Matt Scudder." Maybe that's one of the ways you keep the series fresh—by applying ideas to Matt rather than the other way around?

LB: Maybe. That's right in this case, I guess. The idea just sort of happened. I've never had much luck at forcing an idea. I don't really think of it that way, but maybe.

HC: Any plans on retiring either Matt or Bernie?

LB: No, but I'm sure there'll come a time when I stop writing about them. I think a series can only go for so long. In an essentially static series like Bernie, where the character doesn't change much, there is a real danger that you'll start writing the same book over and over again. The danger in a series like Scudder where your character evolves is that he will evolve to a level of civility where he has a perfectly satisfactory life and then why would he bother fucking around with these cases? That one way or another he's dealt with his issues. One has to be willing to do something else when that happens.

HC: Do you still care what the critics say?

LB: Not very much. I care only in so much as they hurt or help sales. I don't really look for validation there, if that's what you mean. I've had good reviews that haven't changed my life and I've had bad reviews that haven't changed my life and eventually you come to the conclusion that reviews don't change your life.

HC: Deep. Back to the process for a moment. Do you outline? Do ideas strike you with a cry of Eureka or do they take some time? Do you know the ending before you start?

LB: It varies. With *Dance at the Slaughterhouse,* I knew the ending. That's all I knew—I had no idea what book it was an ending for. So I sat down and wrote the last three chapters, and as a result I had a false start. I wrote, oh, 180 pages or so that I ultimately tossed. But that was what I had to go through to find out what the story was really about.

HC: So writing the 180 pages was part of the process. It didn't bother you.

HC: It doesn't bother me now. At the time it pissed me off. Actually, you're right—it didn't really bother me then. I realized that it would work out fine. But usually when I start, I have this feeling that I ought to know more about the story than I do.

HC: But you don't outline?

LB: No. I'm not sure why my work should be that much more organized than the rest of my life.

HC: Tell me a little about creating Matt Scudder.

LB: Scudder was conceived of as a series character, which is not the case with my other characters. Bernie, for example, I wrote one book about him and then I realized I had more to say. But Scudder was offered as a series to Dell. My agent suggested that I make him a tough, New York cop, but I realized almost immediately that he had to be either retired or something that would give me more of an outsider's perspective. That, and I didn't want to learn all that shit about procedure. I find it interesting enough to read but I don't find it interesting to write.

HC: How much of Matt Scudder is Lawrence Block?

LB: When I created him in 1973, Scudder and I shared some tangential similarities. I was living in that neighborhood so I set the books there. I was recently separated from my first wife, that sort of thing.

HC: How much of Matt's life did you plan in advance?

LB: None of it. I had no idea in future books he would stop drinking or move in with Elaine—all of that was surprise to me. And when I finished *8 Million Ways to Die,* I thought I was finished with the series.

HC: Why?

LB: He had a major catharsis, and I figured one to a customer in fiction.

HC: So what happened?

LB: I found a way to write about Scudder without having to figure out what happened next—I set it back in time [*When the Sacred Gin Mill Closes*]. I liked the way that worked but I couldn't do more than one of those. You can't have this garrulous old fart just remembering old cases for the rest of his life. I know too many guys like that. Then one day—you may see a subtle pattern emerge—I was riding a camel in a faraway land. Well, actually I was on the overnight train between Luxor and Cairo, unable to sleep. Everybody on board had dysentery and the facilities on the train were not really, uh, operable. It was a nightmare. And somewhere on that train, I lay on my bunk and came up with the realization that I was ready to do this. I was ready to bring Matt back (in *Out On The Cutting Edge*). It's funny, Lynne and I travel as much as we can—it's one of our favorite things. And I keep going to these exotic spots to find new things to write about and set books there—and then I come back and write yet another book about New York. But I do believe the traveling plays a part in the process. Maybe getting away helps me to see the city with fresh eyes. I don't know.

Robert B. Parker

INTERVIEW BY CHARLES L. P. SILET

obert B. Parker's bestselling and award-winning Spenser series is one of the longest running and most successful in the history of crime fiction. In September 1997 he published Night Passage *and began a second series with another series' character, Jesse Stone, an ex-L.A. police officer who relocated to Parker's favorite turf. The novel quickly made the bestseller list, giving Parker two top crime series. He now plans to release a Spenser and a Jesse Stone novel each year.*

Robert B. Parker was born in Springfield, Massachusetts, in 1932 and he grew up in the area around Boston. After receiving a B.A. from Colby College in 1954, he spent two years in the army. In 1957 he earned an M.A. from Boston University. For the next few years Parker worked as a technical writer and copy editor before finally becoming a partner in an advertising agency. By 1962 he began teaching at schools in the Boston area, finally securing a full-time faculty position at Northeastern University in 1968. He received his Ph.D. in 1971 and became a full professor at Northeastern in 1977. The success of the early Spenser books allowed him to retire from academic life in 1979 to write full-time, a profession he has pursued ever since with phenomenal success.

CLPS: You have started a new series with *Night Passage* with a new character, Jesse Stone. Tell me a little bit about him.

RP: Well, part of what he is is that he's not Spenser. He's at the beginning of an evolution, whereas Spenser is fully evolved. As a practical matter, when you are going to start a new series you don't want to start one about the same guy with a different name. Jesse is younger than Spenser; he's got a problem with alcohol; and his love life is a mess. What seems to keep him straight, or as straight as he can be, is the job. He doesn't have much else so the job matters to him a lot. He probably has good stuff in him and maybe in a while it will evolve out.

CLPS: One of Jesse's background traits is that he was born and raised in the West so when he moves to Boston that gives him an outsider's perspective.

RP: Sure. I used to live part-time in Los Angeles. We had a house in Westwood for awhile so I knew enough about L.A. to do it. I thought it would be interesting to have a countermigration, as it were, from west to east. I play around with the Western, Arthurian, romantic cowboy virtues which is one of the reasons Spenser comes from Laramie, Wyoming.

I remembered John Kenneth Galbraith once said that economists don't make predictions because they know, they make predictions because they're asked. This is quite true of writers, or at least of this writer. Mostly, I just do what seems like a good idea at the moment when my hands are on the keyboard. So when some thoughtful person calls me up and asks, I have to make something up. That's the real truth of the matter, but it makes for a lousy interview.

CLPS: How does Jesse's outsider perspective work for you?

RP: I think that was part of what I was after in the book: the stranger in a strange place kind of idea. While Jesse was born in the Southwest, he grew up in Southern California. This is a complex fate at best. So when he moves east, he gets to see a whole other world that he had never seen before. At the simplest level he experiences the seasons of fall and winter. It gives me another kind of framework with which to look at the familiar New England scene.

CLPS: You mentioned that Jesse drinks too much. What does that give you to work with as a writer?

RP: I used to drink too much in my life so it gives me something I know how to write about. I no longer drink too much. In fact, I'm nearly perfect. When dialogue is easy and you charge along, you have to get in that slow plod of exposition. Among other things, the drinking gives you an opportunity for stage business while you are doing exposition. It also, of course, characterizes the people. Drinkers tend to congregate. For instance, a guy like Jesse, who likes to drink, is unlikely to go out with a woman who doesn't drink at all.

CLPS: Tell me a bit about *Dark Passage*.

RP: I was originally going to call the novel *Stranger in Paradise,* and the publishers didn't think that was a good marketing title. So I gave them a list of thirty titles, some of them less serious than others. One title was *First Jesse Stone Novel,* but they didn't go for that much. *Second Money-Maker for Bob*? One of them was *Night Passage* and the meaning is certainly diffuse. I don't exactly know what it all means so it kind of works with that passage from west to east. It's certainly about a guy who is trying to get himself back after he lost most of what he was. That is part of the passage, too, from what he was to what he hopes to become or is trying to become and which he does become sporadically. Jesse has some of his finest hours there in Paradise. I'm about 130 pages into the next Jesse Stone novel, and we'll find that he hasn't completely conquered his demons.

CLPS: One of the things you do in the novel is to expose the clichés about the small New England village as a paradise. You've dealt with some of the small towns around Boston before. What attracts you to them?

RP: Well, just because they are there and I know them. I've grown up here. I've lived here all my life. I'm sixty-five so I've had a long history here. I lived in a town called Lynnfield, a commuter suburb north of Boston, and I once lived in Marblehead on the coast. Paradise is in some ways an amalgam of Marblehead and Lynnfield in terms of its geography. It's neither, and it's neither primarily because it gives me more freedom. In the second Jesse Stone novel I'm free to put an island where I want it. It's what I need in the novel. If it were really Marblehead, or really Lynnfield, I couldn't do that. I've taken that leeway. I probably don't know more than most people do about the towns around Boston. They're less different than it might seem than the towns around Chicago. We are more alike than we are different in our humanity. I suppose it is still the same old story a fight for love and glory wherever you may be.

CLPS: You show that crime can move out from the cities into smaller communities.

RP: Certainly it is less dangerous in one of those suburban towns than it is in the heart of the dark city, but there is crime everywhere because there are people everywhere. People have certain criminal tendencies, or at least they do in my books. Otherwise I'd be out of work.

CLPS: Why did you begin another series?

RP: Through the years I've filled the writing time with various things, scripts and so on, and it struck both me and Joan, who is my manager and guru, and Helen Brann, who is my agent, instead maybe I could focus this writing time on something more likely to sell. It's not like I was sitting around reading movie magazines. I was writing anyway. I remember I was doing three-hundred-pound bench presses when I was about fifty-eight and someone asked, "Why in the hell are you doing that?" The answer is to see if I can. I guess probably as good an answer as any to why I started a new series is that I wanted to see if I could. Also, it would probably be dishonest if I didn't mention that I'd noticed if I wrote one novel, I'd get one dollar and if I wrote two novels, I'd get two dollars. Certainly it will increase my income with two novels a year on the best-seller list.

Night Passage made the best-seller list, and I was quite pleased by that. We didn't know when we started it if the public would resent it. There is a tendency among readers who are very fond of a particular character in a series not to want to buy another. I would have done that, too. If Raymond Chandler had suddenly written a novel about somebody else, I very well might not have bought it. I would have been sort of mad. Jesse Stone has done about as well as Spenser which suggests that we have conquered that problem.

CLPS: You were a university professor at one point in your life. Why did you leave the academic life?

RP: I didn't like it. I didn't like being a teacher. I didn't like being in the academic community. I didn't like my colleagues much. I didn't seem to be doing anything very useful. I taught in order to write. I always wanted to be a novelist and I had children and a wife early. Thank God. I'd much rather be their father and her husband than Robert B. Parker. But I had to support them all. This was pre-liberation days. Now she works. I had to find a way to make a living and give myself time to write, and with Joan's urging and support eventually I got the Ph.D and weasled my way into the academic world. The academic world gives you a lot of time to write. So I did. As soon as I was able to make a living writing, I quit. I was never Mr. Chips. I only did it in the service of the writing.

CLPS: When you first began writing did you initially think of *The Godwulf Manuscript* as the start of a series?

RP: Yeah. When I had finished the first Spenser novel and had sent it off to the publishers, I started the second one so I was about fifty pages into *God Save the Child* before they accepted *The Godwulf Manuscript*. It wasn't so much that I decided that I would do a series; it didn't strike me that I shouldn't.

CLPS: What are the advantages and disadvantages to writing a series?

RP: I don't see any particular artistic drawback in doing a series. I suppose if you wanted to write a novel in which the protagonist was killed that would be a little difficult in a series. There are certain marketing pluses and minuses. I am very bifurcated on this, but I have no discomfort with it. When I'm working on a book, I'm just trying to make a good book. While I am working on it, it is, to the limits of my ability, art. Once I have finished it and sent it in, I'm trying to sell it and it becomes product which is the bifurcation in the publishing world. The series also limits you in that if you want to do something else there is a resistance in the marketplace. If you are successful in books A, B, and C in the series, then you can pretty well count on success with books D, E, and F. So there's pluses and minuses, but I don't see any particular artistic drawbacks.

CLPS: The Spenser series has now become one of the longest-running and most successful in crime fiction. What do you do to keep it fresh?

RP: I don't do anything to keep it fresh. If it's fresh it's my good fortune. I ponder another novel, and I start writing another novel. I don't think about freshness. I just type away. I type away with good concentration and obviously I'm skilled at this. But if a book isn't fresh, you can't make it fresh. I think that becomes tricks. You introduce a new element or a new girlfriend or the series character stops carrying a gun and starts carrying a cane with a dart in the end. It's

Hollywood stuff. I just don't think about it. The answer to how I keep it fresh is I don't know.

CLPS: Some writers set themselves a little writing task with each novel. Do you do that?

RP: I just try to get it right. I set myself a quantity. I write five pages each day, the five pages that you see—not five draft pages to be revised, but five finished pages. I do that normally five days a week. I'm not obsessive about that. If I have a reason to go visit one of my children or Joan and I have something to do, then I go do it, but normally I work five days a week and write five pages.

CLPS: Why do you think the series has been so successful?

RP: My picture on the back of the books.

CLPS: Buy this book.

RP: Or I'll kill you. Again, who knows. There are a lot of people doing the same thing I do and most of them aren't doing it as well. A lot of people do what Elmore Leonard does but not as well. Consequently Elmore Leonard is more popular than most of the people trying to do what he does. If I could find a way to say so modestly, I would say that about me. I guess they're popular probably because the books are quite well written. I think people like good writing. Also, I think that the kind of character that I write about appeals to a wide readership, but that wouldn't be true just about me, that's true about a lot of people who write this kind of thing. Spenser is free in a way that we're not. He can't be bribed with sex or money. He can't be intimidated by the threat of death. He does what he is going to do and nothing will dissuade him from that. He does what he wishes. That's an appeal, but it's not a new one in the American imagination.

My doctoral dissertation actually wasn't about Hammett, Chandler, and Ross Macdonald. That has become the way it is referred to because of what I now do. It actually was about the American hero and his evolution from the frontier figure into the private eye. There was one chapter on Chandler, one on Hammett. Please do not ask me the title of my doctoral dissertation because I don't know. It was long and it had a colon in it. Colon: "a study." In a sentence the thrust of my doctoral dissertation was the interaction of Protestantism and the frontier in the American cultural experience which produces a particular kind of hero who is especially appealing to Americans.

Spenser is in the grain of the kind of hero figure that Americans have always admired. For more details see my doctoral dissertation.

CLPS: Your series has become prominent internationally. What do you think appeals to people outside this country?

RP: That's a real puzzle. It doesn't appeal to everybody equally. I don't sell well at all in England for instance, but I sell very well in Japan. I am a positive cult figure in Japan. I'd probably say it has to do with the Samurai warrior tradition in Japan which translates so easily into the Western tradition in America. *Seven Samurai, The Magnificent Seven* and all of that. But that's a glib answer. The real answer is I haven't got a clue.

I went to Japan on a combination of book promotion and tourism promotion for Massachusetts. I'm sufficiently popular in Japan so they run Spenser tours to Boston. The state asked me if I'd go over at their expense. I didn't particularly want to go so I told them I'd have to bring my entire family and we'd have to stop in Hawaii. They said sure because no one was paying for it, everything was a boondoggle. So we went and it was quite an arduous experience because I got interviewed endlessly through translators. God knows what they think I said. One of the common themes that I found in the questioning was about the Spenser/Susan relationship. The people that I was with in Japan suggested that it may have something to do with slow emergence of women in Japan and the early stirrings of feminism which in Japan is not anti-romantic but romantic. The claim for Japanese women is more for romantic love than for equality. Anyway, I don't know what to make of it, but quite commonly in Japan their interest was more than anything else in Spenser and Susan.

CLPS: Since we're talking about Susan, how does she work in the books?

RP: She does some of the things that Watson did for Holmes, so does Hawk, in that she explains Spenser. In the first-person narration you can't have some guy walking around telling what he's up to. I said that but deep in my heart I felt blah, blah, blah. That's vomitous. So she explains him to us periodically. She is also the object of his affection. If he is capable of such love for Susan and if Susan is capable in her own and complicated way of loving him back as powerfully as she does, then it tells us about Spenser. People will sometimes say, "Well, I don't like Susan." And I say, "Tough shit." Yeah, she's a pain in the ass sometimes but he likes her. But the books aren't about Susan, and they're not just a love story. Everything in the books tells us about Spenser. All the characters, like Quirk and Belson, they're all at Spenser's service. Everything that happens in the books tells us something about him.

Again, there's the answer and then there's the real answer. The signal event in my life was to meet and marry Joan Hall forty-one years ago. Nothing else comes close to that, so I have all this feeling and this experience with love and it would be very difficult for me to write extensively without writing about it. Susan gives me the opportunity to do that. If you're a writer you get all of this stuff and you use it. That's how Susan works.

CLPS: She's sort of the soft side of Spenser and Hawk is the harder side.

RP: Hawk is the most deadly human being that has ever appeared in these novels with the possible exception of the character in the last novel. If he is so deadly and so dangerous and treats Spenser as an equal, it tells us in some ways what we would otherwise be unable to know which is just how dangerous Spenser is. If a man like Hawk likes and admires Spenser then it tells us a lot about what Spenser must be like. It allows us to understand that Spenser is charming and affable and witty but there is in him a good deal of violence. He is perfectly capable of death. He's a killer. Remember the Warshow essay. He's the killer of men and he will do that. If he couldn't he wouldn't be who he is, and Hawk reminds us of that, I think.

Now and again I get a question about why I don't write a novel about Hawk. The answer is fairly apparent: I don't know enough about Hawk to write a novel about him. We had a thirteen-week television series about Hawk, shot from Hawk's perspective, and if nothing else that proves my point. It was the worst show I ever saw. That's not just because it was from Hawk's point of view, but it was because the producers couldn't do it.

Also, of course, Hawk gives me a chance to have my little say about race just as Susan gives me a chance to have my little say about male/female relationships. I don't know if we are even arguing about anti-Semitism anymore, but if we are she gives me a little chance to dust that off too. The books try not to be about stereotypes. They try to be about actual humans, imaginary humans though they may be. Someone once said to me, "Can you write about life?" My answer was, "As opposed to what?"

CLPS: One of the ways Spenser works against the type of hard-boiled detective is to have him cook. This appears to be something you also enjoy.

RP: Well, I know how. As Henry James said it doesn't matter what kind of experience you have, it's what you do with it. I can cook a little. I was the family cook. Joan can't cook for shit, as she will readily admit. She'll testify to that publicly and is proud of it and doesn't want to cook and never did. At the point where I was home typing and she was at work and the kids were little, I cooked. If you know how to cook, you know it is not brain surgery. Because I am not only a man but a rather large man and I write tough novels, it interests people more than it might otherwise. If Joan had cooked the same things I did, people wouldn't be thinking she was a gourmet. So it's quite deliberate. It softens the roughneck outline a little bit that Spenser cooks. Once again, I know stuff. I know how to cook so I use it. I know how to do carpentry, and you may remember in a couple of the books I use that.

CLPS: You completed Raymond Chandler's *Poodle Springs* and then you wrote *Perchance to Dream,* a sequel to Chandler's *The Big Sleep.* Obviously Chandler is someone you greatly admired. What was the challenge to writing those books?

RP: The challenge was not to make them Spenser. It would have in some ways been easier to finish a novel by Jane Austen because she would be so different from me that I wouldn't have any danger of lapsing into my own voice. The challenge to me was to make it Chandler. So for instance I didn't clean him up. Marlowe and Chandler were people of their time and in their time so they tended to make judgments about people based on race and gender, things like that. The temptation is to fix that now in this new enlightened age, and I did not. I tried very hard not to. I got taken to task for it by somebody in the *Times,* to whom I would say, *phutt.* That's spelled, *phutt.* That was the challenge. The Chandler estate asked me. It wasn't my idea; they came to me. I was flattered to be asked.

CLPS: Do you plan to do any more?

RP: No, that's enough of that. I don't want to be someone whose career is involved in writing some other guy's books. I finished one and I thought one original one would be interesting to do.

CLPS: You mentioned the Hawk series. Tell me a little bit about your experience with film and television.

RP: I can't tell you a little bit. I can tell you a huge amount or nothing at all. It's everything you think it is. I didn't enjoy it much. There's some fun to hanging around and chatting with movie stars so that at cocktail parties later I can say, "Oh yeah, Michael Douglas, I had lunch with him the other day." That sort of thing. It is no place for writers. Pete Hamill said that to me years ago at a party in New York before I had taken a run at it. I thought, "Sure easy for you, Pete." Now I tell people that it is no place for writers. If you remain calm and if you have a day job and don't need it, then there's no harm to play with it.

We're playing now. We have three or four irons in the fire, balls in the air, whatever you want to say, in Hollywood including something with Jesse Stone. By the time this interview gets published that will either have happened or not happened so it is sort of irrelevant. All of that is amusing because I am capable of saying, "Naw, I don't want to do that," and go home. But as long as that goes on, there is a little money. One of the great misconceptions is that for a writer like me to have gotten a television series suddenly made him rich. The television series didn't make me rich. I made ten times as much on books as I ever did on television. The money is good and it is found money. You're sitting around and someone sends you a check, so that's nice. But it does not make you rich. The books make you rich, if you're any good, and successful, if you're lucky. I still occasionally get a check from one of the Spenser re-runs, but they are in the area of two or three dollars now. They're not going to put me over the top. They won't even pay for lunch.

CLPS: Were you pleased at all with the Robert Urich series?

RP: To tell you the truth, I'm not a good person to make that judgment. I knew how much better the series could have been, primarily the writing. If you spend time in Hollywood you discover that people are writing episode television for a reason. They're not doing it because they'd rather. The studio wanted me there working with the writers so I spent about six months commuting every week from Boston to L.A. and back on the weekends. There are writers in Southern California now who are still sticking pins in a Robert Parker doll. They simply couldn't do what I told them to do. It's not like they didn't want to do what I wanted, they couldn't. If it's a sex scene, they know how to have a shower or a massage. If it's exciting, they know how to do a car chase. But they just couldn't do what I wanted them to.

I think the series was probably an above-average television show which is a little like being the tallest building in Iowa City. Nonetheless, it was probably pretty good television, but I knew how much better it could have been without any good reason for it not to be better. The first year was pretty good. The second and third years it went pretty badly downhill. Bob Urich was fine. He's not my Spenser, but he was all right. Avery was a pretty good Hawk. I'm not complaining about the actors. It's really the writing and the production that lost it. They just didn't do as well as they could have done.

CLPS: You have started your own production company named for the wonder dog Pearl.

RP: Well, it's a letterhead and a mail drop, basically. It is just something to refer to. We may someday do something. You know Pearl Productions in association with whatever, a Paramount distribution thing. If you look these days at the way movies get financed you get about fifteen different entities up there on the screen. We don't plan to produce films in any orthodox way. It's just pretty much something to shield me from the public if I want to have letters sent to Pearl Productions instead of me. Joan and I conspire in these matters. She and I work together in the film world. I do the novels myself.

She and I have done a couple of books together. We did an autobiographical book, *Three Weeks in Spring*, which is out of print. We also did together a coffee-table book on horse racing called *A Year at the Races* with a photographer named Bill Stode which was kind of fun. On the screenplays and scripts she and I collaborate. She is not a writer as much as an idea person. She will say why don't we do this and that, and I'm the one who does the actual typing. That works pretty well. Since we have somewhat the same ironic take on it all, we can have a pretty good time in Hollywood as long as we are able to say, "No, no, I don't want the money; I don't want to do that, see ya."

CLPS: You mentioned earlier that you had some things in production. Do you want to talk about any of them?

RP: Well, we sold *Poodle Springs* a long time ago for quite a lot of money. Not the royal "we," I mean the Chandler estate and I. That's probably the single biggest amount of money in a lump I've gotten from the movies. That's the end of that from my point of view. I didn't want any part in the screenwriting or any of that sort of thing. At the beginning at least Robert Redford was involved with it and at that time I thought he might be going to make it. He is notorious for wanting forty drafts of the screenplay. I don't do forty drafts; I do one. I do one-draft novels. As far as I know, it is being made. Tom Stoppard did the screenplay and tells me that they started shooting about two weeks ago in L.A. with Jimmy Caan as Marlowe and directed by Bob Raphelson who once directed *Five Easy Pieces*. But I know nothing about it. I took the money and I ran.

We're playing around with the prospect of a series of movies with Jesse Stone for one of the cable networks, and I think that is probably going to happen but since I don't know it is going to happen I don't think I will mention more than that. I have spent time talking with Tom Selleck about doing three Spenser movies starting with *Small Vices*, on which script I am currently at work. It is on my screen as I speak. But whether or not that will happen we don't know. The odds are that it won't. The odds are that any individual project won't happen. Most scripts don't get made. Most projects don't get developed. Most ideas don't see fruition. But those are in the works at least.

Then there is a prominent actress who wants Joan and me to come out and talk about developing an idea for her as a kind of female Spenser. Since that's so embryonic I don't think I'll tell more than that. We'll probably go out and have dinner at Spago and take a lunch, do meetings, and maybe we'll come up with something. It's just like rolling dice, you know. We have a son in Los Angeles, who is an actor, so it's always a pleasure to go to LA. I didn't enjoy living there very much but I certainly like to visit and I like to visit my son. There is no downside to it. The worst that happens is that you get a free trip to LA., you visit your kid, and you go home.

CLPS: One of your recent projects was to edit a volume on *The Best American Mystery Stories*. How did that come about?

RP: Otto Penzler called me up and asked me if I'd do it. He's a friend of mine so I said OK. Otto did most of the heavy lifting. I think he read five or six hundred short stories and then I winnowed down my favorites out of the field he had narrowed and wrote the introduction.

CLPS: How is the state of the American mystery story?

RP: I think it is probably flourishing. It certainly attracts a large number of practitioners. I am not myself a competent short story writer, and rarely read them except for this. I can't judge by what short fiction is doing the state of the detective story which is essentially in a novel form. Because of commercial circumstances you're not going to make a living as a detective story writer unless you write novels. That may not have been true in the pulp days where there were more outlets for this sort of thing. Being a short story writer is like being a poet. For Christ's sake how are you going to make a living doing that? It seems to me that the form has attracted a lot of quite good writers in addition to Leonard, Higgins, Tony Hillerman, and a wonderful writer, P. D. James, who should be listed first rather than third or fourth. I don't want to keep listing writers I admire because I'll leave somebody out and then they'll be mad at me.

CLPS: Let's talk a bit about *Small Vices*. In what ways is it a part of the series and in what way is it different?

RP: Oh, God, I don't know. I know that this sounds ironic and it's not intended to be, but I've never read my books. I write them in five-page increments. When they're done I send them in and someone publishes them. I don't sit around reading them afterwards. I'm also not too fastidious about reading galleys either. I have a very different relationship with what I write than the reader does who may consume what I write in one or two days. So many of the questions that a reader might reasonably ask I have no answer for. They all seem part of one on-going evolutionary tale rather than a discrete novel which fits in among other discrete items in a series of discrete items. To put it another way, I don't know.

CLPS: How has Spenser changed through the years?

RP: I don't know that either. Again, I assume that he must but I've not reread him so that is something a reader would do better with than I would. I was forty when I began writing about him and my children were fourteen and ten and now I am sixty-five and they are thirty-eight and thirty-four. I have learned an infinite amount from them—more than they ever learned from me—and certainly I would think that in the last twenty-five years that I have probably evolved and as I do it is reasonable to assume that Spenser does too. I suspect that he is less of a wiseguy, a little less inclined to solve problems by punching someone in the mouth. I am. I can't say that for sure because I really don't know. If he hasn't changed what's happened to me?

CLPS: For you what is the most important element in crime writing?

RP: Good writing. It's the most important element in whatever you write, whether it's crime writing or gothic romance. If you can write well and if you can manage the language brilliantly, then you will write a better book than if you don't.

CLPS: What are you working on now?

RP: At the moment I'm working on the screenplay for *Small Vices,* and I have had to put the next Jesse Stone aside. From your point of view however, I am working on the second Stone novel which will be finished sometime in January. There will be a new Spenser in March.

CLPS: What have you not done that you would like to do?

RP: Made a feature film for the movie theaters. Not that it makes a hell of a lot of difference. The real answer is that there is nothing that I've wanted to do that I haven't done. I'm very fortunate in that. I married the girl of my dreams; I have two brilliant sons; I have Pearl the wonder dog; I have done the job I wanted to do; I've made money at it and gotten to be famous; and once I was able to bench press three hundred pounds. What more could one person ask?

Nancy Pickard

INTERVIEW BY ROBERT J. RANDISI

RR: Nancy, how do you answer the readers who say that your books have gotten darker since the earlier ones?

NP: I'd say they're right.

Susan Wittig Albert, the mystery writer, has done some groundbreaking work in the analysis of our genre. She has identified what she calls the "mega-book" mystery series, which she says is a new phenomenon, and which denotes a series of novels which are essentially one long book. Each novel in the series is rather like a "chapter" in the mega-book. My series, according to Susan, may have been the first of these new "mega-book" mystery series.

The reason my books would fall into this new category, rather than into a traditional series category along with, say, Agatha Christie or John D. MacDonald (I should be so lucky), is, in a way, because of those very shades of light/dark that you're asking about. Characters like theirs remained basically, lovably, always the same from the start of a series to the very end. As readers we could count on that, and it was a major factor in their popularity. But in a "mega-book" series, you can't count on each succeeding book being very much like the last. Any given book may be quite different from earlier ones. It's more like real life (if I may presume that any amateur sleuth is *ever* like real life!), because the protagonist goes through some real changes in his or her life and—this is important—character as the years go by. Just as in our real lives we have good years and bad, dark times and light, so does the heroine of a mega-book series. As we (and they) mature, things do tend to assume a more substantial feeling, a weightiness, which can sometimes carry a feeling of greater "darkness." I think I'd call it maturity, rather than darkness, because I don't think we're talking about good vs. evil, for instance, but rather about a feeling or tone generated by a character's response to the events in her life. The truth is that Jenny looks at life in a more complex way now, at thirty-seven, than she did at twenty-nine; she looks deeper, more slowly, and sometimes even profoundly at events, instead of merely coping with them by joking about them. When you're twenty-nine, coping is plenty! But by thirty-seven, we ought to be looking a little deeper, and I think she has slowly begun to do that.

It is, I think, the deepening that is interpreted as "darker."

The lovely irony, of course, is that for any individual—fictional or "real"—it is that very plunge into the "darkness" (the unconscious) which eventually reveals a "light" of greater wisdom, however modest that greater wisdom may be. I think the plunge is well worth the risk, in life or fiction, even if you do lose some friends—or readers—along the way, and you usually do. I certainly lost readers (and reviewers) when I plunged from the lightness of *No Body* into the comparative darkness of *Marriage is Murder*. On the other hand, I picked up new readers (and reviewers) who preferred the change.

Before I knew of Susan Wittig Albert's analysis, I had been thinking that writing the Jenny series was turning into something very like writing the journal of one woman's life. I think that dovetails nicely with Susan's theory. And I suspect—no, I *know*—it is the "journal" that keeps readers coming back to the series. They're not nearly as interested, they tell me, in what murders Jenny may solve next as they are in such questions as: Are Jenny and Geof ever going to have children? Will they stay in Port Frederick, or will they move? Will her dad ever be less of a dingbat? Will her relationship with her sister get better or worse? These are the sorts of "life" questions we ask about our friends, but which we did not, usually, previously ask about mystery protagonists.

I think I should add that in a so-called "mega-book" series, the changes in the protagonist's life may occur relatively slowly, trickling bit by bit through each new book, but that's because that's the way life is, too: We don't have *every* crisis of our life happening to us all in the same year. Alterations to our character, although they may be announced via the trumpets of instant Epiphany, usually take a long time to grab hold permanently. So it is, too, in the lives of long-running fictional characters.

RR: What were your intentions when you first created Jenny Cain, and have you adhered to them successfully?

NP: I didn't set out to write a series, so I didn't have many "intentions." The creation of Jenny Cain wasn't a totally conscious act, anyway. I knew I wanted to write about a youngish female amateur sleuth who would be the director of a charitable foundation, but that's all I knew in advance. When I sat down to write, she just started talking on the page, before I even knew her name.

I do, however, recall a couple of conscious intentions, and they had mostly to do with male/female relationships. At that time, it seemed to me that lasting, loving relationships between American men and women in mystery fiction were about as scarce as flowers on the moon. So, when I did realize that Jenny and Geof were becoming a series, I wanted to give them every chance to love each other for a long time. I couldn't guarantee they would, but I hoped they'd last, and so far, they have.

In addition, I wanted to avoid the incredibly boring scenarios that were being acted out in fiction and real life in which women, trying to make headway in traditional male fields, encountered a lot of head-patting condescension. I found that so annoying in real life that I wanted to skip it as much as possible in my fiction, even if that meant fudging a bit on reality. I decided to try to create a fictional world in which people (men) weren't all that surprised when they discovered that Jenny could actually breathe and speak at the same time. Or, walk and talk. Or, whatever it might be that connotes basic intelligence and competence.

I think I've been more successful in the first ambition than in the latter one. There's still a certain amount of head-patting going on in my series, especially from older men. I couldn't seem to avoid it, and neither could Jenny. Some day, it'll probably make my series feel dated to younger readers, if it doesn't already, and that would just be fine with me.

Another intention I had, starting with the second book, was to give Jenny some black friends—which was unusual at the time among amateur sleuths—because that's how I wanted the world to be. I've also tried to avoid identifying only black people by their color, and have turned the tables sometimes by identifying people as, "a tall white women," or whatever the case may be, in ways actually intended to bring white readers up short. And, in fact, I've been told it does stop them, because they realize they have previously only expected the color adjective to be applied to non-whites. Writing gurus might say this is a bad idea, to halt the reader's eye, but I think some of the most fun you can have as a writer is to dump the reader's expectations completely upside-down.

The only other intention I had from the beginning was to give my heroine a full life, which meant not hiding from the language she spoke in private, or her sex life, or her sense of humor. I didn't want to be straightjacketed by the propriety of traditional female amateur sleuths, even if it meant offending some readers. I wanted Jenny to be a realistic woman like the real women I actually knew, and that meant she'd cuss, enjoy sex and laugh at outrageous things. Even so, I've reined myself in more than I've really liked, but I do have to remember that Jenny has a public image to maintain in her hometown, so I have to behave myself and try not to embarrass her in print.

With the seventh book in the series, I developed an intention to employ cultural references to women, instead of to men, as was the norm. (For instance, on the first page of *I.O.U.*, I purposefully made allusion to Daphne du Maurier instead of to Edgar Allan Poe, although Poe was the easy, obvious, and probably more recognizable, first choice.)

RR: Among your many awards you count a Shamus for best private eye short story. How do you account for that?

NP: I attribute that to the generosity of the real private eye writers.

RR: I know you've just finished your third P.I. story, because you wrote it for an anthology of mine called *Lethal Ladies II*. Are you moving more firmly into the P.I. field? Risking your status as a "Cozy" writer?

NP: I have always loved private-eye fiction, and I've read tons of it, so it was a real kick to try my hand at it with short stories. The truth is, I borrow from all the categories of mystery fiction, and if you look close enough, you'll see certain echoes of private eye fiction in my amateur sleuth novels. For instance, the opening of *Dead Crazy* is modeled on the classic opening for a P.I. novel, with the "client" coming to see the cynical "investigator." I did that on purpose, for my own pleasure. And every time Jenny goes around poking her nose into the affairs of the suspects, she's following the private eye tradition every bit as much as that of the amateur sleuth. None of this means, however, that I will ever be a real private eye writer; I'm a private eye dilettante.

RR: Tell us how that whole Virginia Rich thing came about.

NP: Several years ago, I picked up a mystery called *The Cooking School Murders* by an author named Virginia Rich. I loved it. I wrote to her to say so and to mention some coincidental similarities in our lives and our books. She wrote me back a lovely note in which she mentioned that she was working on a novel called *The 27-Ingredient Chili Con Carne Murders*. Soon after that, I learned that Virginia Rich had died. I was shocked and saddened, as were the thousands of mystery readers who had loved that first book as well as the next two Eugenia Potter mysteries, *The Baked Bean Supper Murders* and *The Nantucket Diet Murders*.

After her death, the three books in her series not only remained in print, but grew in popularity. During that time her husband, Ray Rich, came across boxes full of notes that Mrs. Rich had made for future books she had in mind, and even first drafts of some chapters. He approached her editor, inquiring whether the series might be continued by other writers along the lines that his wife had set forth in her notes. That editor approached my agent who then asked me, "How would you like to write a book by the name of *The 27-Ingredient Chili Con Carne Murders?*"

It felt like fate to me.

RR: Would you take on a job like that again? Finishing someone else's work? Who would it have to be? An undiscovered partial Christie?

NP: I have written another Mrs. Potter mystery, *The Blue Corn Murders*. And I'm under contract for another one after that.

I don't think I'd ever do it for anybody else, however, and *never* for a giant like Christie. It would be like completing a partial Dead Sea Scroll.

RR: If a young writer came to you at Malice Domestic and told you they wanted to write cozies, who would you tell them to read first, and why?

NP: I'd say, "Read the first three Nancy Drew mysteries in their original versions, then read Agatha Christie until you reach the point at which you can tell by the third chapter whodunit. Then start reading the other early British giants: Sayers, Marsh, Tey. After that, read some classic private eye novels for comparison, a few police procedurals, and some classic romantic suspense novels, as well. Once you're well-grounded in the fundamentals, you will have a better understanding of the ways in which contemporary cozies are similar to and different from their ancestors and their close relatives."

RR: Are you a cozy writer?

NP: I don't know what I am. What's in between cozy and uncomfortable? If mystery writers were chairs, I wouldn't quite be a chintz rocking chair, but I wouldn't be a hard metal folding chair, either. A nice, swivel office chair, perhaps? May I make it padded with real leather, and give it a good view out of a wide window, on the third floor? So it feels good to sit down in it, and you're not too high above the action, and you can leave quickly if you need to, and you never know who's going to walk in the door, or what you're going to see from up there.

RR: Who are your literary influences, and to whom are you an influence?

NP: The writers who have influenced me (whether it's visible in my writing or not) have been as diverse as Mildred Wirt Benson and James M. Cain, Raymond Chandler and Daphne du Maurier, James Hilton and Edna Ferber, F. Scott Fitzgerald and Alice Hoffman, Agatha Christie and J.D. Salinger, Robert B. Parker, Sue Grafton, Charlotte MacCleod and P.G. Wodehouse, not to mention a peck of poets and a whole slew of nonfiction writers. It's an endless list of writers whose books have impressed, amused and amazed me.

These days, new writers will sometimes tell me I have influenced them, and that amazes me, too.

RR: Finish this line: "I wish I had never written . . ."

NP: It has never occurred to me to wish that about anything, except perhaps for a certain letter I wrote to a lover just before he broke up with me. Everything else I have ever written, whether it was good or awful, helped to teach me to write.

RR: And this one: "I wish I had written . . ."

NP: *Lost Horizon,* or "A Clean, Well-Lighted Place," or "A Perfect Day for Banana Fish," or *Turtle Moon,* or *The Fellowship of the Ring,* or Emily St. Vincent Millay's sonnets, or "Cossi Fan Tutte" or "Eleanor Rigby," or any number of other deliciously wonderful and perfect pieces of writing or song. It would be lovely, I think, to have true, clear genius, although against that we would have to weigh the possibility of being shot, like John Lennon, or of spending one's life in one's room, like Emily Dickinson. Would it be worth it? I wish we could ask them. (They'd probably say it's the wrong question.)

RR: Where do you see your writing going in the next ten years? More Jenny Cains? Something else?

NP: It's possible that the Jenny Cain series is complete. *Twilight* feels like the end of the "mega-book." But it's also possible there might be another ten of them. Maybe a new mega-book about her middle-age, I should live so long and write so much. The truth is, I don't know where my writing's going, but I do know there are quite a few ways in which I'd like to improve as a writer. I'd like to be a more fluid writer, one who employs a greater richness of telling detail, and one who has more fun playing with language. I'd like to invent more intriguing and complex plots than I do now, and I'd love to soar in my imagination. I'd like to be a test pilot of a writer now and then. And a poet of a novelist. And I'd like to tell short stories that are as full and satisfying as the best novels are. And I'd love to write pieces that are meaningful as well as entertaining. And, after all of that comes true, Ed McMahon will knock on my door with a check for several million dollars.

RR: Please finish this line: "Nancy Pickard has always . . ."

NP: ". . . loved dogs, chocolate and popcorn."

RR: What are some of the more significant changes for women in the past twenty years of mystery writing?

NP: Great numbers of American women getting their novels published and moving onto best-seller lists. Being nominated for and winning great numbers of prizes. Stepping into a proportionate share of the limelight at conventions and other mystery events. Finding each other, which has meant tapping into an incredible sisterhood of women who share similar interests, goals and understandings about the world. Bringing back into the mystery fold thousands of female readers who gave up reading mysteries after they outgrew Nancy Drew. Most important: being able to write from our own voices, instead of male voices, and to write under our own names.

RR: You can point to one woman and say, "Thanks to her, I'm here." Who would that be, and why?

NP: Thanks to my mother, I'm a reader and without that, I'd never be a writer.

RR: And finally, finish this line: "I wish Bob Randisi would ask me . . ."

NP: I wish Bob Randisi would ask me what I think I've contributed to the mystery genre.

I think I helped to introduce contemporary social issues into our genre. Maybe I helped to open the door to the possibility of strong, loving relationships between equal men and women in American mystery fiction. (A man, Robert B. Parker, was the pioneer in this aspect, in my opinion, by creating a true peer relationship between Spenser and Susan Silverman.) If Susan Wittig Albert is right, I (unconsciously and without "aforethought") helped to invent the mystery "mega-book." I hope I helped to loosen the straightlaced bonds that had previously bound the amateur sleuth genre. In sum, I hope I did a bit of pioneering—alongside my friends—for the writers, particularly the women, who've come after us.

Dulcy Brainard

INTERVIEW BY ED GORMAN

EG: I don't know, and I doubt many readers do, how *PW* got started.

DB: We celebrated the 125th anniversary last year. There was an entire issue devoted to its history. Its mission was telling people what was going on in publishing, facilitating the selling of books and promoting a kind of a community.

Its charter today is not so different. What's different is that bookselling itself has changed. The process of getting books into the hands of the reader and the bookseller as a figure are not so clearly definable because the market has expanded so and because of the impact of the media.

There are a lot of alternative markets today. Who's your bookseller? Another change is the Web . . . who's the bookseller then? Is it Amazon.com or Barnes & Noble? Is it somebody who sets up a Web site that links to another bookseller? Many of the independents have Web sites also. There's a huge state of flux. How *PW* fits in requires some flexibility on our part as we try to move with the currents. We will not let go of the goal to address and inform and facilitate the work of the bookseller and to be a kind of central clearing house for information for publishers. Certainly *PW* is read on the West Coast as the film and TV industry mines the literary market for properties. But, basically we're the trade journal for publishing with a real eye out towards the bookseller.

EG: How about some background on Dulcy Brainard?

DB: I've been in publishing since I left graduate school. I started out in educational publishing and moved into trade.

I started reviewing for *PW* in the late seventies. The first book I reviewed was a mystery and that was my specialty after I became an editor here.

Early in 1995, when the lifestyles and the poetry editor left, I took on the editing of those sections, too. I've got this great and eclectic list of categories that I oversee, including cookbooks and gardening and childcare and also the poetry list. I commute from Connecticut and appreciate the train time for reading.

EG: In mysteries, do you see any trends today?

DB: I think the hard-boiled mysteries may be coming back but that could well be a function of TV and movie people looking for properties that will adapt well to their purposes.

There's strong interest in cozies and I think there's a definite surge in historicals. Three of the Edgar nominees were historicals this year.

EG: Why do you think mysteries remain so popular?

DB: Mysteries carry narrative better than any other kind of fiction right now. You have a clear story line. Strong characters and atmosphere. You can do so many different things with the form all the while delivering a story.

EG: Would you track a book for us when it's received?

DB: The publishers submit galleys, that's the pre-publication form of a book, to *PW* three months in advance of the publication. So if the book is scheduled to be published in June, we should see it in February or March. Once a week I go through the new mystery submissions. I look at what's come in, what's being published sooner rather than later and what looks really worthy. I look for titles I believe that the booksellers are going to want to know about. Then I assign the selected galley to a hand-picked reviewer. I have about fifteen regular mystery reviewers.

Each one has a special interest or a special expertise. There's no point in giving a violent, gory, blood-ridden, gritty urban murder mystery to someone who really loves cozies, so the historicals go to people who like them and the cozies go to the people who love cozies. The Conan Doyle specialties go to my Conan Doyle specialist and *noirs* go to the *noir* lovers. The review comes back with the galley in a couple of weeks. I edit the review to make sure that I find the reviewer's assessment is supportable.

If I feel that this reader has not read the story that was written, then we talk. Often I do a good bit of rewriting as a result of conversations with a reviewer. Next I assemble the mysteries that will go in a given issue trying to achieve a kind of balance.

If I've got eight to ten mysteries for one month from one publisher, I'm not going to be able to assign all of them and will pick maybe the five or six most interesting. If a galley comes in that looks sloppily edited or not very well-written, I'm likely to not assign it, rather than to assign it and run a bad review.

There's a compelling reason for that approach. We have limited space in the mystery section and it seems pointless to allot it to a review of a book that I know will be negative. You know sometimes it happens and I make a mistake in my own initial assessment. Exceptions occur, of course; a known author is likely to be reviewed regardless of this given title's merit. Booksellers expect it.

I pay special attention to first authors and mid-list people when I can. The big guys are certainly of interest to the bookseller and we have to pay them attention, but I feel a real responsibility to promote first novels and mid-list books.

EG: How do you feel about unsigned reviews?

DB: I am of mixed mind about that. I would love for our reviewers to get credit in some way. I think *Kirkus's* practice of listing their reviewers but not necessarily with the given review is an interesting possibility. The main reason that our reviews are not signed is that there is a great deal of editing done, generally because of space requirements. It's not that reviewers are not competent. What happens when you review as many books as we do, about 125 reviews per issue, you have to make sure that you're not using the same words, and that the sentences are varied; that there is a way to make the experience of reading all these reviews, which the bookseller has to do, an experience that doesn't send them off to dreamland in two minutes. There's juggling, there's shifting and the truth is, a lot of reviews as they finally appear—they go through my hands and through another editor's hands, and then through copy edit and then through production—may not resemble the words that the reviewer wrote. Given our time constraints, we just don't have the luxury to be able to talk with every reviewer about revisions.

EG: Do you feel that reviews have much impact on the marketplace?

DB: I think for the really established writers, who are going to get attention elsewhere, reviews may be less important in terms of how the book sales will go. But if you rephrase that question, and ask does attention matter, then it does. Attention especially matters for the newer and mid-list writers. It really matters that their names get out there. We take that part of this business really seriously and that's true for every Forecast editor.

EG: There's a commonly held belief that it's better to get a bad review than no review. What do you think of that?

DB: I think it's probably true. A really good writer who gets killed in a review, it's probably not going to make much difference. Patricia Cornwell's *Hornet's Nest* which was not a Scarpetta novel, was panned in almost all media. It didn't make any difference in terms of where it sat in the Best-seller List.

EG: How about the new writer?

DB: But for a new writer to get a *PW* review, even one that's somewhat mixed, is a whole lot better than being ignored. It shows that he or she is a player. I think it's a really reductive statement to say a bad review is better than none but lukewarm attention is better than no attention.

EG: How about publishing giants? When I was growing up, everybody spoke of Alfred Knopf and Bennett Cerf and those folks. Is anybody around like that today?

DB: Well I think that the fragmented nature of this business now precludes that kind of cultural icon. Now there are the bottomline publishers, the marketers who have taken some of the control that Knopf and Cerf and Ian Ballantine used to have. Now we have smaller giants and less visible ones—a function, to my mind, of the expanded nature of media in general. Now we've got TV and movies and cable and video; when Knopf and Cerf were operating it was only books and radio.

EG: Now we have Rupert Murdoch and Ted Turner who own publishing companies.

DB: That's right. It has become a kind of apples and oranges thing. There are some in the small publishing arena who've got some really good people operating and they're not going to make as big a splash but they're in there carrying the torch that was first lit by these icons of publishing.

EG: Do you see small regional presses as becoming a player in mystery?

DB: Small, absolutely but not necessarily regional. The small press has a real chance in this huge marketing-driven publishing industry. The big publishing companies have huge overhead and immense inventory and warehousing expenses. The small publisher can print a beautiful book and sell five to ten thousand copies maybe and not have the returns problem. Better that than having to sell 250,000 copies of a book in order just to approach breaking even.

EG: We're seeing one big advance book after another bomb. Do you think publishers will ever get back to a more basic form of publishing, smaller but more steadier profits?

DB: I don't see it happening right away. But there has to be a retrenching in this industry. There are so many books and I don't think they're being published with the care and the sort of foresight that they used to be. And I don't know how long these big conglomerates can continue to carry their big bombs.

EG: It sounds grim.

DB: It can't be a sound business practice. Some other part of those businesses has to make up for the shortfall. That's why I would much prefer to be a small publisher in this industry right now. You have a great deal more control over what you're doing. In terms of the small publishing, look at Soho.

EG: And Carroll and Graf.

DB: Carroll and Graf, Walker. They're not overreaching and there is something reassuring and solid in that.

EG: That leads into one of my final questions. Are you optimistic that the mystery field will continue to grow and prosper?

DB: This goes back to my belief in narrative. I think the quest for story is written in our bones and mystery is one of the major vehicles of narrative right now. A mystery by its very nature must offer a beginning, a middle and an end. It has to have a resolution, a climax, all the things that I think most human beings want in their reading.

Contributor Notes:

Bob Morrish has had book reviews and articles published in general interest periodicals such as *The San Francisco Chronicle, The Los Angeles Daily News, The San Jose Mercury News,* and *Publishers Weekly;* and in genre-oriented magazines such as *Weird Tales, Cemetery Dance,* and *Rod Serling's The Twilight Zone Magazine.* He has contributed to books such as *The Fantasy Encyclopedia and Fantasy and Horror: A Critical and Historical Guide;* and has had short stories appear in such anthologies as *The UFO Files* and *365 Scary Stories.*

Lee Server is best known for his extraordinary books examining the paperbacks of the fifties in *Over My Dead Body,* the pulp magazines in *Danger Is My Business,* and his prizewinning interviews with early Hollywood screenwriters in *Screenwriters: Words Become Pictures.*

Adrian Muller was born in Canada and raised and educated in the Netherlands. After obtaining a degree in Arts Administration from the Reinwardt Academy for Museology, Adrian moved to the United Kingdom. Living in Bristol, he held various posts at Watershed, Britain's first media center. He has since become a freelance writer specializing in profiles of crime fiction authors. Adrian has also been the Events Manager for the London bookshop Crime in Store, and a contributing organizer for two of Britain's leading crime fiction conventions: Oxford's St. Hilda's Crime and Mystery Weekend, and Dead on Deansgate in Manchester. He is a member of the British Crime Writers' Association, and his work has been published in Australia, Europe, and the United States.

Rylla Goldberg is a freelance writer in Bellevue, Washington, and has written/edited over forty business and technical books. Her mystery writings—essays, interviews and crossword puzzles—have appeared in *Mystery Scene;* her book reviews and word search puzzles have been published in various Washington newspapers. For relaxation she plays chess, teaches piano, and enjoys time with her three grandchildren.

At the tender age of forty-something, **Mike Stotter** has been involved with the Western genre, editing *The Westerner* for some years before selling out to the "big boys." Having written five pulp Western fiction novels, and a children's historical nonfiction novel, he's turned his hand to the crime and thriller genre. Having written for *Mystery Scene* and *The Mystery Review* he now also edits *Shots*—a British magazine for crime and mystery. In what spare time he has Mike writes short stories on the Old West and of present-day crime. Mike lives in Essex and is married with three sons eating him out of house and home.

Charles L. P. Silet widely reviews crime fiction and interviews crime writers for such journals as *The Armchair Detective, Mystery Scene, Clues, Mostly Murder, The Drood Review,* and the Australian mystery magazine *Mean Streets.* He teaches film and contemporary literature and culture at Iowa State University. He is currently editing a collection of critical articles on Chester Himes.

Rick Koster is an arts writer for the *New London (CT) Day.* His first book, *Texas Music,* was published in March '98 by St. Martin's Press. A native of Dallas, Texas, he also reviews books and writes a thrillers column for *The Dallas Morning News* and contributes music features to the *Dallas Observer.* He has also written for *American Way* and *Mystery Scene,* and is finishing a novel about voodoo in contemporary New Orleans. He lives in Connecticut with his wife Eileen and their two greyhounds.

Carol Cope is a Miami-based attorney and author of the critically acclaimed *In the Fast Lane: A True Story of Murder in Miami,* published by Simon & Schuster in 1993. Her second book is *Stranger Danger/How to Keep Your Child Safe, a Handbook for Parents.* In *Stranger Danger,* she recounts the murder of nine-year-old Jimmy Ryce of Homestead, Florida, a case which is set for trial in May. Cope is now at work on a legal thriller set in Miami.

Jan Grape, along with Dean James, is a coeditor of the Edgar- and MacCavity-nominated *Deadly Women: The Mystery Readers Indispensable Companion* (Carroll & Graf). She has eighteen short stories in anthologies, including the Shamus- and Anthony-nominated "A Front Row Seat" in *Vengeance Is Hers* (Signet). Recent releases include: *Midnight Louie's Pet Detectives, Cat Crimes Through Time,* and *The First Lady Mysteries.* Her nonfiction may be seen in *The Mystery Writers Sourcebook, The Fine Art of Murder, Writing the Private Eye Novel,* and *Speaking of Murder.* A regular columnist for *Mystery Scene,* she has written a guest column for the British publication *Shots.* She was editor for nine years of "Reflections in A Private Eye," the newsletter of PWA and is the current V.P. of PWA, and also holds memberships in MWA, Sisters in Crime, and American Crime Writers League. Jan and husband Elmer own Mysteries & More bookstore in Austin, Texas.

Jane Williams is a freelance editorial researcher and writer who lives in London. She contributes interviews and book reviews to *Shots,* a crime and mystery fiction magazine published quarterly in the UK. It's a must-read title for crime and mystery fiction readers and writers. A lifelong devotion to crime fiction began when, as a child living in Africa, she read Sir Arthur Conan Doyle's *The Speckled Bend*—the frisson of terror evoked by the saucer of milk, the dummy bell rope and the ventilator has barely diminished with the years.

Dean James is the manager of Murder by the Book, Houston's nationally known mystery specialty bookstore. He earned a Ph.D. in medieval history from Rice University in 1986, then spent the next ten years as a librarian in the Texas Medical Center before coming to work at Murder by the Book full-time. He is the coauthor, with Jean Swanson, of *By a Woman's Hand: A Guide to Mystery Fiction by Women* (second edition, Berkley Prime Crime, 1996). The first edition of this popular reference book on contemporary women mystery writers was nominated by the Mystery Writers of America for the Edgar Award for Best Critical-Biographical Work, and it won the Agatha and MacCavity Awards for Best Nonfiction. The second edition was nominated for both the Agatha and Anthony Awards. With Jan Grape, he is the co-editor of *Deadly Women,* another volume on women mystery writers, published by Carroll & Graf in 1997. In April 1998, Berkley Prime Crime published *Killer Books: A Reader's Guide to Exploring the Popular World of Mystery and Suspense,* a new reference book which he wrote with Jean Swanson. His first short story was published in the *Malice Domestic 7* anthology, which came out in September 1998 from Avon Books.

Dale L. Walker, a freelance writer since 1960, is author of fifteen books and over four hundred magazine articles and stories. His book column "Westerns" has appeared for ten years in the *Rocky Mountain News*. He is twice winner of the Spur Award from Western Writers of America, Inc., is past-president of that organization and is a long-time member of the Texas Institute of Letters. He lives in El Paso.

Jerry Sykes's short stories have appeared in a number of magazines and anthologies—including *Cemetery Dance, Crime Time* and *Love Kills*—and his short story "Sleep that Burns" is currently being developed for television. He has also edited an anthology of short crime stories, *Mean Time,* based around the end of the millennium for publication in 1998. His interviews and reviews have appeared in *Mystery Scene, The Armchair Detective, Shots* and *Crime Time.*

Winner of the Edgar Award, Shamus Award, and Anthony Award, Harlan Coben is the author of the critically acclaimed Myron Bolitar novels. Since the series debuted in 1995, Harlan Coben has won the Mystery Writers of America's Edgar Allan Poe Award for Best Paperback Original, was nominated for another Edgar, won the Anthony Award at the 1996 World Mystery Conference, was nominated for another Anthony Award, won the 1997 Shamus Award by the Private Eye Writers of America, and was twice nominated for the Dilys Award by the Independent Mystery Booksellers Association. The five Myron Bolitar novels are (in order): *Deal Breaker, Dropshot, Fade Away, Backspin,* and *One False Move.* The sixth Myron Bolitar novel will be released by Delacorte in hardcover in May. Harlan lives in Ridgewood, New Jersey, with his pediatrician wife, Anne, and two young children.

Robert J. Randisi is the author of more than three hundred books, the founder of the Private Eye Writers of America, the creator of the Shamus Award, and the cofounder of *Mystery Scene* magazine. His new novel, *In the Shadow of the Arch,* will be published by St. Martin's Press in 1998. Dominick Abel has been his agent since 1981.

Ed Gorman's name is synonymous with some of the best dark suspense and mystery fiction being written today. His novels *Black River Falls, The Marilyn Tapes, Blood Red Moon,* and *First Lady* have all met with widespread critical acclaim and several foreign sales. He is also the Editorial Director of *Mystery Scene,* one of the top trade magazines of the mystery genre. He lives in Cedar Rapids, Iowa, with his wife, author Carol Gorman.